D1078773

Discover your
psychic
powers

A Practical Guide to Psychic
Development & Spiritual Growth

By Tara Ward

ARCTURUS

ARCTURUS
This edition published in 2008 by Arcturus Publishing Limited
26/27 Bickels Yard, 151–153 Bermondsey Street,
London SE1 3HA

Copyright © 1998 Arcturus Publishing Limited

All rights reserved. No part of this publication may be reproduced,
stored in a retrieval system, or transmitted, in any form or by any
means, electronic, mechanical, photocopying, recording or otherwise,
without written permission in accordance with the provisions of the
Copyright Act 1956 (as amended). Any person or persons who do
any unauthorised act in relation to this publication may be liable to
criminal prosecution and civil claims for damages.

ISBN: 978-1-84837-198-9

Printed in the UK

CONTENTS

INTRODUCTION 5

CHAPTER 1 WHAT ARE THE BENEFITS? 23

CHAPTER 2 KARMA AND REINCARNATION 39

CHAPTER 3 LOOKING AT ENERGY 57
Cosmic Energy 59; Earth Energy 64; Plant Energy 65

CHAPTER 4 HUMAN ENERGY 69
Hand Energies 71; Feeling An Aura 78; Hologram 85

CHAPTER 5 CHAKRAS 89
Chakra Awareness 101; Base Chakra 102; Navel/Sacral Chakra 103;
Solar Plexus Chakra 104; Heart Chakra 105; Throat Chakra 107; Third Eye
Chakra 108; Crown Chakra 109; Choosing the Right Chakra 112

CHAPTER 6 CREATING YOUR OWN SPACE 115
Sad Time 116; Happy Time 116; The Candle 129

CHAPTER 7 BREATHING AND RELAXATION 135
The Diaphragm 139; Arms & Breath 140; Body & Breath 140;
Energy & Breath 141; Balancing Energies 145; Tensing & Releasing 148

CHAPTER 8 TUNING IN 151
Tuning In 151; Cleansing 159; Closing Down 161

CHAPTER 9 THE EARLY STAGES .167
The Letter 168; Connecting With Another Person 172;
The Intuition Book 175; Your Inner Self 176

CHAPTER 10 EXPANDING EVERYTHING 179
Earthing Yourself – Sitting 179; Earthing Yourself – Standing 181;
Expanding Your Aura 182; Lifting & Lowering Energies 185

CONTENTS

CHAPTER 11 YOUR SITTER 189

CHAPTER 12 GIVING AN AURIC READING 205

CHAPTER 13 PSYCHOMETRY 217
Hand Brushing 220; Hand Massage 221; Numbers 222;
Psychometry 224; Finding An Object 229; Focusing On Specifics 231

CHAPTER 14 FLOWER READING 235

CHAPTER 15 SELF-HEALING 247

CHAPTER 16 HEALING OTHERS 257
Healing Preparations: 1 260; 2 262; Healing 265; Absent Healing 273

CHAPTER 17 USING CRYSTALS 277

CHAPTER 18 DISCOVERING AURAGRAPHS 287

CHAPTER 19 PENDULUMS & DOWSING 297

CHAPTER 20 CRYSTAL BALLS 311

CHAPTER 21 THE TAROT CARDS .323

CHAPTER 22 THE RUNES 335

CHAPTER 23 PALMISTRY 347

CHAPTER 24 USING YOUR PSYCHIC DEFENCES 361

CHAPTER 25 THE FUTURE 373

INTRODUCTION

How would you describe our journey through life? A popular analogy would be to compare it to going down a road. There are various forks and turnings on the way, but generally it's a pretty straight route. However, what if there's another route that runs alongside your straight road, mirroring its every twist and turn? Psychic development is like that second road, and you can choose to try it anytime. It doesn't mean you have to abandon your present journey: it just means you can dip off onto it as you wish and then return to your other road whenever you like. The choice is yours. You might find the second journey more pleasing, rather like driving through scenic countryside instead of a polluted city. At the very least, psychic development can be a positive influence on your daily life; at the very most, it can be a spiritual philosophy that has infinite possibilities. Remember, you choose which path to take, no one else. Perhaps that's why you're reading this book right now.

What does the word 'psychic' mean to you? Try saying it to yourself. Does it sound unnatural or odd? Does the the word make your thoughts spiral in new directions? Do you believe you've ever had a 'psychic' experience, or would you call it co-incidence? Has anybody ever told you that you might be psychic or that you have healing abilities? Have you ever experienced that odd sensation of 'déja vu': something happens and you know that it's happened before, either because you've dreamed it or because you simply have a memory of it?

You've just had a lot of questions thrown at you. How does that make you feel? Your ability to question everything is a valuable part of psychic development. This book is going to explore a wide variety of psychic phenomena; some concepts may be new and unnerving. You may find it demanding at times. This is because any form of growth or new awareness takes a certain dedication, a certain commitment. With psychic work, it also takes the ability to open your mind further and expand consciousness onto other levels.

To do this, you need to start looking at yourself and the life you see around you. You need to ask a lot of questions, not only of others, but of yourself as well. You need to be willing to delve into what is going on inside you and get in touch with the real you, not the face you present to others.

If you are willing to take this plunge, then you have the opportunity of discovering a whole new world that is enlightening and energizing. It will change the way you view yourself, other people and the world. Irrevocably. You'll discover new aspects of yourself that will enable you to treat everyone with greater awareness, love and tolerance. In fact, you will benefit in all areas of your life, because you'll gain a true understanding of something important: how everything we give out rebounds and further feeds our growth. It's a process that has infinite possibilities, reaching ever outwards to a world without boundaries.

There is one condition, however. You have to be prepared to put in some work. It may be uncomfortable at times. It may even be distressing. It may feel occasionally as though you're banging your head against a brick wall and you may want to give up. You need to be prepared to accept both sides of the equation to gain from the experience.

Have you an enquiring mind? If you feel daunted by endless questions and probing, then you won't be able to progress very far. You have to be willing to constantly extend your vision and see past the deeply-entrenched patterns that are buried in your thought processes. So many concepts explained in this book, particularly during the first half, may be ideas you've never heard of before. Your first reaction may be 'This sounds ridiculous' or 'This isn't possible'. These are natural reactions to something new and most people initially respond this way. There's a wonderful saying by William James:

'A new idea is first condemned as ridiculous and then dismissed as trivial, until finally, it becomes what everybody knows.'

The secret is to accept that you're feeling very sceptical and then, regardless of that thought, let your mind move on further. The more you practise this, the easier it becomes.

Think of it this way. What would your great-great-grandfather have said if someone had told him that soon two people could be miles apart and yet still be able to talk to each other via a bit of wire? Or that a metal container would lift off into the sky and fly hundreds of people across the world at once? You can imagine his response! Your present disbelief about psychic phenomena is just as understandable. If your great-great-grandfather could see the world today, he would no doubt think of the telephone, plane, radio, television (to say nothing of computers) as the work of aliens.

Perhaps that is rather how you view psychic matters at present: very alien. Just as your great-great-grandfather would find it hard to accept that humans could create all those extraordinary objects, so you may find it hard to accept other abilities that we have as humans. The trick to moving forward lies in accepting that it's difficult to believe and then opening your mind just that bit further to let in the possibility of these new ideas.

You needn't embrace everything without question. (As you've already read, questions are essential for growth). Instead, use your disbelief to question further and probe deeper into these areas. For instance, if your thought on a subject is 'This is ridiculous', then go on and ask yourself, 'Why am I thinking that? What element of this is ridiculous?' Very often, the answer is that it's ridiculous only because it's a new concept! If you break that down further, the 'ridiculous' element can be softened into an 'unlikely'. Why is it then unlikely? The usual response to that is because you can't 'see' the concept.

This is an important area to look at in psychic development. As humans we're programmed to feel comfortable and reassured only after we have physical proof of something. We need to see something before we really believe it. Someone could tell you it's raining outside. Your natural response is to look out the window to check if it's true. If you hit your shin on the coffee table, physical pain tells you it hurts and that's validated by the cut or bruise that ensues.

With psychic work we're dealing very much with the feeling and sensing elements within us and we tend not to trust these as much, although there are exceptions to this rule. These exceptions are our key to understanding more. What about the emotional pain you feel when splitting up after a love affair? There's no visible scar, no real 'proof' of pain, is there? But isn't it as real to you as the pain you felt on physically knocking your shin against the table? Conversely, what about that euphoric rush of utter joy that fills your body when you feel yourself falling in love or when your newborn child is placed in your arms for the first time? You can't see that emotion, can you? But do you doubt that you're feeling it? Of course not. Psychic experiences work on a similar level. The stronger the experience, the easier it is to accept that it's real. You may find it difficult to begin with, because development will take place gradually. For instance, it may take you a while to 'see' universal energy, the aura, or chakras: all subjects covered at some length during the early chapters. However, the fact that you can't see them immediately doesn't mean they aren't there, it just means you can't see them. All you need is the desire to keep trying and a belief that these concepts might exist, to make things happen for you.

There's a wonderful story about the American inventor, Thomas Edison (1847-1931), who invented the electric light bulb in 1883. It's such a common object today that most of us take it for granted. Do you know how many times he is said to have tried to make a light bulb before he actually succeeded? Over a thousand times. Can you imagine the extraordinary determination it took to keep going under those circumstances, with no one actually believing it was possible? It's a fantastic example of a human being who wouldn't give up. This is not to imply that you may have to try a thousand times before you can see an aura! It's merely to point out that if someone like Thomas Edison can keep going without any support or encouragement, there's no earthly reason why anyone reading this book can't start to develop their psychic skills. Unlike Edison, you'll be guided, nurtured and encouraged along the whole route.

Throughout this book, simple exercises have been included to help you expand yourself, using either physical or thought-expansion techniques. Do try these experiments as they crop up; they're designed to help you open yourself up further. Again, some of these exercises may seem odd initially, especially the visualization ones. However, all of them are important and will aid your growth. Don't become confused by believing that a visualization exercise means you should see wonderful images and scenarios. Everyone will have a different experience; whatever happens to you is right for you. These exercises are merely means through which you can expand your consciousness. They do become easier with practice and one of the great advantages with the visualization techniques is their ability to find out about what is hidden deep in your sub-conscious. Nobody else need know what you're thinking and doing, and that freedom can be wonderful for releasing all sorts of old pent-up emotions and thoughts. Remember, this is a book very much about you, and you have permission to take time out just to concentrate on you and nobody else. It's not selfish: it's an essential part of psychic development.

So what exactly does the word 'psychic' mean? If you're considering developing this area of yourself, it would be useful to define it. If you look in dictionaries you'll find a whole host of varying definitions. Here are just a handful:

- *someone who claims to have unusual mental powers*

- *having knowledge and mental abilities impossible to explain using present scientific understanding*

- *concerning the mind rather than the body*

- *of the soul or mind*

Aren't they remarkably matter-of-fact definitions? Now try asking some friends, relations and work colleagues what they think 'psychic' means. Again, you'll no doubt get a wide variety of answers, but it's more likely that this time you'll get a few words such as 'voodoo', 'black magic' or 'witchcraft' creeping into their language. After they finish, you might like to gently point out some of the dictionary definitions, but don't be surprised if they ask for physical proof when you tell them.

With the work you'll be doing during this book, you can help yourself most by thinking of psychic work simply as 'concerning the mind, rather than the body' or 'of the soul or mind'. After all, the word psychic originates from the Greek word 'psyche', which means soul. This is not to say that you should forget about your physical self in preparing for psychic work. This is a common mistake many psychics themselves make. Human beings should never under-estimate the importance of their own physical body. Why else would we be born with this amazingly complex and quite miraculous physical system, unless we were meant to look after it well? The more we nurture our physical body, the more it will aid us in psychic development. Chapter 6 discusses in detail our physical health, as well as our surroundings and their significance. Unfortunately many of us spend a lot of our lives oblivious to the extraordinary body we've been given. It isn't until someone really makes us stop and think about its beauty that we can begin to tune in to it and work with it rather than against it. Yet if you ask most people how 'in tune' they are with their own body, they'd be convinced they are perfectly aware of its capabilities and restrictions. Wait until you try some of the exercises in later chapters before you decide for yourself.

So the physical body is very important, but once you have developed a stronger relationship with it, then you will be ready to move on to explore the inner part of you, or your inner voice, which will guide and protect you. If the words 'inner voice' fill you with doubt and cynicism, call it your soul or mind for now. It doesn't matter at this stage. Once you have spent some time delving into those deeper parts of you, it ceases to be important what you call it. All you will know is that there is something more to you, something that has always been there but you have never tapped into it before, and you'll wish you'd found it sooner! People use various names for this other part of you: higher self, inner voice, gut instinct, soul, spiritual core, intuition. What is it really?

It's the 'real you', the bit you usually hide from people because to show it makes you feel too vulnerable/ frightened/ embarrassed/ emotional or downright silly. It's the bit of you that 'knows' things, not because you're highly intelligent or well-read, but because you are in touch properly with all of you. It isn't even mystical or unfathomable once you've spent some time exploring it, because you suddenly realize it's always been there, but you just haven't realized it before.

You can liken it to having a great desire to fall in love for the first time. Initially, doesn't it seem like some intangible, impossible dream that might happen to others but not to you? Most people can identify with this. Then, when you do fall in love, aren't you overcome with an enormous relief? Isn't there a great sense of joy that you can feel these sensations and doesn't it make you feel like a whole human being? Aren't you relieved to discover you are 'normal'? Then, as more time goes on, you start to forget about how much you doubted yourself in the first place. You start to accept it as a natural event that everyone can experience.

Discovering the inner part of you is very much like that. You start off feeling that it's probably impossible because, although other people might find that magical part inside them, perhaps you aren't special enough to do so yourself. You even wonder if maybe you were one of the few to be born without that special 'bit'. Then, when you discover it, you realize it can happen to everyone. It's this element of psychic development that people resist most: learning to find and develop the inner voice/ higher self. You'll find plenty of exercises to work on that will gradually develop this area in you. When it does start to show itself, it's also one of the most rewarding aspects of psychic work.

Now let's take a moment to look at what psychic work can't do for you. Despite what other people might say, psychic work is not about black magic or witchcraft or voodoo, at least not in this book. You won't find any references to the burning of witches, spells, voodoo dolls or ouija boards. The object of writing this volume is to make psychic work an enlightening and uplifting experience that nurtures you personally and, during that process, also affects others around you in a positive and loving way.

You won't find any references to negative or destructive forces, nor will you find any means of gaining power over people and making them do what you want them to do. This is very important. If you want to embark on an ego-trip and make yourself feel powerful, you'll have to go somewhere else and suffer the consequences. Never confuse psychic work with having dominance over people. It simply doesn't work that way, and if you try to establish power over someone, it will bounce back at you in the most unpleasant and distressing manner. It cannot, repeat cannot, give you power to force people to do what they do not want to do. To fully understand why this is so, you have to look at the concept of karma which is dealt with in detail in Chapter 2. If you really have acquired this book intending to learn powerful techniques to dominate others, please turn straight to Chapter 2 and read it thoroughly before continuing with the Introduction.

This element of not being able to control others is doubly important for another reason. As you start to develop your psychic awareness, you will be tempted to offer advice and guidance yourself. This may not be any conscious desire to manipulate someone: it's simply that you want to help them. However, it can be unwittingly dangerous. This is a difficult area because unless you are speaking from your higher self, or inner voice, you may be giving guidance that is mistaken or unhelpful. With practice, you will be able to tell the difference between your own thoughts and your higher self and it's vital that you learn this. Otherwise, you may pass on advice that harms other people and although you won't consciously have done this, it will still have a karmic effect upon you. When in doubt, you should never try to influence or guide anyone. Fill them with encouragement and love instead.

What else can you not achieve with psychic work? It won't help you to think of it as a fortune-telling tool. This is a tricky area because some people firmly believe that you can see into the future (the possibility of why this might be so is dealt with later), but for any novice it really is impossible to tap into future events. You can make up probability patterns for someone's future and predict likely outcomes, but that is not the same as fortune-telling. Seeing into a possible future comes from one of the highest levels of psychic development and it's not an area you can even contemplate at this stage. Therefore, if you are tempted to predict things during your early work, be aware that you're not working on a psychic level in doing so.

Psychic development is also not a game. It's not meant to be played with as though it were a toy that might afford you some amusement. You won't find any references to 'having a laugh' or 'fooling around' with this work. It's meant to be taken seriously and treated with the utmost respect. This isn't to imply that you have to approach the whole process with a reverential piousness and end up an obsessed bore. Indeed, the actual progress you can choose to make through this book gives you the opportunity to become exactly the opposite: a more open, aware and loving human being. Laughter has its place within psychic development; it's a wonderful release and a means through which you can learn more about yourself and others, but it should come from an awareness that can be shared and never at the expense of others. Trying to fool around with psychic work to have a laugh will cause problems, too. It can be likened to getting into a car and driving it when you've never had a lesson in your life. You'll end up in a nasty accident and possibly hurt innocent others, as well as yourself. Dealing with universal energies can be extremely powerful, and unless the situation is controlled you run the risk of a 'psychic accident'. When the work is treated with respect and sensitivity, accidents are less likely. If something should start to go wrong, you will be able to stay in control and deal with it safely, provided you have studied the ground rules first.

This brings up the fact that you have to read a number of chapters and to try a variety of exercises in this book, before you start tuning in for psychic work and working with others.

Chapters 1 to 11 supply the groundwork you need to cover before trusting yourself with other people: your 'sitters'. The rest of the book details the various forms of psychic expression that can be practised safely with them.

Many of you will be tempted to scan hastily through the earlier chapters, anxious to get to the actual section where you can start working psychically. It's a natural part of wanting to get started on something, rather than waiting. It really is necessary, however, for you to have an understanding of what you are dealing with, before you open yourself up to all the energies out there in the world. You won't realize how strong all these influences are until you are open and receptive, and it can then be a very unnerving experience. It's not a harmful one, however, as long as you have taught yourself how to be protected and how to cleanse away unwanted outside energies. The danger is in believing you know most of it already because it's almost certain that you won't. Arrogance is another trait that can cause many psychic accidents. The book has been shaped specifically to help minimalize any unpleasant effects of psychic development. Protect yourself by giving yourself the best posible chance to work safely and follow the procedures step by step. Also know that by opening up and expanding your conscious mind through all the early exercises, you are giving yourself the best possible chance for obtaining positive and encouraging results with others.

There is another area you can benefit from by considering its relevance. Where does Religion come into the realm of psychic development? In other words, you've been reading about an inner voice or a higher self, so what does this have to do with religious beliefs? The simple answer is as much or as little as you believe. Psychic work is not affiliated to any one religion and it is not intended to be a religious experience. However, many psychics have a deep, abiding faith in God and believe God to be their guide. Others may call the vision Buddha, Allah, Christ, Universal Spirit, Great Spirit, Cosmic Energy, or a whole host of other names. What you call it isn't important because what matters is your own particular faith, and no one else has the right to tell you what that should be. When working on a psychic level, no one should tell you that you must adopt a certain system of beliefs, religious or otherwise. Psychic work operates on a myriad of consciousness-levels and you will find what is right for you through quiet methods of relaxation and meditation. Never let anyone try to regiment you into only one school of thought. Nor should you let go of a faith if you have found one in which you can believe and which affords you peace and comfort. Pray to whatever deity you believe in and always acknowledge thanks in the same way. Throughout the book, it is often recommended you offer your own prayer before starting psychic work and again afterwards. Whatever the source you are drawing upon, it's important to acknowledge its strength and beauty and to continue to ask for further guidance.

There are some organized religions which disapprove of psychic development and believe it to be harmful. They have every right to their opinion and should be heard. However, true psychic work is about loving and nurturing, becoming more aware of everyone and everything around you, and harmonizing with others. It's about developing a deep understanding of people and the world, and discovering levels of compassion and love that transcend the ordinary, material world. It's about letting go of your own ego and seeing beyond our present, troubled earth into a possible future of peace and heightened awareness. It's about letting go of stress and anger. It's about true self-discovery. Can that be harmful or dangerous? Only you can answer that question for yourself.

Everybody is psychic. That sentence deserves repeating and emphasizing. **Everybody is psychic.** Being psychic isn't some special gift of a chosen few; it has nothing to do with social status, intelligence, colour or creed. We are all born psychic but most of us haven't learned how to tap in to that part of us yet. There is a good reason why we aren't all immediately able to open up psychically. As you've been reading, you will be delving into powerful forces, and no one is ready to handle that experience without some time to prepare first. Everyone comes to psychic work when they're ready for it. It cannot be rushed.

Did you know it's a scientific fact that human beings use only a small proportion of their brain? Some say it's as little as 15%. It's said that psychics use a further area. However, even then there is still a huge section of our brain into which none of us have tapped. How does that make you feel? Excited? Unnerved? Intrigued? Daunted? Or a combination of emotions? Human beings are such wonderful entities with endless capabilities, and yet we use such a miniscule proportion of our resources.

Now is a good time for you to try your first visualization exercise. Some of you will find this very powerful. It's a wonderful tool to help open your mind, which, after all, is the very beginning of psychic development. Don't feel you have to concentrate too intently during the process. This is merely an experiment. None of these exercises is meant to be a 'test' and you will find some of them much more powerful than others. So don't worry if it seems difficult this first time, or if very little happens to you. Lots of people don't 'see' anything in a visualization; they only sense or feel. Just relax.

Before you start, ensure that you're warm and comfortable and, most importantly, that someone isn't going to barge in and disturb you. This is crucial for all the exercises. Being disturbed half-way through can be very unsettling and put you off balance for ages. Read through the visualization technique several times before you put the book down, close your eyes and try it for yourself. If you have someone around with whom you feel completely relaxed and happy, then you could ask them to slowly read it aloud for you and take you through it, step by step. For most people, doing something like this for the first time, it's less inhibiting to be on their own.

EXPANDING YOUR THOUGHTS

Close your eyes. Imagine that standing in front of you is an enormously high building. In fact, as you crane your neck to look up, you realize you can't see the top of it. It seems to go on forever and forever, spiralling off into the universe. You're intrigued. You've never seen a building as high as this before and it looks very inviting and exciting. You decide to explore it. You walk through the open door and you're in a light, airy space. It feels and smells comfortable. Then you notice there's a lift in one corner. You go over and push the button beside it, feeling a pleasant rush of anticipation. (Note: if you're claustrophobic, imagine that the lift is large and made of glass so that you can see out all around you. If you suffer from vertigo, have the lift enclosed by solid walls. If just the thought of lifts makes you feel nervous, create a large, open stairwell and imagine a door at each level). The lift door opens and you step in. It feels warm and safe and you have the comforting feeling that someone is with you, filling you with love and peace. You look at the buttons inside the lift. There are so many of them! You see one marked 'Basement' and decide you'll try that first.

You press the button and descend, smoothly. The door opens and you immediately feel uncomfortable. You suddenly see, or sense, things that make you wish you weren't here. There's violence, greed, jealousy and hate in this Basement. You may see images of some of these things or you may just feel them inside you. You may acknowledge times when you have had some of those emotions and not treated others as well as you might have done. You realize you want no part of this floor. It feels utterly wrong. You feel sad, depressed. It's as though you've entered a world belonging to someone else and you know you don't belong there. You close the lift door and as it slides together, you're enveloped by that wonderful, warm, safe feeling once more. As you go to press another button, you realize the Basement button has somehow disappeared from the panel. That makes you feel even better, because you know that part of the experience has now gone forever.

You decide you'll try the First Floor next. You press the button and the lift moves smoothly past the Ground Floor to its next destination. As the doors open on the First Floor you realize this is your domestic life as you know it now. That same familiar feeling you had on the Ground Floor hits you again, but this time your family and friends are here. They're smiling at you, full of love and laughter. You look at them all and realize how much you love them and how special they all are. But you also know there is more you have to explore and you know they will always be there. You can return to this floor any time you want. You return to the lift and press the 'Close' button. Their faces are still smiling as the doors close. You check that the First Floor button is still there and of course it is. The button seems to shine with extra light and you know you'll never have trouble picking it out. You know you want to return to that button a lot, but you're also curious about the rest of the buttons.

What is on the Second Floor? You press the button and the lift glides upwards. The door opens and this time it's your working environment that confronts you. Your image is personal to you and will either make you feel good or unsettled, depending on where you stand with work. Take a good look and you will see there are signs in the room which indicate areas in which you could make changes. You suddenly see possibilities for the future that you hadn't thought of before and you realize you have much more potential than you're using at present. You know you'll return to this floor again to examine it in more detail. You close the doors and notice that the Second Floor button is shining back at you, reminding you it's there for the future.

Then you press the button for the Third Floor. When it opens, it's an empty room! You're confused at first and then you notice that it's a beautiful place. It glows with warmth and beauty. You walk into it because you can't stop yourself and you immediately feel a sense of peace. You feel relaxed but also wonderfully alive and vibrant. The room seems to tingle with a pleasurable air of expectancy. You're all alone but you don't feel in the least lonely. You feel that you've found something very special that is just for you and you feel you want to stay a while. You feel you want to sit quietly and meditate, to drink in the atmosphere. Then you suddenly remember there are all those other floors to discover! You return to the lift and press the button for the Fourth Floor.

The door closes, but this time the lift doesn't move upwards. It stays where it is for a moment and then the doors re-open onto the same empty space of the Third Level. For a moment you feel confused, and then understanding sweeps over you. You need to spend some time on this floor before you can move on. This Third Floor is where you learn techniques that will enable you to explore more of the levels above. You think of all the hundreds of floors above you and know that you want to explore them. There's so much to see and experience! You can't wait to start. In fact, you want to start now by going into this beautiful space again. As you start to move forward, suddenly a gentle, soft voice is calling your name, explaining that your journey is over for now and you must return to your starting place. You ask if you could please stay for a little longer but you're told it's not possible. The time isn't quite right yet.

Reluctantly, you press the 'Close' button and the lift takes you back to the Ground Floor. You walk back through the light, airy space on the ground level and then out through the front door of *the building. You take one last look upwards at that wonderful building and know you will return. Very soon. You slowly turn from the building and walk away. Now take a moment to remember that you are back in your familiar room with a book that you want to pick up and continue reading. When you feel ready, open your eyes and concentrate on your present surroundings again. Look at your book to remind yourself where you are and what you're doing.*

How did you get on? Did it get easier as you went further into the exercise or did you feel immersed in the setting from the very beginning? Were parts of it very uncomfortable? Did sections make you feel really terrific? Did you discover anything new about yourself in the process? Everyone trying this exercise for the first time has different responses and whatever you personally felt is right for you. Try to remember clearly what you were thinking and feeling through each section of the journey. Which sections were the most vivid? Did you want to move on quickly from others? All this will help expand your thinking process to prepare you for psychic work. How much is out there that we don't know about? Can you think of what you might find on some of those hundreds of different levels within the building? Think of what you'd like to find on some of those other floors.

These exercises can be painful sometimes. It's possible to meet people during them that you either haven't thought of for a long time or people with whom you have unresolved conflicts. Often situations will confront you because the time is right for you to deal with them. It's not necessarily comfortable to do so, but it is a vital part of your growth.

Did you hear that gentle voice talking to you? Then you were probably connecting with your inner voice or higher self, the part you might have thought you didn't possess. If you heard nothing and felt very little, that's fine, too. That was only the first exercise and there are a great many more with which you can experiment. Others may prove more inspiring for you. You might also need to spend some time concentrating on your breathing before you can relax enough to let yourself sink into the exercises. Your breathing is a vital mechanism for your psychic development and will be discussed in detail in a further chapter. This is only the beginning for you.

Whilst on the subject of the beginning, you also need to know the level to which this book goes, and why. It's also appropriate, having just worked with different levels of your building, to consider the various areas of psychic development.

Psychic work can be divided into two specific areas: emotional and mental. The emotional level deals with feelings and senses; it covers an extremely wide range of psychic activities. It encompasses auric reading, psychometry, flower reading, healing, pendulums, dowsing, auragraphs, Tarot cards, Runes, crystal balls and palmistry. All these will be explored in some depth during this book (and some of these can overlap into the mental spheres).

Then there is the mental level which covers clairaudience, clairvoyance, trance, channeling, apports, materialization and automatic writing. All of this requires communication with spirit (energy from a life-force which has passed on) and is not covered in this book. It can only be attained through a high form of discipline and study; reading a book, no matter how wonderful or beautifully-written it may be, cannot prepare you for the mental level of psychic work. A minimum of three to five years' constant study is needed before you can progress to any degree of sustained efficiency, and you need to be under the dedicated guidance of a highly skilled medium. It doesn't mean that people won't have sudden flashes of insight and ability to contact spirit before that, but the contact will be short-lived and unsatisfactory. It can also be dangerous, especially if you receive the presence of an unwanted spirit and are not experienced enough to release it back again to its own world. Even a well-trained psychic can sometimes have difficulties in this area.

This is another reason why the ouija board isn't discussed as a psychic tool. Too often people think of it as a chance to have a good laugh and then, once they tap into energies they can't control, they end up with distressing results. It's another reminder that psychic work isn't a game.

If you do have aspirations to become a medium (making contact with spirit), then you need to start by learning how to work psychically on the emotional level. This is the best foundation you can lay for your future work. Once you start working, you will soon realise the emotional level is an extremely complex and wonderful area that is often under-used in our rush to move on. The discovery of how much we can accomplish in this sphere, makes you realize how much you can apply it to all areas of your life to further enrich yourself.

The following is a useful analogy. Imagine you are taking driving lessons to prepare for your normal car licence. You feel confident about your ability to pass because you are working hard. Then suddenly imagine yourself leaping into a double-decker bus or ten-ton lorry and shooting off down the road. Can you picture the mayhem? There's also another matter to consider. You might discover after driving your car for a while, that you have no desire to get behind the wheel of a large bus or an articulated lorry. You might find that ordinary car travel suits you perfectly without going for your HGV licence. Likewise, many psychics choose to work solely on the emotional level and receive enormous job satisfaction from doing so.

Another word of caution before you delve into your psychic development. There are a lot of areas covered in this book and it would be impossible for you to excel in all of them. No psychic is highly skilled in all these areas. It just isn't possible for that to happen. However, you need to try the different areas offered before you know what form of psychic work resonates best with you. If you just read about flower-reading, for instance, and think, 'No, I'm not very interested in flowers, so that won't work for me', then you might be losing a valuable opportunity to discover something new. You have to actually try each method before you know and you need to try each several times. In psychometry, for example, where you hold an object and 'tune in' to its vibrations, you might chose an inappropriate object the first time and feel nothing from it. You need to go on and experiment several more times before you will really know whether psychometry could work for you. When you find areas that simply don't work for you, despite repeated attempts, don't worry or feel there is something wrong with you.

Particularly with enhancement tools such as the crystal ball and the Tarot cards, people can have varying reactions. Some actually find the

Tarot frightening; others say the cards send their minds spiralling onto higher levels of consciousness and they find themselves talking with an awareness they didn't know they possessed. Some people have found they can stare into a crystal ball for long periods and not even see a glimmer of anything; others find it an Aladdin's cave of precious information. The encouraging truth is that there are so many opportunities open to you that, if you persevere, you will find the path that is right for you. You needn't rush the process. You can take as long as you want, because your development is an intensely personal one.

Just think again for a moment about the visualization exercise you've tried. Try writing down what you feel you got from the exercise, if anything. Do you feel you have moved forward a few steps from the place you were in when you first started reading this Introduction? Are there any aspects of life which you're now thinking about and which make you want to learn more? Are you feeling as though a challenge lies in front of you? You decide what steps you take in life. You're being offered a chance to do something new, but only you decide if it's right for you.

This Introduction has only been able to give you a rough outline of some of the benefits of psychic development. Chapter One looks at what it really means in more practical detail and challenges you to ask some more questions about life.

CHAPTER 1

WHAT ARE THE BENEFITS?

So what are the benefits of developing your psychic abilities? The Introduction was a general look at what you might expect, so let's be more specific now. After all, if you're prepared to spend some time and effort doing some soul-searching and mind-expanding work, you want to reap some rewards. If you go to work to earn a living, you reap rewards: a place to live, food to eat, clothes to buy, a certain life-style and social life. If you enter into a committed relationship with someone you reap benefits: companionship and, hopefully, love, laughter, shared burdens and mutual growth.

To look at your rewards with psychic development, you have to start by thinking about the way people and the world have evolved, especially during the twentieth century. In many ways, life was much simpler before we created our highly technological world. People were less demanding; their needs were basic and they asked for little else. Because of this simplicity, it was easier for them to be in touch with themselves and also, and this is a BIG also, to be in touch with nature.

Our rapidly increasing population has led to a frightening over-crowding of our small planet and many of us are struggling more and more to find a quiet oasis where we won't be disturbed and bombarded by modern-day pressures. Everywhere you turn, you see forests and wild-life being trampled over and destroyed in our frantic quest for so-called 'progress': a better way of life. People want faster cars, bigger houses, higher-paid jobs. But is that what they really want? Is it really making the majority of people happy, filling them with peace, contentment and a clear conscience?

This obsession with material things has finally reached such a crescendo, that people are now beginning to pull back, to say *'Hold on, is this really what life is all about?'* People who once held intensely pressurized, high profile jobs are suddenly opting out and choosing to live a modest life in the country. At long last, our awareness is increasing about what we are doing to this beautiful planet; how we are systematically destroying large areas of it, blasting holes in the ozone layer, wiping out entire species of animals, birds and fish, and creating such polluted environments for humans that they're constantly contracting an ever-widening and bewildering array of illnesses. Living in over-crowded conditions has made humans claustrophobic, aggressive, depressed and angry.

Is all this sounding very negative?

There is the 'upside', too. True to the laws of nature, the negative always has the positive attraction. It's wonderful that we now have levels of hygiene that weren't even dreamt of a century ago. The majority of us wouldn't chose to live without our toilet, bath, hot running water, clean water to drink or our centrally-heated houses in which to take refuge. Our medical break-throughs have led to prolonged life and less physical pain. Not many of us would choose to be without our telephone for contact with the outside world, or our television or radio. An ever-increasing number would find it difficult to cope without their fax, mobile phone or computer systems. Indeed, writing this book without the aid of a computer would make it an exceedingly laborious and far less pleasurable task. How many of us rely regularly on our various forms of transport without which we'd struggle to cope? Be it bicycle, motorbike, car, train, bus or plane, we have now come to depend upon our mobility as a means of life and to be without would make every-day tasks very problematical.

So we have much to be grateful for in this modern existence but, as with everything, it's a question of balance, and we seem to have become badly imbalanced. The good thing is that a lot of us are finally acknowledging this and we're trying to address the situation. There's nothing wrong with enjoying the benefits of our technologically advanced civilization, except that we now need to look at the other side of ourselves to balance life again.

What is the other side? Our spiritual self. Our soul. It's the part of us that, amongst other things, is nurtured and uplifted by walking through a still forest, by strolling along a beach as the waves pound onto the shore, by rowing a boat through a calm stretch of water, by sitting in an empty garden, by finding time for ourselves that is meditative and still.

Stillness. Silence. How often do we achieve that in our life? Try this quick exercise to see for yourself.

STILLNESS

Wherever you are right now, close your eyes for a few minutes. What can you hear? Obvious sounds are road traffic, distant planes, trains, a dog barking, the hum of a refrigerator or a heating system, distant voices or music. Now concentrate even more. Is there a clock ticking? A creak of a floorboard? Can you hear someone's footwear clicking on the pavement outside? Is there a tap dripping? Is the wind rustling in the trees? If you hear a distant voice, try to work out what kind of voice. Male? Female? Child? Adult? What is the tone of voice? Try to really listen for every possible sound around you and analyse it. The deeper you concentrate, the more you will hear. If you concentrate enough, you will hear your own heart beating gently. You'll feel it pulsing through various points in your body, too: chest, neck, wrists, maybe even your fingers and feet. Feel the rhythm of your heartbeat and then take a few slow, deep breaths. Don't strain, just breathe as deeply as feels comfortable for you. If you're relaxed enough, you'll feel your pulse slowing slightly. Take a few more comfortable, slow breaths and then open your eyes slowly. Re-orientate yourself by focusing on an object until it becomes clear to you.

Were you surprised by how many sounds there were when you really stopped to listen? Most people can't believe how many sounds surround them, until they try that exercise. Did it take you a while to hear them all and then, just as you thought you'd acknowledged them all, did you become aware of yet another noise? Perhaps you even heard another sound after that point. What happened when you started becoming aware of your heartbeat? Did the other sounds fade into the distance? Most of them would have still been around you, but did you stop focusing on them? Was it easier to shut out the other noises as you took more deep breaths?

Stillness and silence are hard to achieve in our modern world and it gets harder each day. Most of us can't physically create that around us, so we have to find another way to still ourselves, to slow ourselves down. Only through doing that, can we find our inner self, our spiritual being. How we breathe is a major part of that process. The one exercise above can't accomplish it on its own but it can set you on a new path.

Our breath is our life force and it is also the means through which we accomplish a great deal in psychic work. You need to start becoming more and more aware of your breath and how it affects your body. You need to start acknowledging its tremendous strength and beauty. Further exercise will help develop this appreciation.

How often do you find time for a moment of peace? This doesn't mean sitting in front of the television, reading a book, chatting to a close friend, knitting, or making love. The above are all highly pleasurable past times and they have their place but they are all geared to stimulate various parts of you. They can't offer you a moment of stillness or peace. If you practice yoga, you will have experienced what is being referred to, or tai chi, or any other form of holistic exercise that deals with the mind, body and spirit.

Most of us never take time for ourselves. We feel it's selfish or wrong. Or we don't think we can fit it in to our day, which is crammed full of the practical things like working, eating, sleeping and socializing. Those are the things most of us think of as important. It's self-indulgent to contemplate spending ten or fifteen minutes each day devoted to nothing but being alone and 'doing our own thing'. As for the thought of spending as much as half an hour! It's impossible, isn't it?

This is where psychic development can make an enormous difference to you. It can persuade you to slow down for a small part of each day and teach you how to rejuvenate yourself. You can start with just a few minutes spent in relaxation, in the form of a visualization or a meditation exercise. (Don't worry if you're now thinking that you don't know how to meditate: exercises throughout this book will gradually introduce you to this experience, without specifically using the word meditate. You will be doing it before you know it!)

Perhaps you hadn't realized that renewing your tired energies is also part of the plan and one of its benefits? You see, it's not a selfish act of only thinking of yourself. Setting aside a small time each day to relax and renew yourself will enable others to appreciate you more. Which would the people around you prefer? A tired, grumpy person who flops in front of the television to relax, incommunicative and disinterested in them? Or would they prefer someone who spends a quarter of an hour alone somewhere and then re-emerges to greet those they love with a relaxed attitude, full of warmth and enthusiasm? The difference can be as powerful as that, it really can, provided you are prepared to work at it a bit. One session on your own won't necessarily turn you into a more contented human being but several of them can. Regular trips into your peaceful, spiritual self can accomplish miracles that influence others, not just you. Also, don't under-estimate that whoever you might live with, would also welcome some space sometimes. Have you ever argued over a television programme that one wants to watch but not the other? What a perfect opportunity for one of you to retreat for a little meditation. It can suit both parties.

Is all this making you feel a little more interested? There's a great deal yet to discuss, so read on. (If you're still busy thinking that you can't fit daily meditation into your busy life, try to let that thought go for now. Discussion and exercises will help you later in this book).

If you think about how most people live their lives in the Western World, we are not geared towards spending time with our inner selves. Much of what is discussed in this book has been followed by Eastern philosophies for centuries. It has just taken us a while to catch up. You go to a doctor for your physical problems, a psychiatrist for your mental or emotional problems, but who can you go to for your spiritual problems? Yourself. A wonderful advantage is that meeting your spiritual needs is very likely to improve your other states as well. Many emotional, mental and physical imbalances stem from lack of contact with your inner self. Some people would go so far as to say that all illnesses are as a result of someone not getting in touch with their spiritual self. You don't have to take that on board as a belief but you might like to think about it for a moment.

Another area that psychic development has an enormous effect upon is your sensitivity. In fact, another word for a psychic or medium is the word 'sensitive'. Sensitivity doesn't just mean instinctively knowing more about someone's present state, it means improving your first five senses: touch, smell, taste, hearing and sight. You had an example of intensifying your hearing by doing the Stillness Exercise. Now you can try one that relates to your touch, sight, smell and taste all in one.

FRUIT

Choose a piece of fruit on which to conduct your experiment. (An apple is used in this example but you can use whichever fruit you want). Firstly, hold the apple in your hands and close your eyes. Now, feel it all over; examine every part of it with your fingers, especially using your finger tips because they're an ultra-sensitive part of touch. Is the skin as smooth as you first expected? Is the apple cold or hot? Is it springy or firm? Don't rush any part of this exercise. The more you relish each section, the more you will get out of it.

When you feel you really know what it feels like, move it closer to your nose and, still keeping your eyes closed, smell the apple. Take a deep breath in and feel that breath being sucked all the way down into your stomach, so that you're actually drinking in the smell of it. Is it a sweet smell? Or is it sharp? Are you aware of a slightly chemical odour? Keep taking deep breaths and wallow in the experience of really smelling every nuance of scent. Does the stem part of the apple smell differently from the base?

When you feel you know its odour thoroughly, then open your eyes. Now look at an apple properly, as if for the first time in your life. Study the shape of it. Is it symmetrical? If not, how is one half different from the other? Look at the colour of it and notice how different shades run around the apple. Then look at where the stem grows. Study it intently. What about the base? Now turn your attention to the skin itself. Look at each line and ridge, each tiny indent. Study it for as long as you like. (This exercise can go on for ages. If you've the time, let it). You should now know this apple intimately. You should feel that if you put it in a bowl of apples and got someone to hand you one at random, you'd know straight away if it was yours because you now know there is no other apple like it in the world. No two apples are exactly alike; it's impossible.

Once you feel you could pass that test, then take a bite of it. (As this stage, some of you may feel rather attached to your apple and even feel guilty about eating it! Remember it's only an experiment and apples are nature's gifts, intended for consumption). Bite into it slowly, feeling the juice splash up against your lips, noting the crispness of the flesh and the different texture of the skin. Hold it in your mouth for a moment before you chew, closing your lips together. It's hard to do this because your natural reflexes are to chew. Can you taste much in this state? If so, what? Hold your nose closed for a brief moment. Now can you taste anything? Breathe again through your nose and start to chew, but very slowly and deliberately. Again, this is hard for many people because they usually eat at such a fast rate. Try to chew it for at least thirty chews; it will probably take a great effort not to swallow it before then. Can you define what it tastes like? Most people would just say 'it's an apple taste, that's all', but what is an apple taste? Imagine defining it to a person who has never experienced an apple before. As you swallow, really feel the apple sliding down into your system, feel it nurture and enrich you.

Now you've started eating the apple, you might as well finish it, so as you continue eating, let your thoughts dwell on the apple's origins. It started from a tiny seed, planted in the earth. Think about planting that seed in the soil, covering it and watering it. Think about how the plant was nurtured, drinking in the sun and rain and *goodness from the soil, slowly growing and expanding. Think about the blossoms that came, how they died away and how small apples started to form. Think about their growth, their eventual harvest and the possible journey they made to arrive in your hands. Have you finished the apple now? Open up the core and look at those tiny seeds. If you feel the urge to plant them in a small pot of soil and nurture them, why not do so?*

How did all that feel to you? Strange? Wondrous? Does it make you contemplate all the other things around you that you never fully observe, smell, touch or taste? Do your senses feel slightly heightened now? As you look around you, do colours seem brighter? Do certain objects seem more interesting? Are you aware of new smells in the room? Touch any item around you with your fingertips, perhaps a particle of your clothing. How does that feel? This exercise can go on forever and, in a way, so it should. You have the opportunity to increase your five senses in a practical, day-to-day way. Everything around you can be seen in a new light. After a while you may discover certain items haven't as much appeal to you as before. Or you may find out that you would like some different clothes or objects – or even fruit! You can do this experiment on everything edible and then take away the taste element for other objects. If you have a partner with whom you're comfortable and uninhibited, it's a wonderful means of increasing your awareness and appreciation of each other. The possibilities are endless and as you open your awareness more, you'll discover new elements for yourself.

Now, apart from these five senses, you actually have another two. These probably aren't developed in you, at least, not yet, but they can be. You need to have an understanding of them before you can start discovering them.

Different people and philosophies have various names for these two senses (and some believe there are even more) but it will probably clarify it best to use the words 'Intuition' and 'Knowing' for them.

You may already know a bit about the intuitional sense. It's also sometimes called a kind of gut instinct, a 'feeling in your water' or a 'mother's sense'. (The last seems unfair, as men also possess and demonstrate extraordinary depths of communication with their children.) This intuition comes from contact with outside energies and probably most people have experienced it at some time in their life. Did you know the phone was about to ring even though you weren't expecting a call? Did you know who was calling even though there was no obvious reason for you to know? Have you ever looked into someone's eyes and known that you've met them before? (This often happens when you look into a very young baby's eyes.) Have you ever had a vague sense that something nice was about to happen to you without having a concrete reason for feeling that way? Or, conversely, an uncomfortable premonition that something not so great was going to occur? In case you were wondering, this latter experience is nothing to do with voodoo, black magic or fortune-telling; it's you tapping into energies that are all around us. This is explained in more detail in Chapter Three.

For most people, this intuitional sense usually comes out in short bursts and is not sustainable or reliable. Sometimes we're sure we know something instinctively and we're proved wrong. Then we dismiss our intuition as nothing more than guesswork or co-incidence and we shut down that part of ourselves because we feel inadequate or silly. However, you can learn how to appreciate the difference between guessing something and using your intuitional sense. It's a skill you can develop, just like driving a car or learning to ski, but instead of needing tools such as a vehicle or skis, all you need is yourself and a little quiet time.

The sense of 'Knowing' is more difficult to explain and it's also more difficult to develop. Some of you may have experienced moments of it before but thought it was intuition because you weren't really aware of what was happening. For others, it will be a hard concept to grasp. If you are using your knowing sense you are in communication with your inner self or higher self and there is no element of doubt or any conscious thought in the process. You know because you know and it comes from a deep core within you that is pure and clear in its intention. In fact, the knowing sense isn't related at all to our physical and thought states. It's on another level and until you have experienced

31

it for yourself, you won't quite know what it is. Once it has happened to you, it is unmistakeable and you will always recognize it when it recurs. It's not a sense that can be taken lightly as in, 'I know what that person is like. I just know it'. It's not connected with earthly relationships because it's purely spiritual in nature. Don't worry if this paragraph seems incomprehensible right now. It's enough for you to be willing to acknowledge the possiblity that this sense exists at all. If it doesn't seem remotely possible to you, ask yourself what element of it seems so unlikely. Again, it may just be the newness of the concept that is unnerving you.

So, you're reading that psychic development can increase your five known senses and possibly give you the ability to develop two further ones. How does this relate to you or benefit you in a practical way?

Have you ever wished you could understand people better? If you have a healthy, enquiring mind, you may already have studied people on different levels. Perhaps you are interested in psychology and have already learnt a little about what people's physical mannerisms and speech patterns say about them. You may be interested in design and notice people's clothing and how it relates to their personality. Or you might be able to understand a fair amount about people from their homes and what they choose to have around them. The relationships they choose, their parents and children are all contributing factors, too. If you're a doctor, studying their physical condition can reveal a lot. A dentist can know about their eating habits. A therapist can unravel some of the mysteries of their mind. If you're involved in business communication, you may have spent time on various workshops and training courses where you've discussed people and how they interact and have been able to learn a tremendous amount from that. All these are invaluable aids in understanding people. However, you can spend all your life studying all the above and still be missing a link to understanding people. Why? How can this be?

It's because you're not looking into their soul. You can't look into a person's soul by taking an X-ray or studying their physical, emotional or mental habits. Their very physical experience on this earth is not the same as their spiritual core. There's a good saying:

'We're not physical beings having a spiritual experience.
We're spiritual beings having an earthly experience.'

Again, this is a challenging statement and many of you may not agree with it or be willing to embrace it wholeheartedly: at least, not yet! Chapter 2, in discussing karma, goes into this in more detail. Yet, if you could accept this belief, doesn't it help explain why all the study in the world about people doesn't fully satisfy your feeling so far as wanting to know and understand people more deeply?

This book is about helping you work towards achieving that greater level of understanding. It's about releasing energies trapped within you and enabling you to connect with everyone. It's about experiencing love on a new level, where you love unconditionally. It's where you love everyone, irrespective of their personality, behaviour or physical condition. It's about true acceptance of people exactly as they are. Does this sound impossible? Does it seem unrealistic to strive for this? It's only because you're trying to limit yourself. People thought that Columbus was crazy for saying that the earth was round, that Edison was incapable of creating this new-fangled light-bulb, and that Gandhi and Nelson Mandela had pie-in-the-sky dreams that would never materialize. In fact, look back through history and most of the amazing events, revelations and inventions were initially ridiculed. People used to say the television would never last! We are a cynical, suspicious species, aren't we?

Think back over the intuitional sense you've been reading about. Did you know that extensive studies have been carried out on animals and there is now clear evidence that a wide range of animals have a highly developed intuitional sense? Recently a series of experiments were carried out on pet dogs and their owners, to test animal behaviour under controlled conditions. A camera was placed inside a front door where a dog would lie in wait for its owner's return. The owner was then instructed to return home at varying times of the day, deliberately avoiding the usual return time. They also made the owner return from different locations, too, not their normal place of work, requiring different lengths of travel time. An astonishingly high proportion of the dogs reacted by either standing up, moving to the door, barking, or scratching and sniffing at the door, often wagging their tail furiously. When did they do this? At the moment the owner was thinking of, or in the early stages of, preparing to return home, not as the owner was approaching the front door itself. It wasn't possible to dismiss the tests as co-incidence because so many were carried out on a variety of dogs.

Animals haven't been instilled with human cynicism. They are instinctive, not reflective, in their behaviour. We believe certain things won't work, usually because other people tell us they won't, so we programme our brain not to respond and pretty soon that area of our brain is shut down and becomes rusty.

There is another part of us that also needs rejuvenating. It was touched on briefly earlier in this chapter: appreciation of nature, a fundamental life force of this planet and one we abuse and disregard constantly. Animals, especially in their native habitat, respond to and interact with nature with an instinctive, reflex action. As humans we also have that ability, but we have buried it through generations of supposedly refined human progress. When you read earlier that people of a few centures ago were more in touch with themselves, that wasn't to imply that they went around discussing each other's souls and consciously developing their psychic awareness. They worked on a more instinctive level. More often than not, they had to work the land to survive, by building their own homes from natural, available materials and growing their own food to eat. Their very beings were steeped in appreciation of the earth and nature and how it would nurture and support them. They had to harmonize with it to survive. That is the element we have mostly lost in our modern world and we need to recapture that awe, that appreciation.

Did you have a flash of that wonderment when you were nearing the end of the Fruit Exercise and you started to think about the apple's origins and its progression through to your hand? It's a powerful thought process for many people. Whether or not it touched you, if you want to develop psychic awareness, you need to spend time developing your appreciation, and understanding, of nature. You may already be someone who loves to walk in the woods or the park, or who enjoys walking along a seashore or who get pleasure from taking off in a boat somewhere. In fact, almost everyone enjoys that sort of experience when they manage to find time for it. It leaves them refreshed and revitalized and also helps lift depression and stress. Do you know why nature has this effect? It's because we are unconsciously drawing its healing energies into our system. It's those very energies that you will be using to develop your psychic abilities. Does that sound too simple? It's true. The discipline required to work with those energies is the more complicated area: learning to control and shape that energy.

Next time you take your walk or sit quietly in your garden, try applying the Fruit Exercise to what is around you, but do include the Stillness Exercise as well. This will enhance your ability to appreciate nature and you may find yourself slipping into a higher level of consciousness without even realizing you are doing so. Remember to keep asking yourself questions about everything you see, hear, smell, touch and taste.

There is one more benefit to consider before we leave this chapter: your ability to help others through psychic awareness. Obviously, this is an enormously important benefit. You will be given the opportunity through this work to help people on many levels; healing, flower reading and auragraphs can be particularly powerful areas. You will have the wonderfully uplifting ability to comfort, nurture and love others in a deeply satisfying way. Very few human experiences can surpass the joy that brings. However, this benefit has its other side; it can be dangerous. It needs to be treated with the greatest respect and sensitivity because, with that growing ability to help others, comes an overwhelming responsibility. The content and phraseology you use with people has to be considered closely before you start practising, because otherwise you will end up in distressing situations. This won't happen if you observe a number of ground rules and never swerve from them. They're listed in detail in Chapter 11 and you need to read and then re-read them until they're imprinted in your brain. You must never forget that you are completely responsible for someone's well-being when you are giving them a reading, whatever level you are working on. Failure to do this, will result in unpleasant forces bouncing back at you. Remember the brief discussion on karma? That is the subject of the next chapter.

So, to sum up, here are the benefits you may reap from entering into psychic development:

- *the opportunity to discover new areas of yourself, including your inner self*

- *how to relax and let go of stress*

- *the chance to be a better companion to those around you*

- *expanding your consciousness to encompass new concepts and beliefs*

- *seeing people and the universe in a much deeper context by the purpose of life*

- *the higher development of your five senses*

- *the discovery and development of your two further senses*

- *a more intimate relationship with a partner*

- *a greater appreciation of nature and its power*

- *the chance to experience universal energy and to learn how to channel and control it*

- *respect for people as a whole*

- *an unconditional love for people and the world*

- *developing a deep gift to comfort and nurture others.*

It's an impressive list. Psychic work can offer a great deal. Not that every one of you reading this book will necessarily end up experiencing all those benefits. You also have some work to do before you can go out and practise on other people. And only you can decide if you're ready to take this plunge or not. Perhaps you should just read through this whole book before you make up your mind. However, what you should know is that, if you faithfully follow the path laid out for you in this book, you can do it; everyone can.

It seems fitting to close this chapter with a saying from Goethe (although you don't have to believe it!):

> *'Whatever you can do, or dream you can, begin it.*
> *Boldness has genius, power and magic in it.'*

CHAPTER 2

KARMA AND REINCARNATION

So what is karma and why is it so important to know about it before you start psychic development? Karma is the law of cause and effect; understanding this law and its repercussions will protect you and, hopefully, prevent you from making any dangerous or foolish mistakes. Grasping the concept of karma is also another means through which you expand your awareness levels.

The word karma is from the Sanskrit meaning 'action' (some translate it as 'deed' or 'fate') and it's said to have originated in India between two and three hundred years before Buddhism. The law of karma states that as we sow, so shall we reap. In other words, everything we think, say and do becomes part of an energy or force that we send out into the universe, and that energy will then return to us. Put simply, if you do harm to others, harm will come to you. If you give out love, then love comes back. It's also said that whatever you send out, comes back to you with doubled intensity. If you haven't spent much time considering karma before, then your initial reaction is likely to be one of cynicism. That's fine, but now start to think a bit deeper.

Go over areas in your life where you can see a possible 'cause and effect' scenario. It might be in the workplace, where you treated someone badly in your effort for promotion. Did someone then treat you in a similar fashion? Have you been the one to break up a relationship, perhaps not handling it very well, and then had your next partner end the relationship, treating you in a like manner? Did you have a difficult relationship with your parents and do you now have difficulties with your own child? Have you ever stolen from someone and then had a commensurate item stolen from you? Have you started the day in an angry mood and noticed how other angry people are attracted to you? Likewise, if you feel particularly loving one day, have you had others be very loving in return? A good example is if you're in a rush to get somewhere and you need a helping hand: a driver to give way at a busy crossing, or a train to come along swiftly. Have you noticed whenever you're in this situation that if you're irritated and tense, everything goes wrong? However, if you remain calm and focused, refusing to panic, does the situation smooth itself out? If you feel an argument brewing with someone and you're both getting more and more worked up, are you not simply giving out anger and receiving it back? What if one of you suddenly backs down and refuses to fight, expressing instead their love and concern for the other person? Do you think it's very likely they'll still retaliate angrily? Love is a very powerful force.

These are simple examples but karma is a little more complex than that. It's been embraced by a wealth of influential people since its conception. Everyone from Pythagoras and Plato to our modern-day Theosophists have lived their life adhering to its law, as well as many millions in between.

To explain the concept a little more fully: karma is basically carried with us, and is the effect of all that we have thought, said and done both in the present and from our past. So it isn't just how we treat people and the world today, it's also an accumulation of everything we did in the past. Everything remains with us, good and bad, until we choose to look at it and change the balance by our present and future thoughts, words and deeds.

Karma contains three elements: the initial thought, the will to put it into action and then the union of the thought and will which transforms it into action. Here's a very basic example. You feel incredibly angry towards someone and you think of killing them. At this stage, only the thoughts are going out into the universe as a force or energy. Then you decide you will kill that person. At this level, the energy changes again as you prepare for what you intend to do. Then your thought and will are united if you finally kill that person. The energy level increases accordingly. Those three separate levels determine the intensity of your karma. In other words, hatred in the heart is not so heavy a karma as hatred which has been transformed into physical or verbal action. It doesn't mean that carrying hatred around with you is acceptable, whilst killing is not. Any destructive emotion will only help destroy you, not someone else.

In fact, do you now see how futile our negative emotions and behaviour are, if you look at it on a karmic level? If you're carrying resentment, fear, anger or frustration around with you, how does it affect anyone but you? You may resent a parent for not raising you as you would have wished, you may feel let down by a friend, you may loathe your partner for leaving you for someone else, you may be angry you didn't get a job that you wanted. What benefit does it have for you to hold on to all those emotions? Can you think of any, apart from revenge? Yet how does revenge prove to be an answer if it's all going to rebound back on you, anyway?

If you're now starting to think it might be nice to release some of those negative emotions, keep reading, as further exercises will suggest ways you can start to do this.

Do you feel you are developing an understanding about karma? If the word itself puts you off, you can always think of it simply as energies that we give out and that hang about before returning, rather like an atmosphere or an odour in the air. You don't have to embrace it completely and decide to live your life by it, but it's important that you're willing to consider the possibility of its existence and effect.

Where does karma relate to psychic work, apart from the obvious warning that if you intend to use psychic skills for power or domination, you'll be in for some nasty experiences? After all, most people reading this book will intend their work for positive purposes, not negative. Karma is relevant to psychic work because it will help you understand your responsibility to the people with whom you're working. It's part of the human conditioning for survival, that if we know any action may harm us, we think twice before acting. Your intention will, hopefully, be to offer helpful readings at all times, but intending to do a good job isn't the same as believing it's vital for you to do so.

As mentioned at the start of this chapter, you can also use the concept of karma as a mind-expanding tool and for meditative purposes. Below is a good exercise with which you can start. Remember to ensure you won't be interrupted half-way through the meditation. You need to be alone and to feel safe and warm before you start.

KARMA

Choose one person towards whom you know you want to change your karma. It doesn't matter if they are young or old, a close friend or a casual acquaintance. It could just be a work colleague you snapped at recently, or a friend whose actions have irritated you recently. Try to be gentle with yourself for the first attempt. If, for instance, the thought of someone brings up very strong emotions in you, then leave them until later. Choose a person with whom you'd like to sort out a few things, but not heavy issues.

Now settle yourself comfortably into a chair and close your eyes. You can lie down if you prefer. Start by taking a few deep, slow, comfortable breaths. Don't force them, just feel your body relax as you breathe in and out. Concentrate on your breathing and let outside sounds drift off into the distance.

When you feel relaxed, imagine you are sitting in your ideal setting. This could be a beach, a forest, or by a waterfall. Perhaps you want it to be a building which represents a sanctuary to you; it doesn't matter where, as long as it makes you feel good. Try to make it as vivid as possible. If you choose a garden, what flowers, bushes and trees are around you? Is it all grass or are there paved areas? Spend time creating the setting exactly as you want it.

Now move yourself into that space and sit or stand or do wherever feels right for you. Maybe you want to lie in the grass or swim in the sea. You have the freedom to place yourself wherever you want, provided it makes you feel good. As you settle yourself, feeling happy and content, you then see the other person approach you. Instead of feeling anger or fear or resentment, you are pleased to see them. You want to sort out the conflict. As they come closer, you realize how special they are. You see into their soul and appreciate their beauty. You smile at them and they smile back at you. You ask them to come and join you. You may even want to hug or kiss them. Then say whatever you need to say to sort out the problem. Sometimes, it feels unnecessary to say anything; sometimes looking into the other person's eyes and then hugging them says it all. If you want to do more, then explain how you were feeling or why you did what you did. They may just smile back at you, or they may even reply. They may explain what was happening to them or why what you did doesn't matter now. Keep talking until you feel you have sorted out the conflict. All the time that you are looking at them, you realize more and more how special they are, and how you didn't truly appreciate that before.

When you know that any negative emotions have been wiped away, explain you must leave now, but you will see them again soon. Say good-bye in a loving way that seems appropriate for you both, and then see them turn and walk away into the distance. You may then choose to stay by yourself in your sacred setting and reflect on what has been said.

When you feel ready, move yourself out of your picture and then return to where you were when you started the meditation. Take a few comfortable breaths and remember where you are now, before slowly opening your eyes and re-orienting yourself. Don't get up or move suddenly when you open your eyes. It's important you give yourself time to adjust again.

That meditation can have powerful results, particularly the more you practise it. However, it's very important that you start by looking at people with whom your conflicts are small. Were you surprised by the strength of your emotions during it? What often happens is that we discover that the person with whom we were having problems isn't the cause of our emotion. We realize we may have off-loaded some feelings onto them, but they originated from another source. Powerful insights can occur and they can give you food for thought about yourself and how you treat others. It also gives you the opportunity to experience compassion for someone, looking past their physical being, into their soul. Of course, this may not be possible on your first attempt. You may even find you can't rid yourself of the conflict initially and that is fine, too. Remember you can go back there at any time and continue sorting out problems. Once you feel you can handle your emotions on a deeper level, you can then tackle someone with whom you know you have a lot to sort out. Then it is unlikely you'll be able to clear everything up in one meditation. The joy of it is that no one is watching you or judging you and you can take as long as you like. This can be an ongoing project in your life, that you delve into when you feel the time is right.

A word of warning. This meditation isn't meant to replace sorting things out with people in a physical, literal sense. Just because you now feel good about someone, doesn't mean they necessarily feel that way about you! After all, they haven't been party to your experience. So you still need, next time you see them, to speak to them, or offer them a hug. What you may find is that something unusual does happen when you next see them. This is quite hard to explain, but you may find that they aren't as upset as you expected, or that they have a softer, more understanding response than the one you were anticipating. This is because you have already set in motion the possibility of the energies changing between you. This is hard to believe in the beginning but once you have done a few meditations and seen the results, you will know it really does happen. Your thought process alone has started the ball rolling. In a further chapter, you'll read about Absent Healing, where you can send healing to someone without their realizing it. The results then can also be wonderfully rewarding and it works on a similar principle. There is nothing like seeing the karmic law in action for you to appreciate it and to want to pursue its power, by introducing it into all areas of your life.

As you've been considering the concepts outlined in this chapter, have you also been thinking that something isn't quite right? Have you been thinking about people you know who are terrific souls, and yet they seem dogged by bad luck? People who, no matter what they do, seem to have a tough life? What about young, innocent children who do no wrong and yet are abused or mistreated? What about wars, when scores of innocent people are tortured and killed? You'll no doubt be able to think of many occasions when life isn't at all fair. So how can karma then work on that level?

You now need to go into this more deeply by introducing the concept of reincarnation. This is the belief that when our physical body dies our soul lives on and is then re-introduced into other physical bodies. In other words, our soul is separate from our physical being. Our soul is ever-lasting and constantly in a state of growth and change. We live different physical lives because our soul has many lessons to learn and cannot learn them all in one lifetime. You will probably have heard of reincarnation before but may not have spent much time thinking about it. Now is the chance for you to consider it on a deeper level. Reincarnation is harder to accept only because we haven't concrete proof of it. We can experience karma because we can watch it work during this lifetime, but most of us have no conscious memory of previous lives, so how can we be sure?

The answer lies in looking within rather than seeking physical proof. The belief in reincarnation can develop slowly from total disbelief, to a very vague possibility, to a glimmer of insight, to increased understanding, to deep interest, to a higher level of appreciation, through to an unshakeable sense of knowing (as opposed to believing). The process may be gradual or accelerate at speed. Some of you may remain at the vague possibility level with the occasional insight to keep your interest alive. If you are stuck in total disbelief, it will make your psychic development slower, but it won't make it impossible. You will only be able to work at a certain level, i.e. the emotional level discussed during this book. Any experience on the mental level wouldn't work for you because communication with spirit would be hampered by your lack of belief.

What can you do to help your understanding of reincarnation? (Again, reincarnation is another wonderful tool for mind-expansion, all part of your psychic development.) Consider the following questions. Have you ever looked into a very young baby's eyes, as young as a few months, and been overwhelmed by their wise, knowing eyes? Or have you seen a three or four-year-old utter or do something that is far beyond their present level of comprehension? Might it explain child prodigies, past and present, and where their abilities have come from? Do you have any fears or phobias in your life that you cannot explain using rational terms? In other words, do you have a fear of something such as water without having had any distressing experience related to water during your life? Have you ever travelled somewhere new and then had the unmistakeable sensation that you've been there before and know it quite well already? Have you met someone and felt on the very first meeting that you've known them before and have some indefinable connection with them? Have some of these questions started to make you consider the feasibility of reincarnation?

The hardened cynics among you will want to find rational, earthly explanations for all the thoughts above. You'll want to say it's coincidence that babies look wise; child prodigies are just smarter-than-average children; human fears are just about being human, nothing to do with past-life experiences; feeling you've known someone before is only about chemistry between people. So you need to look deeper.

For instance, why has this concept been believed by so many people for so long? Surely, there must be some good reasons for so many to follow its teaching. You can go back as far as the ancient Greeks. Pythagoras, Plato and Plotinus were all convinced of the truth of reincarnation and it's been adopted by equally influential people throughout history, right up to our present day. It's spanned many professions: scientists, doctors, philosophers, psychologists, politicians and poets. Here are some of them: Dante, Kant, Goethe, Blake, Napoleon, Schiller, Nietsche, Franklin, Emerson, Thoreau, Whitman and Jung. Teachings based on are followed by a wealth of religions. To name but a few: Hinduism, Buddhism, Taoism, Native American, Shamanism and Theosophy. In fact, until a couple of hundred years ago, when science and materialism began to take over, reincarnation was virtually a universal belief. Again, this is another example of humans losing touch with their spiritual being through our so-called progress. So rather than reincarnation being a new concept to grasp, it's more a question of re-discovering what is already deep inside our sub-conscious. If you're willing to take on board the concept that we have a spiritual being, an inner self, that is not our physical body, then can you further expand your thoughts to consider that although our physical body disintegrates, our soul may not?

To quote a passage from the Bhagavad-Gita, which is part of the Hindu Scriptures:

'As man casts off his worn-out clothes and takes on other new ones, so does the embodied soul cast off its worn-out bodies and enters other new ones.'

References to reincarnation are found frequently in poetry throughout the ages. Do you know the often-quoted passage from William Wordsworth?

'Our birth is but a sleep and a forgetting:
The soul that rises with us, our life's star,
Hath had elsewhere its setting,
And cometh from afar.'

Perhaps you know those lines but have never connected them with the concept of reincarnation. If you start reading more poetry, you'll probably be quite taken aback by the constant references to an after-life and to the effects of karmic law. Why is it found so often among poems, in particular? Perhaps it's because poets are often soul-searchers and use their work as a means of expressing their inner self. Also, as poetry is often a very lyrical form of expression, do we not find it easier to accept than if the words had been written in a factual book? Perhaps we should all read more poetry to improve contact with our own spiritual selves.

However, on to a more factual aspect of reincarnation. What about some of the experiences that have taken place under hypnosis? There are countless examples of people who have given detailed accounts of past lives whilst under hypnosis, revealing precise information that they could not have gleaned from reading historical books.

Possibly one of the best-known cases is the account of Bridey Murphy. Bridey Murphy was believed to be an Irish girl, born in Cork in 1798, daughter of a Protestant Cork barrister, Duncan Murphy. She was supposedly reincarnated in the twentieth century as Mrs Virginia Burns Tighe, and it was Mrs Tighe, an American, who gave six sittings under hypnosis to Mr Morey Bernstein, during the 1950s in the U.S.A. Her account under hypnosis contained so many small, highly detailed incidents and colloquial expressions peculiar to that period of history that it's impossible for Mrs. Tighe to have known them from her life in America. Although there are earlier reports of hypnosis revealing possible past lives, Bridey Murphy's account was the first to receive wide-spread publicity and, as a result, thorough scrutiny. It definitely remains one of the most thought-provoking studies on reincarnation under hypnosis. Of course, there are sceptics who believe Mrs Tighe's experience was connected to the fact that she was part-descended from the Irish; possibly her account was connected with some telepathic or clairvoyant experience, as opposed to having anything to do with a past life. However, if you read details of the case, the evidence remains overwhelming.

A more modern experience of reincarnation has been documented by Jenny Cockell in Britain. Ever since she could remember, Jenny Cockell had clear memories of her past life as another woman called Mary, who died more than twenty years before Jenny was born. What makes this case particularly interesting is that Jenny actually managed to trace Mary's remaining family through her strong memories of past events, and met up with them. Her extraordinary account is detailed in her book, 'Yesterday's Children'. Jenny Cockell's experience also helps to clarify a problem many people have when it comes to reincarnation. So often people discount the possibility of having lived before, because they argue that everyone should be able to remember past lives. Jenny Cockell's strong memories of a previous life caused her great distress and confusion for much of her present life, enabling her neither to enjoy her present existence nor to understand her past. It's a good example of the effect of conscious past-life memories. Most of us have enough difficulty coping with our present life, without dragging up another complex scenario of a previous life. However, these past-life memories remain within the subconscious and can be tapped into under controlled conditions.

There are a number of books available, detailing other people's experience of past lives and if you feel you want to know more, most bookshops and libraries will have details.

Embracing the concept of reincarnation, together with karma, gives a shape and purpose to our lives. If we believe our karma travels with us from life to life, it also explains why some people lead troubled lives now, without apparent explanation. They are following their own karmic route, influenced by past lives, details of which they probably don't recollect. It makes you take responsibility for your own existence and gives you a desire to want to learn, to want to achieve higher levels of consciousness. You see why it is such an important part of psychic development.

If you believe we are only given experiences that will enrich and nurture, no matter how tough those experiences may seem, you can then learn an acceptance of what is around you and what is happening to you, rather than descending into bitterness and resentment. If you choose to react angrily and vengefully towards what life throws at you, you will only attract more of the same experiences until you truly learn and grow from the process.

It's not always an easy path. Lessons are hard to learn sometimes and we often want to give up en route and go back into old, familiar patterns, even if they do make us feel miserable. At least we feel safe with them. Yet psychic development is not about diving off into the unknown abyss: it's about re-discovering what is already within us. As Marcel Proust said:

'The real act of discovery consists not in finding new lands but in seeing with new eyes.'

To finish off this chapter, here are two exercises that will further assist your thought processes. You don't need to do both; choose the one you feel most drawn towards. If both interest you, then try them on separate occasions. They are also geared towards relaxing you and freeing tension.

THE BIRD

Choose a bird with which you feel the greatest affinity. (It must be one that can fly). If your mind draws a blank, choose from one of the following: sparrow, robin, crow, eagle, or owl. Close your eyes, and imagine yourself stepping outside your front or back door. As you do so, the bird of your choice flies down and lands in front of you. It asks you to hop onto its back. It seems natural that it's talking to you but how could you possibly fit onto its back when it's so tiny and you're so large? As you're pondering the problem, you are suddenly on its back, resting comfortably on its soft feathers.

It takes off into the air and you suddenly realize there's a magnetic force between you and the bird such that, however it moves, you move with it, as though you were both one and the same. Knowing that, you relax into its feathery down and enjoy the exquisite pleasure of flying off into the sky. To begin with, your bird stays quite close to the ground, but you feel so secure you want it to go higher. It circles above where you live, gradually climbing higher and higher. You look down on where you live. It's getting smaller amd smaller. How does that make you feel? You see the other buildings around it and see it in a different perspective. What about the lives of all those other people? You're climbing higher now. The air feels softer, fresher. You feel it caressing your skin and then, as you breathe in its fragrance, you feel it filling the inside of you. It feels warming, revitalizing. The higher you climb, the freer, the more alive, and the more relaxed you feel.

Your home is but a dot in the distance now as you break through into the clouds. They feel like soft cotton wool brushing gently against you. The bird pauses to rest on a cloud and you watch the world swirling below you as the cloud carries you along to different areas. You see land masses and mountains and bodies of water. You realize how vast the world is and what an infinitesimal dot your home is on the earth's landscape. You start wondering about all the other countries and their people, about their customs and beliefs. How many of them have spiritual values that you've never considered before?

Your bird now takes off again, higher into the universe. Everything is becoming brighter and lighter and even more beautiful. You see stars and planets. You are drinking in the beauty of the universe when you become aware of something more in the far, far distance. Is it a new planet? An undiscovered star? You strain your eyes to see it, but it remains elusive. You know that something new is out there. You know it's something very special, something you want to experience. You ask the bird to fly nearer, but he explains that he can't. Not yet. Your curiosity is aroused. What is that new and unexplored something? You are drawn powerfully towards it. You ask the bird why it's so important. It explains that the entity in the distance is Enlightenment and you can only reach it when you are ready. Your journey has started but you still have a distance to travel. You don't have the means to complete that path yet. The bird gently informs you that you must return to your home now. Slowly, it starts its descent.

You reluctantly leave the planets and stars behind as you fly back, through the clouds and down towards your home. The bird gently lands at your door and as you step off, you are back to your earth size and the bird is now at your feet. It explains that you can call on it any time you want to explore further. All you have to do is call it. You ask the bird its name and it tells you. This is the name you use to call it in the future. You thank him for the journey and watch as he flies off into the sky. You are sorry to see him go but you know you have work to do on this planet. You know you can't reach Enlightenment until you have completed more of this life's experiences. You feel refreshed and re-energized by your flight; you have a renewed sense of purpose and an increased confidence in the future.

You walk back in through your door and return to the start of your meditation. Breathe slowly and gently for a few minutes before you open your eyes and re-adjust to your surroundings.

Have you ever flown in your dreams before? If so, the sensation in this meditation won't be new to you, but it'll no doubt prove just as enjoyable. This is an especially good exercise to do if you are feeling weighed down by mundane, routine tasks. It puts them into perspective and lets you analyse your life on a more objective level. Spend as much time as you like looking down on your home before the bird takes off any higher. At that moment, you may gain valuable insights into what is and isn't important in life and how you can rebalance some of your priorities. Your bird is a valuable friend and guide, so get to know it well. As you fly more, it may want to talk and discuss aspects of life with you. Open yourself up to your new friendship and let it enrich you.

Now, here's the second exercise for you to try when you feel ready.

THE FISH

Close your eyes and imagine you are on a beach and it's a hot, sunny day. Create the beach as you want it: sandy or pebbly, large or small, with trees or rocks. You're lying on the beach, enjoying the feeling of warmth and peace. No one else is around. After a few minutes, you realize you're quite hot, so you decide to have a swim.

You walk down to the water's edge and put your toes into the water. It feels refreshingly cool and tingly on your skin. Slowly you walk in, enjoying the sensation of the water lapping around your skin. You start to swim, conscious of the lulling sensation of the waves. Lazily, you turn over onto your back and gaze up at the rich blue sky. A few gulls are flying overhead. Everything feels peaceful and soothing. You float in the water, feeling all the tension and stress oozing from your muscles. Each ripple of the water against your skin makes you feel more comfortable and contented.

As you lie there, you become conscious of something nudging against you under the water. You turn over and see, just below you in the water, a fish. The fish is whatever species, size and colour you want it to be. You might prefer to make it a mammal instead, such as a dolphin. Create what feels right for you. As you look at your fish, you realize it wants you to swim under the water with it. It explains that you'll be able to breathe. It wants to show you the wonders of the sea. You watch its beauty as it swims smoothly below you and know you want to experience what it's offering.

You slide onto its back and hold onto its fins or gills. Then you glide effortlessly under the water. The water all around you feels wonderful as you realize you can breathe normally, just as the fish said you would. Your new friend swims slowly, gently down into the deeper water and you stay on its back without any difficulty, as though you were moulded together as one object. You are stunned by the beauty of this new world. You are passing different plants, a myriad of other fish and sea-life and banks of coral as you head down onto the sea bed. It is unexpectedly colourful, vibrating with a wonderful energy, and heavenly in its silence.

You reach the bottom of the sea and slide off your fish so that you may sit on the bottom of the sea for a while. Your fish understands your need and swims quietly nearby. You watch all the sea-life around you and marvel at its existence. Why have you not realized before just how amazing this world is under the sea? Why have you never stopped to think of it in the past? You notice all the sea creatures seem to communicate with one another without any sound or movement. They seem to have invisible links that connect them; an energy seems to flow through and around them that renders verbal or physical contact unnecessary. You know that humans could achieve that same state of communication if they only spent more time observing these creatures and learning from them. You soak in this sensation of peace and perfect harmony and determine that you will start to create that in your relationships with others. You realize this silence and stillness is an essential part of you and you want to spend more time in this state. You start thinking about how you might attain this high degree of communication with people. Is it not about awareness and sensitivity to others; isn't it to do with an appreciation of everything around you and how it all vibrates and resonates together?

You are still mesmerized by the beauty you have discovered and your new insights when your fish gently nudges you, brushing itself against your skin. It's saying you must now return. You have your work to do outside the seaworld. You slide onto its back again and enjoy the pleasurable sensation as you glide up through the water. Again, you feel connected to your fish, as though you were both one. You realize you have discovered a harmony, a spiritual connection with your new friend that enables you to relate to one another on a deep level. You realize that you haven't been speaking to your fish at all; your conversations have been taking place through a form of mental telepathy. You understand each other without words because words aren't necessary.

The fish gently deposits you on the surface of the water again and, as you bob up, you feel the warm sun shining down on your body. You turn to your fish under the water and, without speaking, ask its name. It answers in the same fashion and you repeat its name, knowing you can call to it when you next want to travel to that wondrous world of the sea. The fish glides off into the waters' depths and you slowly turn and swim to the shore. The sun feels comforting and welcoming now, without feeling too hot. You lie down to let your skin dry off and contemplate what you have just discovered. You think more about how you can create communication without words or touch and resolve to increase that awareness of people and nature.

You know you are dry now and slowly get up, returning to the start of your meditation. Breathe deeply for a minute or two before you open your eyes. Then focus on a nearby object and remember where you are and what is happening around you, before you get up.

If you haven't experienced deep-sea diving before, either first-hand or on television programmes, then you'll probably be amazed by the beauty you witnessed. You see, your knowledge of the sea's beauty was already there in your sub-conscious; all you have to do is call upon it when you feel the urge to do so. Your fish can become a friend and guide, just like your bird in the earlier exercise. You should feel refreshed after both exercises, energized by your thoughts and discoveries.

A little while later, you may find your usual pattern of nagging doubts come creeping back to haunt you. You may wonder if you were only day-dreaming and if your new thoughts about karma and reincarnation are just silly. Remember that every new concept is usually ridiculed initially. You're only behaving in a very human fashion. To help rid yourself of these doubts, keep questioning your life and your actions. What further examples of possible cause and effect can you find in your day-to-day existence? Read other, more detailed books on reincarnation and what has been discovered under hypnosis.

Lastly, can you think back to any occasion when you saw a lifeless body? It needn't have been a human body; you can have the same experience by looking at an animal after it has passed over. If you have, you may already understand the following sentiment. Looking at a lifeless body, you suddenly realize the person you once knew is simply not there any longer. Their shell, their outer case, may lie there, but their soul is not present. You can tell it has actually departed from the body itself because their very essence, their very being, is no longer around. Highly skilled psychics talk of actually witnessing the soul leaving the body upon death: a fine, vibrational energy that slowly separates from the body and drifts upwards into infinity.

So what is the actual definition of this word 'energy' that has cropped up rather a lot in this book? You've been told that karma can be likened to energy. Is this the same energy that psychics see at death? Aren't there different kinds of energy? How does it affect us? How can energy be so powerful that we can use it in psychic development? This is the next topic under consideration in Chapter 3.

CHAPTER 3

LOOKING AT ENERGY

There are different types of energy and you'll need to have at least a basic understanding of them to progress psychically. For work in this book, differentiating energy into three groups should be sufficient. You will need to use all three during your work.

Firstly, there is the energy that you will use in opening yourself up to prepare for psychic work. You learn to draw upon this energy by visualizing it. You then bring it down into your own system, and thereafter learn to control it and move it through your body as necessary, depending on the level at which you're working. This will still sound fairly impossible at this stage, but further exercises will show it to be less daunting than it sounds. This energy is pure, infinite and of the highest vibration. It's often called cosmic energy.

Secondly, there is the earth's energy. This emanates from the earth's very core and resonates around and through every part of what we would call nature: every stone, blade of grass, flower, plant and tree. You could call this the energy of Mother Nature. Psychics use this as a means of grounding themselves during work. As the cosmic energy (mentioned above) is a very powerful, heady substance, the earth's energy is needed as a balance to help you work effectively. Remember earlier discussions about how we should never forget that our physical body is just as important as our spiritual self? Earth energy is part of that grounding, physical process. It is through this grounding that we also increase our connection with our inner self. To repeat, it's part of the balancing act we need in order to work properly. This energy is often called universal energy but because to many people that implies the universe, as in the cosmos, it's being called earth energy to help avoid confusion.

Thirdly, there is human energy, often called the aura. This is our own energy that we carry around with us and it is therefore emanating from us at all times. Psychics tap into this energy during a reading, to understand and to 'read' others. This energy is constantly changing and is extremely complex in its entirety. It is made up of many influencing factors and the study of it is a lifetime's challenge. There are seven layers of increasingly finer and higher energies but you will only have the opportunity to look at the first few layers during this book. Many highly trained psychics can't even see the sixth and seventh layers. The human aura is given a chapter of its own but in this chapter you'll be looking at cosmic and earth energies.

Let's start with cosmic energy. This is the most difficult energy to define, the most difficult to actually see and yet, paradoxically, probably the most easy to draw upon and use as a psychic. As you've already read, it is pure, infinite and of the highest vibration. It comes from the cosmos and pours down in abundance. You can use it at any time, not just to increase psychic awareness, but as a cleansing and re-energizing experience. You may initially find the concept of its existence hard to accept but just one opening up session in which you feel the energy for yourself is quite sufficient to assure you beyond any doubt of its presence.

So where does it come from? Many people say this source of pure white light and energy comes from God. Others use their own word for God: Allah or Buddha, for instance. However, you do not need to affiliate this to any religious experience. As mentioned in the Introduction, psychic work is not an exclusively religious phenomenon: it's a spiritual path. If you are now opening your mind to belief in a soul as well as a physical body, if you are beginning to grasp the concepts of karma and reincarnation, if you are feeling that there may be some great, higher consciousness out there, related to our souls, that can offer supreme wisdom – then why not believe this pure energy comes from that source? You don't have to call it God, unless that feels true to you. If you want to put a name on it, you can use a non-religious title, such as Great Spirit, Universal One, Supreme Soul; you can make up a name that seems appropriate to you.

No psychic teacher should decree this source has only one name. For example, a group of psychics are working together in one room. They all call upon the energy in their own way; one silently calls upon God, another thinks of Heavenly Father, another calls upon the Great Universal Spirit. Their names make no difference to the energy that streams into the room; it pours down from above as powerfully as ever. It can be any name that resonates powerfully for you. It's the thought process that creates the power and you have to learn to connect with the right word for yourself. Try saying a few names out loud to yourself: God, Buddha, Allah, Great One, Universal Spirit, Heavenly Soul. Do any of those feel right to you? Don't worry if nothing happens. In time, you may make up your own name. What is important is that you acknowledge, appreciate and respect its divine power and give thanks for its presence.

When starting psychic development, many people think that calling on this pure energy must be extremely difficult. They feel it ought to take them a long time to connect with it and, although it might happen to others, maybe they won't experience it. It's rather like that earlier quoted example of thinking you'll never fall in love. So, before you start to build up any more blocks in your thought process, try this first simple exercise to experience the cosmic energy for yourself.

COSMIC ENERGY

Sit comfortably in a chair but choose a padded upright one, not an armchair into which your body will sag. Keep your back as straight as feels comfortable, have your legs uncrossed and put your feet flat on the floor. Let your arms relax at your sides and have your hands unclasped, resting loosely on your thighs. Close your eyes and concentrate on your breathing for a moment. When you feel ready, breathe a little more deeply, really drawing the breath down into your stomach.

Wait until your body feels nicely relaxed, and then imagine the ceiling is lifting off the room in which you're sitting. Either have it roll to one side like an awning, lift off into the air, or disappear like magic. Now there is the rich blue sky above you and warm light is streaming into the room. Concentrate on that warm light and realize it's pouring in as a rich stream of pure white energy. It's a never-ending waterfall of light, streaming endlessly from its source. As you see it even more clearly in your mind, it gets even brighter and lighter and more intense. It's the most beautiful light you have ever seen in your life. It makes you feel wonderful. Let it pour into your room and have it cascade over and around you. If you feel like it, even have it pour in through the top of your head and feel its energy cleansing and refreshing your entire body. The more you visualize the energy, the stronger it gets and the more refreshed you feel. Its intensity and purity is energizing on a level you've never experienced before.

Enjoy it for another moment longer, and then start to concentrate on your physical body again. Remember how you are sitting in your chair and feel your weight resting on the chair seat. Be aware of your breathing and feel its comforting rhythm. Slowly put the ceiling back on your room again and know you are safely enclosed, back in your earth world again. You might want to thank the spirit or force for the opportunity to feel its heavenly strength and love.

Before you open your eyes, concentrate on your feet which should still be resting flat on the floor. Notice how heavy they feel and imagine there are long roots coming out of the soles of your feet, anchoring you to the floor again. When you are really aware of the weight of your body again and feel properly grounded, then slowly open your eyes. Wait a few minutes before getting up out of your seat.

How did that feel? Did you have a sense of that white energy? It doesn't matter if it wasn't an overwhelmingly powerful experience for you. If you felt a tingle, a sensation of light and energy, that is fine. The more you visualize the cosmic energy, the more intense it becomes. Some of you will find it immediately powerful, probably those of you who have spent some time thinking about and acknowledging energies before. Some people find it quite a holy, reverential experience. The acknowledgement of something more in our universe is always mind-expanding and exciting.

Whilst this energy is very beautiful and enriching, it is also very accessible. The energy can be created very quickly, once you have practised it for a while. You can call upon it literally at any time you feel you need a boost. You may be tired at the end of a long day, or you may start the day feeling exhausted after a disturbed night's sleep. Simply create the white light above you and then feel it streaming down around you, energizing and uplifting you. Further exercises will go into this in more detail. If, at any time during the exercise, you feel light-headed, remember to bring your attention back to your physical body and to concentrate on how heavy it feels. Always be aware of your feet resting securely on the ground.

This connection with the ground is the second energy you need to know about, the earth's energy. As already mentioned, this is also called the universal energy field. This energy is a little easier to relate to, partly because it has been studied, measured and talked about for thousands of years. Over five thousand years ago, India coined the word 'prana', meaning the basic source of all life. Ever since then, a vast number of words have been used: the Chinese call it 'ch'i' and talk further of feminine and masculine energies that are, respectively, 'yin' and 'yang'; the Greeks refer to it as 'vital energy'; research carried out by various enquiring individuals have created words such as 'iliaster', 'monads', 'magnetic fluids' and 'odic force'. You may already be familiar with some of these words.

What is it? This answer can go on for a long time and become so involved, that you'd need another lifetime to study it. The description in this book is a very simplified version, to help you grasp it as a concept and then use it constructively within your psychic development.

This earth energy is composed of matter, but it is so fine, so subtle, that most of us don't see it. The fact is that you can train yourself to do so; exercises follow shortly. Those who can see this pulsating energy in considerable detail say it is a supremely organized design, consisting of spirals and little dots with webs of lines, sparks and clouds. It is everywhere, flowing between every animate and inanimate object on the earth, actually connecting everything together, with varying degrees of intensity. It is said to be influenced by consciousness, from primitive to highly developed. The apple seed planted in the ground doesn't 'know' that it has to grow into a tree: a primitive energy force propels it into that cycle. Likewise, much animal behaviour is instinctive and unconscious, coming from a primitive pattern of thought or energy. You also have the other spectrum, with humans trying to attain levels of sensitivity and awareness that require heightened consciousness.

This energy is indeed a vital life force, and its unique beauty and complexity make it an invaluable source of strength and power for us. Certain phenomena create particularly powerful energy patterns. That is why different locations have a very different 'feel'. You are responding to the energy within that area.

So how is the energy created within an area? It's a highly complex series of influences, but here are some: the combination of the organic and inorganic elements in the earth itself, the energy of the flora and fauna in the area, the presence of different human and animal forms within that space, the energies from the solar system and power of magnetic fields which direct lines of cosmic energy. Are you feeling confused? You don't need to study all these factors in detail: all you really need to do during this book is to start thinking about the earth's energy with an ever-expanding series of questions.

These varying earth energies also explain why some of us prefer different area to others. As each person is unique, our individual make-up dictates which geographical area we feel best in. It's to do with us balancing our own energies with the earth's energies and creating complete health and a true sense of being. For instance, are you somebody who must live near a stretch of water? Others feel they must be in the mountains; others need the sea; some crave the close presence of large trees. It isn't coincidence you feel this way; you are reacting to your own energies and wanting to harmonize and balance with others.

Weather is another enormous influence and people, again, have different needs because their make-up is different. Some people feel charged by constant sunny weather; others feel drained of energy.

Moist, humid climates can benefit those whose energies resonate with that field; constant cold conditions suit others. Electrical storms are another good example; energy fields flow faster during that process. Does this excite you? Some people are deeply frightened by it because they don't like the sensation of the sudden change in energy flow.

Do you see now why connection with what you might call nature is so essential for your psychic growth? You need to connect with these energies and you need to get to know yourself better through the process, by experimenting and working out what earth energies complement and strengthen you.

Whenever possible, take the chance of increasing your contact with what is around you. At least once a week, more often if possible, make contact with different earth energies. It doesn't have to be a lengthy drive to the seaside. It can be a simple gesture. For example, the next time you are near a tree (and preferably alone) put your arms around its trunk and hug the tree. You may feel silly initially, but close your eyes and rest your face against the bark. What can you feel? Try to connect with the tree's energy by relaxing and breathing deeply. Trees have a wonderful energy of their own. Run your fingers up and down the surface of the trunk, smell it and look at it closely. This is you connecting with the earth's energy. You can do the same with a flower or bush or rock, or even a blade of grass. The more you practise, the more powerful it becomes.

Wildlife is another wonderful opportunity to communicate with other energies and feel their influence. Have you ever lain in the grass and watched a tiny ant pursuing its day's tasks? Ants have a highly developed, intricate social structure and consequent set of behavioural patterns. Yet who taught them that existence? Can you imagine them all sitting down in a circle to discuss who is going to do what and why? Their quite extraordinary, specific behaviour is yet another example of the effect of the wondrous qualities of earth energy. If you have any domestic animals, they too can provide fascinating study. Although some of their instincts have been bred out of them, they still resonate with their own energy. Observing them and appreciating them gives us access into another realm of awareness.

In fact, appreciating the energies of each species of animal, each form of plant and mineral life, gives a richness to our own levels of understanding and gives us the chance of ever-evolving growth. You should never under-estimate the power of that sentence. Once you have spent some time working with your own personal psychic development, you'll appreciate the sentiment even more.

You were promised exercises to help you see this earth energy. Two examples follow. The first is to help you see a general level of energy that exists through everything. You may be able to perceive some of the beautiful, intricate patterns that were mentioned earlier. If your sight isn't yet finely tuned enough to see those details, you should still be able to see part of a pattern. You need to be outdoors for this exercise and you need a sunny day to help your vision. If it's a cold day, make sure you're wrapped up warmly. Once you start this exercise, it can be so fascinating that you don't want to stop!

EARTH ENERGY

Find a quiet spot outdoors where you won't be disturbed. Lie on your back and gaze up at the blue sky. Keep gazing at it, feeling relaxed as you do so. Take a few deep breaths. After a while, you may see something making a sort of pattern against the blue sky. It will look a bit like squiggles at first and then you may be able to make out little white balls that suddenly appear for a brief second and then disappear again. As they disappear, they leave a pale trail behind them, but that quickly vanishes as well. This is the earth energy. Study this phenomenon for a few minutes and then as you widen your gaze, you may be able to see that the whole expanse above you is actually pulsating with these small balls of energy. If you are relaxed enough, you will see it cover your whole field of vision. The more you look at this energy, the easier it is to see it. When you feel confident, take your vision away, down to the grass or your clothing. Close your eyes for a moment. Then focus again on the sky. How quickly can you see the energy again?

Now try focusing your gaze on a nearby tree. Study the edges of the tree. Can you see a sort of green or pink haze around the perimeter of the tree? Have the tiny balls of energy suddenly disappeared at the edges of the tree? Now look a little more closely at the haze around the tree. If you are watching closely enough and tuned in to its vibrations, you will see that the balls of energy are outside the haze but then they actually slip into it and disappear into the tree. So the tree is absorbing some of the earth energy! The more you're able to see of this activity, the more you'll want to stay observing everything around you. Remember to keep yourself warm if it's not summer.

Did you find that exercise relatively easy? Most people expect it to take enormous concentration and when you do see the tiny balls quite quickly, you then feel sure that you've imagined it. You haven't. In fact, after a while, you'll see it when you're not even thinking of it. When you're sun-bathing, for example, and gazing lazily upwards, you'll suddenly see the familiar tiny dots. Or it might happen when you're swimming under a blue sky and you turn over to rest on your back. This energy exists everywhere, of course, not just against the backdrop of a blue sky. However, it's certainly easiest to start this way because a blank expanse helps you to focus. That's why a cloudy or rainy day would make it difficult for you, although the energy is still there, whatever the weather.

The second exercise requires a houseplant. You could use a piece of fruit, if you prefer, but it seems that a plant's energy is more accessible to the human eye. You could try both and then experiment with other objects.

PLANT ENERGY

Take a houseplant and place it against a plain, dark background. It helps most if the overhead lighting in the room is quite dim. Then, take a bright light and shine it directly onto the plant. Now stand back a little way and observe the outline of the plant. What can you see? Is there a sort of hazy glow around its edges? What colour is it? Is the energy uniformly distributed around the plant? What about the base? The stems? The leaves? Try moving your gaze just a bit further from the immediate energy field. Can you see anything else? What other colours are there? Is this energy moving or travelling in a specific direction? If you can move closer to the plant and still see its energy, do so. Now try placing your own hand near the plant, without physically touching it. Does anything happen to the plant's energy? Move your hand around to different areas of the plant. Then try gently stroking a leaf. Is there any change?

You won't necessarily see a change in the plant's energy from your touching it, although you will have altered its energy state. As energy vibrates at different frequencies, you won't probably be able to see the whole energy of the plant. It takes considerable time and study before you can understand energy at all its levels.

To give you an indication of the level at which an experienced psychic can work, consider the following experiment that has been carried out by various people who have a high degree of sensitivity. The leaf of a plant is observed by a psychic. The energy emanating from it is seen to be blueish-green in colour. Half the leaf is then cut off from the plant. The psychic then observes that the energy has changed to a rich maroon in colour: the energy of the plant has been disturbed. A short while later, the plant's energy will stabilize, returning to its orginal hue. However, where the leaf has been cut, a long, thin streamer of energy is now in evidence. The plant is 'missing' part of itself. Sceptics might be tempted to dismiss this experiment as fanciful thought on the part of the psychic. However, a Russian called Kirlian actually spent a great deal of time photographing the effects of this 'phantom leaf' phenomenon. The photographed results bore out the experiences of the psychics. Kirlian is mentioned further in the next chapter about the human aura, as he spent a great deal of his life investigating it.

So, hopefully, you now have an understanding of the cosmic and the earth energies. Do you understand how differently the two energies operate?

The cosmic energy is an unchanging constant, an ever-lasting and divinely pure source of white light. It is always there, existing above us, waiting to called upon, and is not influenced by any human or earthly behaviour. It is truth and strength in its highest form of consciousness.

The earth energy is from the earth and its inhabitants and is influenced by everything, animate and inanimate. Earth energies resonate at different vibrations in different areas according to a wide range of influencing factors.

It would be fair to consider that cosmic energy may influence the earth energy but the reverse is not possible.

So where does human energy, or the human aura, come into this newly defined world of energies?

CHAPTER 4

HUMAN ENERGY

You've been reading about a powerful source of energy from above, as well as an earth energy that resonates around everything. So what about us, as humans, amongst all this energy?

Our energy is most often called the human aura, so we'll just use the word, aura, in this book. It will crop up a great deal throughout all areas of psychic work, so you need to work with it and learn to understand as much as you can about it.

In Chapter 3 you experimented with looking at a plant's energy, or, as we'll now call it, aura. You could probably see some of that aura, albeit hazily, as you went through the exercise. Every human being has their own aura, too. In fact, every living object has its own aura. (So do inanimate objects, but that energy is slightly different and is discussed later in this chapter).

Our aura is our own, highly individual band of energy that surrounds us. It's a very sophisticated band with at least seven different layers. Each layer deals with a different aspect of ourselves. Our auras constantly change, expanding and contracting, as we go through life. You may not have seen a human aura – yet! – but you will almost certainly have felt one before. You just didn't realize what it was at the time.

Have you found yourself in any of these situations? You're in a room with other people around you. Someone new enters the room and suddenly the whole atmosphere changes. The room may suddenly become bright and feel charged with energy, or you may feel the energy level suddenly plummet as a depressed person walks in. You greet a friend and immediately know that something is different about them. They look exactly the same, but somehow they 'feel' different. It turns out that they're about to become a parent or they've been offered a new job. Your partner comes back from work and you know, before you even turn around and look at them, what sort of day they've had because you feel their emotions.

You may also have felt you've seen someone's aura, through colour expressions that have become part of our language. Have you noticed a 'black temper' around someone, 'red anger', an 'in the pink' feeling of well-being, the 'golden glow' of love, or 'green jealousy'? (The latter would be a dark, sludge-green in hue, not bright grass-green, which reflects other states.)

Another very strong energy within the aura is fear. Animals, in particular, have the ability to sense this in auras. You've probably been affected by it yourself. Have you ever sat in an audience and watched someone, who is very nervous, get up to give a speech or presentation? Can you not tangibly feel their fear? Sometimes your own heart will start to beat faster in sympathy. Or you may be party to an argument that is taking place between other people. As you watch, can you not feel the waves of anger emanating from their auras? Sometimes those waves can hit you, as you get caught in their cross-fire. Does it make you feel uncomfortable, as though you want to beat a hasty retreat?

Perhaps the strongest auric force of all is love. If you've ever spent time with someone who gives out unconditional love, you'll know how nurturing and powerful that can be. You are literally encompassed by their loving energy, protected and supported by them. A good parent will, hopefully, be able to offer this. Or, if you spend some time in the company of a couple who are very much in love with each other, can you feel their waves of warmth and joy?

You've already experienced seeing part of a plant's aura. Perhaps it's time you experienced part of your own aura. The easiest way to start, is with the energy between your own hands. This exercise starts with feeling the aura, and then progresses to trying to see it.

HAND ENERGIES

Hold your hands up in front of you, arms bent to avoid any strain. Now turn your hands so that your palms face each other, ensuring there's at least twelve inches of distance between them. Your fingers need to be straight, with no space between them, although you don't want to hold them open so tightly that they ache. Now, slowly and smoothly, start moving your hands towards each other. You need to go slowly or you won't be able to feel anything. Remember to take a few nice, deep breaths, especially if you're feeling uncertain about your own abilities during these exercises. Take at least ten gentle breaths, in and out, as you move your hands together. At some point, before your hands touch, you should feel something. It will be stronger for some people than others. Your hands could start to feel very hot. You may feel tingly. It might seem as if something is tickling your palms, like a butterfly delicately brushing its wings against your skin. For others, it will be a stronger sensation of pressure and you'll just want to stop moving your hands together. Whatever it feels to you, that is your own energy fields meeting one another.

Move your hands a little further apart now. Can you still feel the energy, although it's finer and lighter? Keep moving them apart. When can you no longer feel a pull? Now cup your hands slightly (still keeping the sides of your fingers touching to avoid gaps) and move your palms closer together. Is the energy stronger this time? Move them quite close together now. Does the energy feel hot or uncomfortable? Move your hands back and forth a little more quickly and 'play' with that ball of energy you have created.

You can then try feeling energy just between one finger of the left hand and one finger of the right hand. This is finer and lighter, but you may still be able to feel it. Then take a finger and try tracing a circle in the palm of your other hand, but without physically touching it. Does it tickle?

Once you have experimented with feeling your own energy, you can try to see it. This may be more difficult for some of you, so, to help yourself, hold your hands in front of a dark surface and have a bright light shining from behind you (as you did with the Plant Energy Exercise). Practise the same exercise again. Can you see anything happening between your two hands? If you can't, then try using just one finger of each hand and move them back and forth towards each other. Now can you see a stream of light? Now hold your hands up in front of you so that you're looking at the back of your hands. Have your fingers straight but with a little space between them. Whilst keeping your palms facing outwards, rotate your hands inwards so that the tips of the middle fingers just touch. Slowly move your hands apart again. Can you see anything now?

Don't worry if you see nothing. It is often more difficult to see your own energy than other people's. If you were to practise by watching someone else playing with their hands' energies, you might see more then. If you want to, ask a friend if they'd like to experiment with you and try the Hand Energy Exercises again.

Whatever you see during these experiments, will almost certainly be part of the first level of the aura. There are another six levels of increasingly finer vibrations, that also exist.

As we go further into discussions on the aura, the words 'vibrations' and 'frequencies' will be used quite a lot and they may initially confuse you. How is one vibration, one pulse of energy, finer and higher than another? Why can you see the first layer of an aura but not necessarily the following six?

A good analogy to help you grasp this concept is that of an electric fan. Imagine that a large fan with propeller blades is about to be switched on. The blades sit there, motionless, and they're very easy for you to see, aren't they? You turn the machine on to 'low', and the blades slowly whirr into action. They move quite slowly at this speed, so you can still see them, but their edges are a little hazy. Their individual shape isn't as easy for you to distinguish, although you know they're still there. Now you turn the fan up to 'medium'. The blades twirl more quickly now and they're even more blurred, so you can no longer make out their shape clearly. In fact, the blades look as if they've become paler and lighter because of their speed. Now turn the machine to 'high'. The blades seemed to have disappeared! They're turning at such speed that you can't make out anything except, at best, some blur of movement. The blades themselves are no longer visible, yet you know they must still be there.

Does that make more sense now? Our human energy which, like all energy, is made up of a very fine matter, is twirling at different speeds. It can be seen as seven separate levels, radiating out sequentially from the body. There's a diagram on the left which demonstrates this. Each level, as it builds outwards from our body, becomes finer and subtler in quality. Therefore, it becomes harder and harder to see it, because we haven't adapted our vision yet to see those very fine vibrational frequencies. You can train yourself to do this. Anyone can see auras. However, to tune your energies to such a fine degree that you can see the highest levels of the aura, is not a quick task.

So, what is contained within these seven levels of the human aura? Basically, it's our whole life and more as well. It's further proof of how extraordinary all people are.

If you've had a look at the diagram, you'll see that the first level tells you all about your physical state. Inside this band, a psychic can find information about your physical sensations, both pleasant and unpleasant. If you're an athlete, this level would be particularly strong. If you're someone who is very much in touch with your physical self and enjoys sexual activity, physical touch, eating and sleeping, then this section of your aura would also be bright. Psychics say this level radiates shades of blue, depending on a person's physical condition.

The second level relates to your emotions and feelings. This isn't about how you relate to others, it's all about how you feel about yourself. If you feel good about yourself, if you honestly love and accept yourself as you are and can express your emotions, then the energy would flow well within this band. If you keep emotions bottled up inside, if there are areas of yourself you don't like which cause you distress, or if you just don't spend any time looking at emotions and feelings, your energy will be sluggish in this second level. Most people have emotional areas which they block, not wanting to look at them, and this restricts the natural energy flows within and around you. Apparently, all colours can be seen in this section.

The third level is associated with the realm of mental and rational thought. If you are mentally alert and agile and have a clear mind, that will be evident from this area. Mental sluggishness, a lazy mind, will show up. Also, any negative thought processes that we have accumulated over the years can be seen. How many of us have acquired those? How often do you make negative or disparaging comments about other people? Those negative mental processes are only damaging you, affecting the flow of energy in your third level. It's said that yellow is the predominant colour here.

The fourth level is about your relationships to others. It's to do with how you relate to everything: not just people, but animals, plants, inanimate objects and, literally, the whole universe. If your relationships are strong and happy with your family and friends, if you love people and everything around you, your energy will be strong. This level is very much about love of, and appreciation of, everything. If you are a loner and lack communication with anyone, your energy will be blocked. If you go around feeling jealous and envious of everyone, you'll restrict the flow also. All colours have been seen in the sphere.

The fifth level becomes harder to explain. Remember, each frequency is becoming higher and harder to see. Likewise, our ability to grasp its meaning may also start to diminish. This section is called divine will. It's to do with you knowing that you have a place and purpose within the world that is related to a great, universal plan. It's to do with your understanding a pattern of evolution and a meaning of life, that enables you to resonate and react and learn from everything around you. It's how you connect with this divine will and use it as a means to further enrich your life. This is not about living as social etiquette may demand; it's to do with creating your own special place within this world, and aligning yourself to a universal energy in the process. Cobalt blue is used to describe the colour of this field, although it is more complex than simply seeing one colour. If this last paragraph has confused you, you might want to re-read it before moving on.

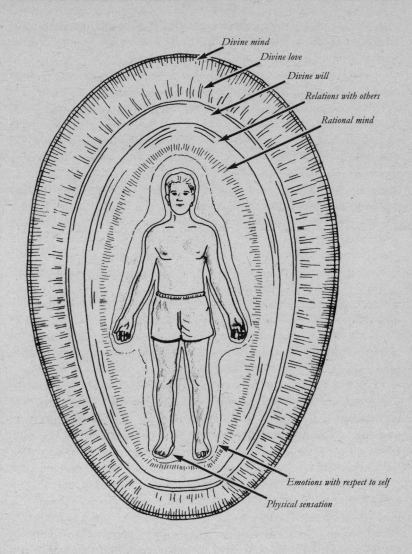

Divine mind

Divine love

Divine will

Relations with others

Rational mind

Emotions with respect to self

Physical sensation

Seven Levels of Human Aura

75

The sixth level is called divine love. This is not about our love for ourselves or others: it's on a higher level of consciousness and relates to true spiritual love. This encapsulates what for many people are, as yet, unknown degrees of love: bliss and elation. It can only be achieved through a deep stillness and by silencing our active mind. If you have little energy in this area, it isn't just because you haven't experienced this state, it's because you won't have any belief in spirituality. You will never have had an insight or moment of enlightenment before, nor will you believe any to be possible. Please note: this isn't to imply that you're a bad person! It simply means you haven't explored all of yourself yet. This level can pulsate with a vibrant energy when you take a little time to meditate and get in touch with your spirituality. Quietly watch a beautiful sunset for five minutes and you will be recharging your energy. Psychics describe this level as the most beautiful explosion of rainbow colours with streamers of billowing colours, radiating pure love.

The last level is the seventh level and it's related to the divine mind. This is about our conciousness and understanding of the universe of the divine mind. Here we know we are part of the great purpose or pattern of life. We know we can communicate with this divine mind, blend with this higher consciousness and become part of it. A belief in the above will stimulate this energy. A continual desire to seek for higher truth, and then a desire to live by that truth, will create a flowing energy. Again, meditation is important for this process. This band is described as golden and egg-like in shape. As it is the last layer, it actually supports and protects all our other layers. The outside edge of the seventh level is said to be extremely strong and regulates how much of our energy we give out into the world. It also protects us from unwanted, outside influences penetrating our aura.

Now that you have read about everything our aura contains, does it not make you feel deeply grateful that not everyone can automatically read your aura?! Can you imagine sitting on a crowded train and being able to immdiately see everything about that person? It would be the equivalent of everyone sitting there naked and utterly vulnerable. Most of us aren't ready for that level of scrutiny and wouldn't know how to handle it. That's why psychic gifts are meant to be developed slowly.

As your sensitivity to these energies increases, so can your sensitivity as to how you handle everyone.

A highly developed psychic is capable of seeing the whole aura. A further few are able to work with healing techniques to help blockages within your aura.

Does reading about the levels of the aura also help clarify the concept of balance within our energies? All seven levels of the aura need to resonate and flow with unhampered energy, for us to truly experience being 'whole', feeling complete. If certain levels are much stronger than others, we become imbalanced.

For example, consider a person whose third level is particularly vibrant but their second level is weak. They will operate on a highly successful mental level. They'll be quick thinking and technically analytical; they may hold a position of great authority in some academic institution. However, they will have little contact with their own emotions and feelings. They won't be in touch with what is going on inside them and they are therefore unconsciously blocking part of their own energy.

What about a person who has a strong energy within their seventh level but a very weak first level? They will probably be superb at meditation and contemplation. They may have a deep grasp of higher consciousness and an ability to communicate with a higher source. Yet their own physical body will be lacking in energy. It won't support them through their physical tasks on this earth and they'll have no interest in earthly pleasures such as invigorating exercise, nourishing food, and the rejuvenating pleasure of sleep.

Can you think of other examples by imagining people with different energy patterns within their aura? Is all this making you think of your own aura and what that might look like? Most people find as they read through the different levels, that they identify with various aspects. It's not always a comfortable feeling but it may offer you some insights into your own life.

If you're now wondering about how on earth you are going to learn to see all those levels and then be able to interpret what you see, you can relax. This book is not about literally seeing all those levels and analysing them. It is about tapping into them on a feeling, sensing level and this is what you will be able to accomplish through studying this volume. By understanding that all these levels exist and vibrate constantly around everybody, you will know what it is you are tapping into. Knowing this helps to erase the uncertainty and unknown element of psychic work. You can think of the aura as a video that doesn't quite work in your normal machine. You have to find another machine to be able to play it. Likewise, you are re-programming your mind to be able to play your psychic video.

So, if you're going to be sensing this aura, what does it actually feel like? Now you could try actually feeling someone else's aura, provided they are agreeable. This isn't what you would normally do during psychic work with someone; this exercise is designed purely to expand your awareness of the human aura. Firstly, you need to find a willing friend. As it can be a strange experience, you need someone with whom you feel comfortable being alone in a room. If you choose someone who's highly sceptical, they may end up making derisory comments and you may lose confidence as a result. Read through the exercise first to understand what is involved before you choose someone.

FEELING AN AURA

Ask your partner to stand in the middle of the room, arms by their side, with their eyes open. (If they close their eyes, they may feel off-balance once you start moving around them. This is because your energy may be responding to, and affecting, their aura). Explain to them that everyone has energy radiating from their body and you are going to try to feel it. Emphasize that if they feel uncomfortable at any time, they should tell you so immediately.

You should start off by standing well away from them; you need to hold out your hands and have them be at least three feet away from the other person's body. Take a few comfortable breaths and feel as relaxed as you can. Now start to gently move your hands around this field. Don't linger around their heart area or over the top of their head. (Reasons for this are explained in a later chapter). A good place to start is around their stomach but do remember to keep your distance. Can you feel anything? If nothing is happening, try moving in towards them a fraction, and continue moving around their energy field. Now can you feel anything? Everyone's aura is different; some are wider and bigger than others. When you do feel some sensation, stop, and don't move any closer. What is it like? Slowly move your hands back and forth a little, analysing how it feels. It will probably be a bit like touching a very light, frothy marshmallow, or you may feel heat or a tingling sensation. Continue moving your hands over their body. Does it get hotter, or colder, at certain spots? Where? Are there areas where you feel you should back off more and others where it feels safe to move in a bit closer? Remember to keep breathing and remember to keep that distance. It's very easy when you do feel something, to find it so exciting that you unconsciously move in towards them. You must be sensitive to them at all times. You're actually touching their energy and you know now what is contained within that field, even though you can't yet tap into it.

When you have moved around their whole body and experienced different sensations, then step well back, out of their aura, and ask for some feedback. How did they feel during the exercise? Did they tell you if they felt uncomfortable? Many people won't. What other sensations did they have, if any? Did they feel pulled in any direction? Was there any feeling of heat or cold for them? Or did they feel comforted at any point? Make sure you thank them at the end.

It's a strange feeling, when you first feel someone's aura. You normally feel as though you are intruding. If you do, that's very appropriate and it shows your sensitivity. Also, most people are nervous on the first occasion, both the subject and the feeler, and auras contract when people feel anxious. If possible, try this experiment with different people. You'll be amazed how utterly different each aura feels. Some people make you feel you ought to stand six feet away; others make you move to within a foot or two. Once you have tried this a few times, your own nervousness will disappear and you will instinctively know how close to stand to someone.

Start becoming aware of your own aura, and others, on a day-to-day basis. You will soon realize how you have been reacting and responding to auras in a variety of situations. Do you know certain people who always seem to stand too close to you, making you want to back off a few step? That's because they keep intruding into your aura and it feels unwelcome. Usually, these are people with whom your energies aren't naturally harmonizing, and that is what makes you feel hemmed in. There's the other side of that experience, when you just want to be physically close to someone. You needn't necessarily be touching or hugging them, but their close presence makes you feel good. Their energies are nurturing yours. Does being in a crowded bus or train make you feel claustrophobic and irritated? It's no wonder, when all those energies from all those different auras are whirling together in close proximity, mixing with and reacting against each other. A large group of people together can also have a very uplifting and energising effect, when they are involved in sharing a pleasurable experience: a music concert or a religious gathering, for example. As you go about your daily tasks, start questioning how your aura is reacting to people and situations. Start really becoming aware of others and notice when you feel you have stepped inside their aura.

If some of you are still feeling uncertain about how energy has been discussed so far in this book and sceptical about human auras, it might help if you know that energy and auras were studied by scientists as long ago as a hundred years. Some of them were convinced that the aura was an objective reality and could be monitored, long before it was socially acceptable to think along those lines. It's worth taking a brief look at this section of history. Even if you already find it easy to accept the existence of energy fields, it makes interesting reading.

A brilliant German scientist, Karl von Reichenbach (1788–1869), spent over twenty years studying energy, despite ruthless criticism and constant ridicule. He called energy the 'odic force', named after the Norse god, Odin. His investigation involved tests with over two hundred individuals who had 'sensitive' powers. What he discovered was that these people, whilst in total darkness, could see emanations from crystals and magnets. He then devoted himself to studying these visualized manifestations of energy and their relationship to electricity, magnetism and chemistry. Although we now acknowledge the value of his research and can validate his claims, he was never taken seriously during his life.

Walter J. Kilner (1847–1920) was a physician who was familiar with Reichenbach's work. He devised a method for making the aura visible, by creating spectacle screens or goggles impregnated with the chemical dicyanin. Through his work he was able to perceive three levels of the aura and to directly relate illness to imbalances within the aura. His work was considered highly controversial, although he didn't receive the same degree of derision suffered by Reichenbach.

You earlier read a brief reference to Kirlian photography. Two Soviet scientists, Semyon and Valentina Kirlian, have done extraordinary work during this century to strengthen our understanding of auric energy. In 1958, the husband-and-wife team discovered a technique whereby they could convert the non-electrical properties of an object into electrical properties. This lead to endorsement of their work by Soviet authorities and they were subsequently provided with a new laboratory to develop their work. Over the years, their work has gained increased recognition and now many people are familiar with Kirlian photography. A popular example is their photograph of two leaves. They look identical but one shows up in the photograph as having a very weak energy field; the other is strong. This is because one leaf was diseased, the other healthy. They could therefore make strong links between health and the aura. One day while Semyon was repairing an instrument, he noticed tiny flashes of light between some electrodes and a person's skin. This started his experiments with human energy, where he used his own fingers to photograph his own energy. Today, this form of Kirlian photograph is used throughout many countries as a diagnostic tool to promote holistic health.

It isn't just the Kirlians who have done fantastic work during this century. Our present-day research into the human aura has escalated, with increasing emphasis being placed on how we can relate to it scientifically. In other words, it has moved on from the realms of being purely a spiritual experience and is now being acknowledged as a tangible phenomenon. Individual studies have resulted in different words and different areas being discussed: electromagnetic fields, life fields, thought fields, bioplasma and biofields. Delving into all these areas would necessitate a further book on the subject, but it's important for you to realize that the energies that are used constantly in psychic work are in no way a wild figment of a few people's imagination. They are scientifically recognized energy fields about which we're learning more and more all the time. No doubt, there is still a great deal more we have yet to discover, but at least we have started on the path.

You may now believe that every live object has an aura, but how could an inanimate object have one, as mentioned at the start of this chapter? Surely if an aura is the energy emanating from a living object, something that is inanimate should have no aura? That seems to be logical, but there is one aspect you've not considered. What about the energies with which that object comes into contact?

Have you ever gone from one room to another in a house and been forcibly struck by the change in atmosphere? Or have you noticed, when you go into different people's houses or offices, that each feels quite different from the other? The air in the room has absorbed the different energies of the people who have spent time in that space. If the finer substance of air is capable of absorbing these vibrations, is it not feasible that physical objects, which are made of denser matter than air, should also absorb that same energy?

Why is it so touching when a child hands you a drawing they have done? It's not just because they've made something for you: it's also because that picture is vibrating with their energies. That's why we can't bear to throw away the things they have made, or the clothes they wore when they were tiny, or the toys with which they played. All those inanimate objects still resonate with their energies and experiences. You thought it was pure sentiment, didn't you? There's an element of that involved, of course, but your subconscious was also working on another level.

The same can be said of family photographs. They aren't just about nice memories, they're about the energies you share with your family, and your friends. A simple object given to you by somebody with whom you share a deep love, is a powerful manifestation of their energy. The material value or size of the object is irrelevant. Have you had someone with whom you aren't naturally compatible, buy you an expensive gift that means less to you than a tiny item given by a trusted friend? If the object is a leaf, or piece of wood, or stone, then the energies are further charged by the earth's energy. Not only are we given items which carry their own energy before we get them, but we then continue to imbue the object with our own energy. It becomes a constant, ever-increasing cycle. Every object is affected by the different people who actually handle it, and the different atmospheres and situations through which it passes. Can you imagine what energies might be imprinted on a small coin in its journey through life? If you purchase an old item from an antique shop, what possible energies may it hold? (If you're now thinking you never want to go into an antique shop again, further exercises show you how to tune in to receive information about an object's energies. You can learn to be your own judge of what is right for you. You can also cleanse objects.)

Can you now see that a cluttered, unclean environment doesn't help you or your psychic development? If you want to improve the flow of your energies, it would help you to improve the energy flow within your own living space. If you live with other people, this doesn't mean you have the right to go around getting rid of items which they might want. However, if you have the opportunity to create a small space just for yourself, then you would benefit from carefully considering how you want to fill that space. Chapter 6 goes into this in more detail.

Being scientific for a moment might help you grasp the concept of inanimate objects absorbing energy. You may already be familiar with atomic structure and know atoms are contained within both animate and inanimate matter. Each atom is comprised of electrons and protons which are magnetic and electrical vibrations. Our human aura is basically a strong electromagnetic field; we give off (electrical) and receive (magnetic) energy. Therefore, as we go through life we are leaving our traces and imprints everywhere we go and on everything we touch. Certain objects absorb more energies than other. Tests have shown that natural fabrics absorb more than synthetic materials; metals are good conductors of electricity but wood is a little more difficult to leave a strong imprint upon. All this is very relevant to work with psychometry, which is when a psychic tunes into the vibrations of an inanimate object.

There is one last subject to cover concerning energy and consciousness: the Hologram Theory. Considerable research has taken place over recent years in this field. It's important to look at the basics of this theory because it offers a possible explanation for the sometimes unfathomable power and accuracy of psychic work. It takes away much of the mystic element in doing so, and makes understanding of psychic phenomena more accessible.

You are probably all familiar with a hologram and have the memory of seeing one. It's a flat picture that, when you look at it, projects a three-dimensional image of a something that stretches into infinity. As you move the picture slightly, you see the image from a different angle, but the whole image still remains. They're fun as well as fascinating objects. However, did you know that if you took a hologram picture, cut it in half and then looked at each half, the whole image would be visible in each of the two pieces? It would be slightly less clear, but there would be two identical, whole images now. Cut it into a quarter, and the images are hazy, but there are four, complete images. Cut it into yet smaller pieces; each piece retains the whole picture. No matter how small a piece you are left with, the whole image is there, albeit hazier in shape. What does this mean and how can this relate to energy?

The hologram shows that no matter how small a fragment you take from the whole, each tiny bit contains the whole. Think about that fact for a moment and then try and relate it to human energy. The Hologram Theory states that each part of our energy contains the whole. In other words, if our fingers brush past an object, it doesn't matter that only our fingers touch it, because in that touch is the energy of all we are. If this isn't clear, re-read those two paragraphs again. It's an important concept and, once you start really thinking about it, the implications become enormous.

Remember how hazy the images of the small pieces were in the hologram? A touch of our fingers might make a hazy impression, too, but it would be a complete, hazy image. Now think of what happens when you put all those tiny pieces together to make it a whole. It becomes a crystal-clear image, bright and sharp. Therefore, if all the energies within us are fitted together in their proper place, can you see the implications for us as human beings? With scattered energies, we're an indistinct, vague pattern of the whole. If all our energies are combined properly, then we have the opportunity to vibrate in complete harmony. This is the true meaning of 'holistic' health.

Once you have really grasped the possibilities of this theory, endless new realities come into focus. Ask yourself what would life be like if you really believe that you're a hologram. Try this exercise below to help you focus:

HOLOGRAM

Sit comfortably in an upright chair, legs uncrossed, feet flat on the floor, and your hands resting on your thighs. Close your eyes and concentrate on your breathing for a few minutes. Feel each breath coming right down into your stomach. As you exhale, imagine any stress or problems being released with that air. Create a rhythm of breathing that feels comfortable for you. Don't rush. Take your time. Wait until you feel relaxed before you move on.

Now imagine the ceiling opening up, as you did with the Cosmic Energy Exercise. As it's removed, the warm light floods down and fills the room. Concentrate on that pure white light and feel it increasing and growing stronger with every breath you take. Bring it right down into the room and feel it flooding around you. Now imagine the top of your head is opening up and let the white light filter into you, warming and refreshing every part of you. Actually feel it trickle through every part of you. As it does so, it's removing any tension or worry. Luxuriate in its presence and comfort.

When you feel thoroughly revived and relaxed, think about the word 'hologram'. See it written in front of your eyes in large letters, or take an imaginary pen and write it for yourself. What does the word say to you? Really look at it and concentrate. Are there bits of other words in it? What does it make you feel? What other images does the word conjure up for you? When you feel you have explored the word itself, take an imaginary eraser and rub the word away.

Now create an image of a hologram. The image is of you, floating, suspended in that picture. You are suspended in infinity. The hologram represents all of everything. Everything means all you can grasp of the world and everything within it. The hologram is the whole planet and solar system, every part of earth and all its inhabitants, including all animal, plant and mineral life. It contains every thought, word, action and energy within the universe, including all forms of higher consciousness and supreme beings. You are therefore everything. Let that image fill you as think about it. What does that mean for you? What are your possiblities if everything is you and you are everything? Let your thoughts spiral onwards and outwards as you become the hologram. You are whole. You are everything. Fill yourself with the knowledge that you are everything as your thoughts expand ever outward, seeing new realities everywhere. Let this take as long as you want, or as long as you can.

When you feel you have really explored the experience then, slowly, remove yourself from the hologram. Let the image fade gently from your mind, knowing that you can call upon it in the future. As the hologram fades into the distance, become aware of your physical body again. It feels heavy and solid in the chair. Your feet feel planted firmly on the ground. Concentrate on your breathing. Let the white light wash through your body again, if you want to wash away any other thoughts or images.

When you feel grounded, slowly open your eyes. Focus on a nearby object for a few seconds, remembering which room you're in. What day is it? What is the time? Make sure you are well grounded back in our earth reality before you continue your day.

You will probably have discovered some new thoughts as you were going through that exercise. Some may have been very powerful and thought-provoking. Others will seem to be a confirmation of what you already know, or what you already suspected. Some of you may have felt confused during it, in which case it's because you haven't given yourself enough time to grasp the Hologram Theory. Re-read the paragraphs several more times. You can think about the concept and then come back to this exercise later on. The more your thoughts are focused on it, the more you see amazing possiblities in life because of it.

Here are a few further thoughts to think about. This doesn't mean you should embrace every one of these as being the truth and that you must adhere to their teaching. These are meant to expand your awareness. You may consider some of them to be false, but at least you can think about them.

If humans are holograms, then some of the possiblities are that:

— *psychic work is not about tapping into unknown energies, it's about awareness of our own energy*

— *we affect everything and everything affects us, because everything is connected to everything else*

— *we have access to all knowledge in the universe*

— *we are responsible for everything that happens and we have the ability to change anything*

— *every part of us is contained in each of our cells*

— *we exist in all of time, not just in earth time*

— *by connecting all our energies together, we can create a clearer, stronger 'whole'*

— *by human energies joining forces to make positive changes together, we make our energies more powerful*

— *we have created all disharmony in the world and we can create complete harmony again.*

Some of those statements are very powerful. Do they make you feel even more certain that you want to tap into psychic awareness and development? You are already well on the path by having absorbed these first four chapters. By now you'll be appreciating that we can only increase our awareness by strengthening and re-arranging our energies. To be more effective in this area, we need to look at 'chakras' and see how they're an invaluable part of our development.

CHAPTER 5

CHAKRAS

By now, you may really be appreciating how complex our human energies are. You've read about seven different levels within our aura, each level radiating different energies which connect to different aspects of ourselves. It makes you wonder how on earth you're supposed to get in touch with all that energy, doesn't it? After all, until reading this book, you probably thought of energy as being what you use to lift your arm or turn your head. So, now you want to start working more with these finer, subtler energies because, until you do, psychic work will be difficult.

It might help if, for a few moments, you compare psychic work to the mechanism of running a car. Everyone knows you have to fill the tank with petrol before the car works. Our body needs psychic petrol for the same reason. This takes the form of the pure cosmic energy mentioned in detail in Chapter 3. You've had a brief experience of this energy through the Cosmic Energy and Hologram Exercises. However, just by taking in some of the pure white energy through the top of your head, did you feel able to work psychically? The energy probably refreshed you, cleared your mind, helped relax you, and gave you a focus for your thoughts. That isn't the same as using the energy to make our psychic engine run. Just as the car needs a key in the ignition, so we need our own psychic key and ignition. The key to the ignition is the focusing of our mind. The mind has the power to turn the key. However, unlike a car which only has one ignition, human beings have seven! These seven ignitions are called chakras. It's no co-incidence that there are also seven layers of the aura. They are connected; the first chakra relates to the first layer, the second to the second, and so on through the seven layers. However, it becomes more complicated than that, which you'll understand as you read on.

Chakras are energy centres, or openings, through which we receive energy in to our body. We don't just have the seven, but these are considered to be the major centres; there are also twenty-one minor chakras and a veritable host of other smaller ones.

The significance of these chakra centres is determined by the number of lines of energy that cross at that point. We have a massive number of energy, or electrical, currents that run through our body. A major chakra is defined as a point where there are twenty-one rays of light or energy crossing each other; the minor chakras are positioned at locations where fourteen energy lines cross. Other chakras are created where seven energies cross, and then there are even smaller vortexes of energy after that. You may already know of acupuncture and acupressure. The energy points used in these techniques are where seven lines of energy cross each other.

In this book, you'll be studying the seven major ones. If you look at the Chakra Diagram on the right, you'll see that these seven chakras are all interconnecting centres which flow through the body. Each chakra is cone-like in shape and, when opened, allows streams of energy to whirl in through its open cone and to flow through into the body via its connecting pipe. You will see that the first and seventh chakras (base and crown) connect straight through to each other, with energy swirling up from the base and down into the body through the top of the head. The other five in the middle open both back and front through the body, so each of those has two openings. The second chakra goes through your navel area, the third through your spleen, the fourth through your heart, the fifth through your throat and the sixth through your forehead.

Now you know roughly where they are in your body, let's look at what a chakra means. Firstly, it comes from the Indian Sanskrit and means 'wheel'. It's a useful analogy, because as you open each centre it does spin, albeit on a high frequency. As you move through the centres, the higher you get, the finer and faster the frequency becomes. Remember

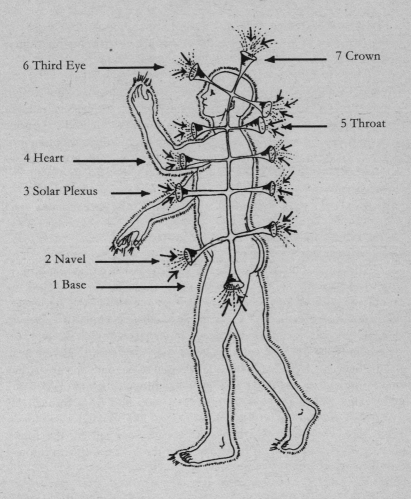

6 Third Eye

7 Crown

5 Throat

4 Heart

3 Solar Plexus

2 Navel

1 Base

The Seven Chakras

the concept of the electric fan? All our energy centres spin at a frequency which we find difficult to actually see, but the experience of opening and closing them enables us to appreciate that they do exist.

The chakra is also referred to as a lotus flower, which is equally apt. If you aren't familiar with the shape of a lotus, it's similar to a water lily, with many beautiful petals which open. In Greek legend, eating the fruit of a lotus was supposed to induce a dream-like state; lotus-eaters are referred to in the 'Odyssey'. You may also have heard of the lotus position in yoga. The reason a lotus flower seems appropriate is because opening a chakra can be likened to the petals of a flower slowly unfolding.

As these chakras are the means through which we open up our energy channels, and our energies are our path to everything we are, they're often called 'gateways to the soul'. In working with your chakras, and other people's, respect is of the utmost importance. These precious energy centres have been revered for centuries and, many years ago, their presence was considered so sacred, so holy, that information about them was only handed down from a teacher to his pupil in a secretly guarded tradition. Discussion of the chakras only took place in spiritual retreats or holy shrines, so that the knowledge was protected and continuously respected. Over the years, that reverence has all but disappeared; almost any book you pick up on psychic subjects will refer to the seven centres and describe them in a very basic, matter-of-fact manner. Of course, it's wonderful that we are all now developing an understanding of the chakras and the way they can influence and enrich our life, but there are problems in making them sound so ordinary. You can lose your appreciation of their very deep spirituality, their unique power and beauty.

To understand the true significance of all the chakras and their individual strengths, a great deal of study and meditation is needed. This book tries to explain them in as thought-provoking a manner as possible, but it still has to revert to basic colours and descriptions. Whilst reading through them, it will help you to always remember that these chakras are our energy centres of consciousness. Many would say that our path to a holistic existence lies in the way we work with these centres. Everything you read about them is but a simplification of their very intricate, soul-enriching powers. Meditation exercises later in this chapter will help your appreciation and understanding.

Each chakra is associated with a colour, although psychics who see these energy centres say that each is a myriad of colours. Assigning each their own colour gives you a better focus; it's a learning tool for you, rather than something to be taken literally. Every chakra is connected to separate elements of our emotions and actions, and each is related to a different part of our anatomy. Most are allocated an animal and elemental symbol to increase our relationship to those different energies. There is a varying number of lotus-flower petals for each chakra and corresponding mantras and yantras (mystical dialogues between divinities) for meditative use that aid enlightenment.

You aren't expected to remember all aspects of each chakra. There are basics you do have to remember for psychic development, however. You need to know the name, location and associated colour of each chakra, together with how it opens (i.e. front and back, or up and down). If you can remember just this much, you can start working. Nevertheless, the more you study these chakras, the more you understand about each of them, the more powerful you will be in your psychic work and spiritual growth. It's suggested you read through this chapter several times and practise the exercises at the end more than once.

The first chakra is known as the base. Sometimes it's also called the root chakra. It's located at the base of the spine and its associated colour is red. The base chakra has only one opening, which is pointing downwards towards the ground; the energy is therefore drawn up into the body with this chakra. It's related to the spinal column and kidneys and governs the adrenal glands. As its name implies, this is about the rooted, physical part of us. Survival and primal instincts are governed by this chakra. This is about how well we respond to our physical body and our relationship to nature, earth's bounty. Do you live in harmony with nature, or are you oblivious to it? This chakra has four petals, as the number four is often used to symbolize the material world. It also refers to the four directions: north, south, east and west. Its associated element is, not surprisingly, earth, and the animal connected to it is the elephant, Airavata. He is the king of the elephants who belonged to the earth god, Indra. He is often depicted with seven trunks, that signify the seven minerals necessary for physical life. He also has a heavy black collar around his neck to remind us of his ties to earth. The elephant is the largest land mammal; he represents physical matter itself. There is also a coiled snake within this chakra. This refers to a latent energy which, when the seven chakras are operating fully, can awaken deep within us. This energy is known as kundalini and is explained in a later chapter. It's an energy with an intensity of power that most humans can't relate to; it can only be aroused and used under strict tuition. It's enough to know that it rises from this chakra, once all are open. The strength of this energy is another reason why the existence of the chakras was only known originally by highly trained spiritualists. This is your starting point along the discovery of the chakras. Its associated action is 'I have' and its connected sense is one of smell. It is indeed your 'root', for you can be likened to a tree that will only grow tall and healthy if it has strong roots. Some of the physical dysfunctions that can occur from blockages within this chakra are: irritable bowels, spastic colon, stiffness in the joints, sciatica, constipation and haemorrhoids. The psychological functions associated with this chakra are your will to live and your amount of physical energy.

Chakra awareness doesn't come easily and quickly, but you can start along this path gradually by asking yourself questions about how you relate to aspects of each chakra. Exercises to clarify these areas come later.

The second chakra is called the navel or sacral. It's located just below the navel and it's associated with the colour orange. This chakra opens both front and back through the body. Its physical connection is to the reproductive system, and the glands affected are the gonads (ovaries in women, testes in men). As you might expect, this relates to your feelings about your own sexuality and your relationships with others. It's not just abut sex, but also about your ability to form intimate, non-sexual bonds. Are you good at sustaining long-term friendships? This chakra is depicted with six petals, each representing a level of a thought which stimulates the mind. The element is water;

this is because our emotions are fluid in movement; they're constantly changing. The animal in this chakra is a mythical 'makara', a half-alligator, half-fish, that lives in deep water. This symbolizes our own emotions which run deep, and our need to delve into the subconscious mind to increase awareness. It also reminds us of the respect we need for all chakra work; they have hidden depths and power which we must appreciate. This chakra is said to contain seeds of our karmic path and, because sexuality is an extremely sensitive area for most people, meditation on this chakra must be gentle and gradual. Its associated action is 'I feel, I want' and it's connected to the sense of taste. Possible physical misfunctions that may arise are: impotence and frigidity, infertility, hormonal imbalances, and fungal infections. Psychologically, this chakra is associated with your quantity of sexual energy and your amount of love for the opposite sex. Just to repeat, delicacy is essential in this area as particularly strong emotions are aroused here.

The third chakra is the solar plexus. It's located below your breastbone and slightly to the left. This is related to the colour yellow and opens both front and back though the body. Its body functions are the stomach, liver, gall bladder and nervous system and its associated gland is the pancreas. This chakra is about your will-power and determination in life, as well as your own sense of destiny. It's about how you feel you fit into the world. The yellow is a reminder of the sun and its energy and strength. The petals now become ten in number and represent a smoky rain cloud. This shows how we cloud our own vision and need to use our own bright sun to burn those clouds away. It's therefore suitable that the element associated with this chakra is fire. You could call your fire your sense of will, your sense of determination. The animal connected to this chakra is the ram, which is sacred to the god of fire, Agni. Most people see the ram as a stubborn creature. Are there areas of your life where your stubborness stops you from seeing clearly? This chakra is also about prana, the life-force, and how we digest that into our system. It's a reminder about how we eat and how we use our energy. Its associated action is 'I can' and it's connected to the sense of sight. Blockages within this chakra often relate to stomach disorders: ulcers, diabetes, chronic indigestion, gastritis and eating disorders. The psychological functions here are healing, your intentions towards your own health, pleasure in expanding awareness and a consciousness of who you are within the universe.

The fourth chakra is the heart chakra. It's situated in the middle of the breastbone, above the chest. The colour used here is grass-green and it opens back and front through the body. The body functions are the heart, blood, vagus nerve and circulatory system. The gland affected is the thymus. The heart is often associated with love and that is true of this chakra, but it's a wider encompassing of love. It doesn't mean the love you have for your partner or child; it's about a universal, unconditional love. This is the level when the vibrational frequencies start to become faster and lighter. We are moving higher into the realms of spiritual consciousness. This is not about needing and demanding love; it's about an unselfish, ever expanding outpouring of love from you towards everything. You give love and expect nothing in return. Have you ever experienced that degree of love? The petals have now increased to twelve and the associated element is air. That's because air is ever-present, our very life-force that is shared by everyone and yet it is invisible. People in the Western World are very suspicious of what they cannot see. Perhaps that is why many have problems with the concept and expression of love. The animal is now the gazelle, sacred to the goddess, Kakini. If you think of the gazelle as it bounds gracefully through the air, it can be said that we also jump up into spiritual awareness and then return to the earth again. There is also the symbol of two interlacing triangles within this chakra. This is meant to show the place where the spiritual and physical may meet and harmonize. The centre of the triangle shows a drop of pure nectar which has fallen from the moon. True, unconditional love generates a compassion which leads to universal awareness and growth. The associated action here is 'I love' and the sense is the sense of touch. Physical dysfunctions within this chakra may show up as: heart problems, high or low blood pressure and allergies. The psychological functions of the heart chakra are your openness to life, your truly loving feelings for others, your ego and your will towards the outer world.

The fifth chakra is the throat chakra. It's positioned at the hollow of the throat and is associated with the colour blue. This is a sky blue, not a dark blue. This chakra opens front and back through the body. The connecting parts of the body are the bronchial and vocal apparatus, lungs and the alimentary canal. The affected gland is the thyroid. This is about purity of speech and clarity of communication. Again, as the vibrations become subtler and lighter, this is not about talking as we normally know it. It doesn't mean how we enunciate words or what accent we use. It's about considering carefully the content and meaning of our words and knowing when is the right time to speak and when we should remain silent. This chakra is also about our hearing; how we hear and interpret words and the power of sound and silence. How can we hear our inner voice if we are not still? The petals have now inceased to sixteen and we are shown a new fifth element 'akasa', which is demonstrated as a circle, with a triangle inside it pointing downwards. This is symbolic of a gateway into liberation. The colour blue is significant here, reminding us of the sky, which is limitless. Expansion is important. Again, the elephant, Airavata, can be seen here but this time he no longer wears his heavy black collar. He is no longer restricted to earth and bound by ties. This chakra is about how transforming speech and sound can strengthen you on your spiritual path. Its associated action is 'I speak' and its sense is one of hearing. Possible disorders from blockages in the throat chakra can result in: sore throats, laryngitis, tonsillitis and tinnitus. The psychological functions of the chakra are considered to be how you take in and assimilate things and your sense of space, relating to your position within society and professional work.

The sixth chakra is known as the 'third eye'. Many of you will have heard this expression before but not known what it really means. It's found in the middle of the forehead and is represented by the colour purple. It opens front and back through the body. Physically it relates to the lower brain, left eye, ears, nose and nervous system. It's associated with the pituitary gland. As we move higher, so we enter further into the realm of the higher consciousness. Cognition is talked about with this chakra but it doesn't mean knowing in the sense of being worldly-wise or well-read. It's about transcending physical knowledge and reaching into spiritual enlightenment. Rational thoughts are not needed because direct knowledge is taking place. It's referred to in our discussion about the knowing sense. Here there are two large white petals, flanked by a circle. They represent the two halves of the pituitary gland, with the brain in the centre. It symbolises harmony of mind. Opening this third eye chakra is about visualisation of higher concepts. There is no element or animal associated to this chakra because it transcends the physical and ordinary in every way. In the centre of the circle there is a triangle, representing three levels of energy which will be discussed in a later chapter. There is a also a golden spot which is to remind us of the energy from which we come and to which we will return; birth and death are but transitions. A quarter moon is barely visible, to symbolize the subtlety of the energy. This third eye chakra is affiliated to the action 'I see' but transcends our five known senses. Physical dysfunctions can be any of the following: disturbed sleep, nightmares, snoring, migraines and dental problems. The psychological functions are summed up as your capacity to visualize and understand concepts and your ability to carry out ideas in a practical way.

The seventh chakra is the crown chakra. Its location is at the top, or crown, of the head. Its colour is violet, although it is often described as white, symbolising purity of the highest level. This chakra opens upwards from the top of the head to allow the cosmic energy to flow in and down through the body. The body areas affected are the upper brain and right eye and it's connected to the pineal gland. This is the highest and finest of all vibrational frequencies and it pertains to a level of consciousness which most of us cannot yet grasp. This is about self-realisation on the highest level which creates fulfilment and a state known as 'bliss'. From the base chakra, the simplest and most instinctive level, you have now reached the crown, the most complex chakra which transcends almost everything we think about in the Western world. How can one grasp ultimate perfection if you have never experienced it? It can only be an ideal to which one aspires at this stage. The path to enlightenment on this level is a slow one. It's also a deeply personal journey requiring both courage and determination. In this chakra the petals are now a thousandfold and they cascade in a lustrous white light down over the top of the head. In the centre of the flower are the symbols of the sun and moon representing the universe. There are no elements or animals associated with this chakra, nor any mantra or tantra. It is simply too high a vibration to be touched upon in any physical sense. It transcends all others. Many spiritual teachers are silent about the wonders of this level; this is said to be because it is beyond description. Its related action is simply 'I know' and it again is beyond any of our five known senses.

If you have managed to read through the descriptions of all seven chakras without taking a pause, you have done remarkably well! This really is an area of psychic and spiritual development that cannot be rushed. These energy centres are your doors into a new world and they won't necessarily open easily and quickly. When they do open, you won't immediately be able to assimilate all the information that is contained within each. It's a lifetime's study. However, there are certain basics you must commit to memory, because these are elements you will use and refer to in almost every aspect of your psychic work. Here are the basics for you to memorise:

1. *Base. Red. Base of spine. Opens downwards to the ground.*

2. *Navel. Orange. Just below navel. Opens front and back.*

3. *Solar Plexus. Yellow. Below breastbone and slightly to the left. Opens front and back.*

4. *Heart. Grass Green. Centre of breastbone, above chest. Opens front and back.*

5. *Throat. Sky Blue. Hollow of throat. Opens front and back.*

6. *Third Eye. Purple. Middle of forehead. Opens front and back.*

7. *Crown. Violet or White. Top of head. Opens upwards to the sky.*

You also need to know that the base and crown chakras are always open in us to allow a flow of energy through our body. However, they normally spin at low speed and when you open up for psychic work, they need to be turned up to vibrate faster. The other five chakras are all closed during normal day-to-day activities and when preparing for psychic work they have to be opened completely. It is therefore essential that they are also closed down thoroughly before you face the outside world again. The method through which you open and close these chakras is explained in a later chapter.

Now, you can do some visualization work with chakras. Although some of you may find it easier than others, this is usually a very emotional experience. These energy centres are very powerful and can trigger off a great deal of hidden feelings. For this reason, you haven't been given the related mantras to chant or details of how to consciously open the chakras. It really is enough, at this stage, for you to think about each chakra and spend a little time looking at emotions and actions related to each.

If, during any of the work below, you feel upset or distressed in any way, either physically or emotionally, stop your visualisation by releasing the thoughts connected with your upset out into thin air. Then concentrate on the beautiful white light above you and draw it gently into your system, using it to cleanse and rejuvenate you. Focus on your breathing and take comfortable, slow breaths. Cleanse for as long as you like, really enjoying the sensation. Remember to always think of your breathing and notice how it is calming and soothing you. Then spend a few minutes focusing on your feet and the weight of your body, before opening your eyes. These exercises are meant to make you think more deeply, but no one should decide that you ought to get upset over something. In all these exercises, you are in control and have the right to stop them at any time. If you feel that by shedding some tears, you can release tensions and improve your state of mind, then that is up to you. Only you know how much you want to delve into different areas of your life. You are in control and can stop at any time. It's important for you to really acknowledge that. You are in control. No matter how freeing, how uninhibiting these visualization techniques may make you feel, it is always you who control and shape them. Restrict your thought processes if you don't yet feel ready to look at certain parts of your life. Remember, you can always go back to the chakras and look at other aspects when you feel ready. There is no rush in this process because there is no timekeeper. Be gentle and remember to love and respect yourself during your spiritual growth and psychic development.

CHAKRA AWARENESS

Firstly, you need to make sure you won't be interrupted at any time during this. Choose a quiet room and lock the door. If you can't lock it, then put a note outside, firmly requesting not to be interrupted. Put the answerphone on; make sure no animal is in the room. Try soft lighting, perhaps a candle, but make sure it is secure in its holder. Ensure you are feeling warm. Lie down if you prefer, although you may find yourself drifting off to sleep. If your powers of concentration are good, you may be fine. If in doubt, choose an upright chair but make sure that it has a comfortably padded seat.

Now settle yourself down, legs uncrossed, feet flat on the floor, hands resting loosely on your thighs, and really concentrate on your breathing. Start off slowly and gently and then gradually breathe more and more deeply, until you feel as if each breath is filling every part of you. If you become aware of any tension in your body, imagine that your breath is going to the spot that aches and then, as you exhale, feel the tension leave your body. Wait until you feel in tune with your breathing and completely relaxed before you move on.

When you feel ready, then lift the ceiling off the room in whatever fashion you choose. Feel the warm light spilling in to the room, filling your space with peace and comfort. Remember to keep concentrating on the light and feel it become stronger, whiter, brighter. Feel it streaming down from above and know it is endless, infinite. Now feel it streaming down into your head through your crown chakra. Now you know there is an energy centre there, and that it is always open, it feels perfectly natural to bring the light into yourself. Imagine the light as pure, holy water if you like that image. Let it fill all of you, and then let it sweep out down through your arms and legs and out of your fingers and toes. Keep this cycle going for several minutes. Let go of every troublesome thought and image, feel it all washing out of you, so that you feel clean and whole. You don't need to rush this process. Wash everything away. When you feel ready, tune in to the first chakra.

BASE CHAKRA

Think of where this chakra is in you; it's situated at the base of your spine and is very much about the physical part of you. What is the spine connected to? What activities take place in that area?

Now think of the colour red. What does red mean to you? What images does it conjure up? What emotions? Concentrate on the colour red and think of how many objects you know that are that colour. Man-made or natural, it doesn't matter which. Think of both. Think of everything you can.

Now think about your physical body. Do you like exercise? Are you good at finding time to exercise all of your body? Do you like your body? What bits do you not like? Why? What do you think about when you think of the parts of your body that you don't like? What emotions or thoughts crop up for you? Realize that every part of you is beautiful just as it is. Realize that you can love all of you.

Now consider how you feel about what you are doing with your life. Do your job and your lifestyle make you feel secure? Do you work at a job you love, or is it simply a means of survival? If you could choose to live another way, what would that be? What does it take to make you feel secure?

Move on to your relationship with nature. How often do you find time to go for a walk or visit the seaside? When was the last time you watched a sunset? Try to remember how you felt when you last experienced these things. Do you have plants in your garden or in your house? How do they help you?

What do you think about your relationship with your mother? Would you describe it as strong and loving? Is there a lack of communication? Think about the memories you have of your mother during childhood. How have those experiences affected you through into adulthood? Concentrate on your mother and know that she loves you in her way. Know that she is doing the best that she can. Send her loving thoughts.

When you feel ready, you are going to leave the base chakra. To do this, create a ball of red colour in front of you. As you watch it, it slowly moves out into the distance and disappears into the universe. You know you can call it back when you next want to meditate on your base chakra; you want to return some time, to look at it further. If you feel you have now done enough exploring for one day, then concentrate again on your weight in the chair and your feet flat on the floor. Tune in to your breathing again and become aware of its comforting rhythm. Before you put the roof back in place, let the white light come down in through your crown chakra again and feel it washing away any unpleasant residue from your meditation. If you are feeling tense, let it wash away the tension. When you're ready, then open your eyes and take several minutes to re-orientate yourself.

For many people, it's enough to concentrate on one chakra at a time. Many are surprised by the unexpected emotions that crop up. You are using your breath, your life-force, to focus your mind and work on new, higher levels of awareness. Development work on your chakras is the start of a deeper expression of yourself. That's why it can be painful at times. It can also be very comforting and rewarding.

Move on to the second chakra when you feel ready. This second energy centre deals very much with your sexuality and relationships. If you don't want to delve into that area at present, that's fine. You can still tune in, but only look at the aspects you feel comfortable with. Perhaps just think about the colour orange and what it means to you. Stop whenever you feel you have done enough work or when you feel you've had enough self-enquiry. Always remember to cleanse thoroughly with the white light and to ground yourself before opening your eyes.

NAVEL/SACRAL CHAKRA
Think about the location of your navel chakra; it's just below your navel and is concerned with relationships. What do you feel about your own navel? What is connected to it? Does thinking about that area make you feel vulnerable or uncomfortable?

Now think about the colour orange. Do you like oranges? Think

103

about other objects are orange. Do you ever wear clothes with orange in them? Think about the emotions you conjure up with orange. Have you got the colour orange around you in your home? Not necessarily on the walls, but in pictures, ornaments and fabrics. Do you like those objects?

Now concentrate on how you feel about sex. (Skip this section if you wish). Do you enjoy love-making? Are you content with your present sex life? Is sex an important part of your life or do you feel sex is somehow dirty? Ask yourself if you feel confident about your sexual abilities and your own sexuality. Does making love make you feel closer to someone, or do you use it as a means of avoiding discussions? Do you find intimacy exciting or intrusive? How many non-sexual friendships do you have? Are they important to you? Consider if you feel comfortable discussing sexual feelings.

When you feel you have delved enough into your sexuality, then create an orange ball in front of you. Watch as it slowly bounces away, disappearing into the distance. It will return on another occasion, when you call upon it. Now you can return to the outside world, using your cleansing and grounding techniques; or you may choose to move on to the third chakra.

SOLAR PLEXUS CHAKRA

Your solar plexus chakra is near your spleen. It is just below your breastbone and slightly to the left and is very much connected to your sense of will-power. Think about your spleen area. What do you know about the spleen? What do the words 'solar plexus' make you think of? What activities take place in that section of your body? When would you feel the need to protect that part of you? Why?

Now concentrate on the colour yellow. What images come into your mind? How do those images make you feel? Try thinking of other objects that are yellow. Do you like some of them? Do you have them around you on a day-to-day basis? When do you not like having yellow around you?

Now think about aspects of life that matter to you, whatever they may be. Do you feel very strongly about them? How strong is your willpower? If you set out to do a task, will you always complete it? Is having a conscience, a sense of what is right and wrong, very important to you? Are you more interested in pleasing others than in listening to your own conscience?

Now think about the word 'power' and what it means to you. Move on to the word 'authority' and how that makes you feel. Do you feel others have power over you? Does that make you angry or sad? Is ambition a positive or negative trait to you? Ask yourself if you are an emotional person. Do you express those emotions clearly or do you try to bottle them up? Can you say 'no' to someone and not feel awkward about it? Do you believe that you truly belong in this world, that you have a special place within the universe which is uniquely designed for you? Are you a workaholic? Consider what possibilities you shut out from your life by your working so hard. Are you frightened of looking into those areas?

When you know you have probed enough into the solar plexus chakra, then decide to let it go. Create a ball of bright yellow and then release it up into the air. Watch it slowly fade away. Did you feel some emotions being released with it? You can look into your solar plexus chakra again, whenever you feel the time is right. Let the images you have created wash away, using your cosmic energy to cleanse and refresh you. Wait until the thoughts have cleared before you move on. Then ground and re-orientate yourself, or choose to tune in to your fourth chakra.

HEART CHAKRA
This chakra is all about unconditional love. Think about your heart. Become aware of it beating against your chest. How is it making you feel? Think of some of the functions of the heart. Do you look after your heart and nurture it? How are you not kind to it? Think of ways in which you could respect and cherish your heart more. How are those thoughts making you feel now?

Then concentrate on the colour green. Visualise it as vibrant grass-

green. What does that colour remind you of? How much of nature is coloured green? Think of as many areas as you can. Then think of fruit and vegetables. Do you like eating those that are green? Then consider other things in life that are usually green in colour. What does that say about those items? Do you choose to have green around you a lot? If you wear green, how does that make you feel?

Now concentrate on the word 'love'. Do you love your partner, children, family and friends equally? Do you love life, nature, the universe? Do you love yourself? Do you feel you should be perfect, so that others will love you? Have you had a moment in life when you felt so full of love, that you felt your heart might burst? Remember when it was, then re-create the moment in your mind and feel the sensation again. Do you believe you should love people as they are, without trying to change them? Can you love yourself, exactly as you are? Do you believe it's possible to love someone without asking for love in return? Try to imagine loving everyone and everything within the universe, realizing that everything is as it's meant to be. Now imagine everyone else loving everyone and everything. Fill yourself with that concept and then hold on to it for as long as possible.

When you feel ready, prepare to move away from the heart chakra. Imagine an enormous green ball is in front of you, pulsating with vibrant, green energy. Give it a gentle tap and see it bounce away into the distance. As it does so, see streamers of pure green light radiating out from it in ever increasing brightness. As the ball fades into the distance, the streamers of green light remain, reaching out and touching everyone and everything with love and light. The green streamers fade away slowly, but you know they are still there, pulsing, unseen, through everything. You will return to your green ball often in the future. As the green light fades into the invisible, cleanse and renew your energy with the cosmic light. When you feel refreshed, choose to either ground yourself and return to the outside world, or move on to the fifth chakra.

THROAT CHAKRA

This chakra is about communication. Focus on your throat. Swallow. How does that feel? What muscles can you feel being used? Think about what your throat connects into. Think about what you choose to put down your throat each day. How does that nourish you? Are there other substances you're not eating that might benefit you? Tune in to your throat and think about what else it needs.

Now concentrate on the colour sky-blue. What sensations come over you as you do so? Think about the blue sky and its limitless expanse. Think about bodies of water: oceans, lakes, rivers and streams. Imagine being the sky, imagine being a large body of water or a trickling brook. How does that expand your thinking? What else is blue? What do those things signify to you? Where have you chosen to have blue in your home? Are any of your clothes blue?

Now consider speech. How often do you really think about what you say before speaking? What might happen if you did? How often have you wanted to say things but not done so? Consider how you felt by not speaking up. How often do you discuss aspects of life which really matter to you? Do you talk openly at work, or with your family and friends? Think about what is left unsaid in these areas and how you might benefit from discussing them. How good are you at being spontaneous? Think about embracing new concepts and notice how that feels.

Now spend some time thinking about sound. Is the thought of complete silence a pleasant or unwelcome state? Do you like listening to music? What do you like/hate? What is it about that music that you respond to? Think about peoples' voices and what you find attractive/ unappealing. Can you think of moments in your life when you have craved silence? Imagine a world where everything was silent. Do you like that idea? What sounds would you miss the most and why? If you were to spend time in silence, what could you learn from the experience? What new and higher levels of awareness are attained through stillness?

When you are ready, slowly withdraw from the throat chakra. Create a ball of sky blue in front of you and then let it float gently off into space, reaching out into, as yet, unfathomable areas of consciousness. As it finally disappears completely, you know you can call it back again. You know that you will, when the time is right. Now bring down the cosmic energy into your crown chakra and feel all thoughts and worries wash out of you. Feel re-energized as you do so, ready to either ground and re-orientate yourself, or to move on to the sixth chakra.

THIRD EYE CHAKRA

This chakra is very much connected to higher spiritual awareness. Concentrate on the middle of your forehead. Can you feel a very light, virtually imperceptible pulse? What does the forehead tell us about people? Think about how your forehead feels and what is behind it. Think about how little we know about the brain and its functions. What else is it capable of? Imagine a world in which everyone uses all of their brain. What might it be like? Realize that you are using more of your own brain as you study this thought.

Now think about the colour purple. What is there in the world that is naturally this colour? What do you have that is purple? Did you acquire the object because you liked its colour? When do you most feel like having purple around you? What effect does it have on you?

Now think back to your concept of the universe before you started reading this book. Has it changed in any way? How? Do you now see yourself differently within this universe? Ask yourself if you have ever had moments in your life when you knew something because your instinct told you, rather than someone else. Do you think we block ourselves sometimes by rationalizing too much? What would happen if everyone opened themselves up to spiritual awareness, instead of concentrating solely on the material world? See a future world where this happens. Let your thoughts dwell on all the problems that would no longer exist, because we would all be taking responsibility for everything. Imagine this awareness spreading to every corner of the earth and how everything would change. Create a clear picture of this state in your mind and know that it is possible.

When you're ready, slowly withdraw yourself from this chakra. See a purple ball, bright and vibrant, in front of you. You may not have to consciously visualize it; it may suddenly be there for you. Notice how beautiful it is; it shimmers with an incandescent richness that is almost overwhelming. Reluctantly, you watch as it slowly glides away into the universe. Know that you can call it back again. Resolve that it will be soon. Wait until the pulsating purple has blended invisibly into the universe, before you become aware of the pure white light again. Then draw the white energy down into you, letting it refresh and re-energize you. When you feel that your energies are properly renewed, close down, or move on to the seventh chakra.

CROWN CHAKRA

This chakra is related to enlightenment, leading to a state of bliss. Think about the crown of your head. What does it feel like? Do you like wearing headwear or does it make you feel restricted? Ask yourself when you would actually want to have something over your head. Did you know that a large percentage of our body heat escapes from the top of our head?

Now concentrate on the colour white. What does white symbolize to you? Can you think of things in the world which are naturally white? What do they mean to you? Now think of how we use white in our every-day life. Think of what it means to different people. Why is white important in a hospital? Why do certain religions use white? Look at where you choose to have white around you in your home. What does that say about you? Consider situations in which the colour white would be important to you.

Now concentrate on the hologram you were working with before. See it in pieces in front of you. You can still see every part of you in each small piece, but the image is blurred. Slowly put all the pieces together to make a whole. Take your time. You may want to move the pieces around for a while before you find the right combination. When it is finished, hold it up in front of you. Looking at it gives you an incredible feeling. Its beauty astonishes you. It is shimmering with gold light and its clarity and radiance overwhelms you. You see how beautiful you are. You see that you and the universe are all one. You know you are connected to everything and everything is connected to you. A feeling of peace and joy sweeps over and through you; it's so intense you can hardly withstand its strength. You feel as though your soul is reaching everywhere, touching everything. You know everything and understand everything. You are lifted into a realm which you canot describe because it transcends everything that we know on earth. It is infinitely more wondrous than all the powers of nature put together. You have the supreme sensation of 'being'. You experience true ecstacy. You have reached complete bliss. You are part of the white cosmic energy. You have become pure light. You rest in this state for some time.

Then you start to remember the earth. You remember that you are also a physical being and you are on earth for a purpose. You now understand your purpose and know you must continue your work. Your task is not yet completed. As you realize all this, you feel your physical body reforming from the white light and you start to become aware of your position in your chair. Feel your weight become heavier and heavier in the seat; your feet are resting firmly on the ground and they are feeling heavier and heavier with each breath you take. You appreciate how heavy your body is now, but it feels warm and relaxed. It tingles with the earth energy, although you know you are also the spiritual energy. Feel the white light cascading over and through you and know you are part of that light, but focus your attention on your physical body. Concentrate on the earth and the jobs you know you must accomplish during your time here. Think about how you will accomplish these tasks. Feel roots growing from the soles of your feet, anchoring you deep into the earth. Feel completely connected again to the earth energy. Let it sweep up through the soles of your feet, up into each part of your body, revitalizing you. Let it flow up through you, all the way up your spine and then down into your shoulders, arms and hands. Feel it trickle out of your fingers again. Let this process happen several times, until you feel thoroughly grounded and re-orientated.

Keep your eyes closed for several minutes afterwards, and concentrate on your breathing and how each breath feels going in and out of your body. When your body feels heavy, slowly open your eyes. Choose one object and focus on it. Concentrate on it until you feel ready to get up and continue with your day.

How did that last exercise feel? Obviously, that is the most difficult chakra to work on. It's the one we understand the least and the concept of working with the unknown is very daunting. If you only felt a slight tremor of excitement, or pleasure, as you were working with the crown chakra, that is quite enough. It's not suggested that you should work a great deal on the seventh level, as most of us aren't ready to deal with it yet.

Remember, the first and seventh chakras are always open in us. They are the energy centres that need to remain open for a healthy flow of energy within us. Although we can open them more for psychic work, they can not be closed down at the end in the same way as the other chakras need to be.

It's important that you realize that all the chakras are of equal significance. It's easy to think of the lower chakras as being the lower part of us and that we know all that already, therefore we need to concentrate on the higher chakras to increase our spiritual growth. It won't work that way. Remember our hologram? Every piece is needed to form a truly clear picture. We need to be as much in touch with our physical, emotional and mental needs, as we are with our spiritual needs. All must operate and function in harmony together, to create a truly holistic experience.

Earlier in the book, you were reading about two basic expressions of psychic work; they are the emotional and mental levels. These levels require different use of the chakras. The emotional levels are what you will be studying through this book and they require full use of the first four chakras: base, navel, solar plexus and heart. The mental levels require use of all the chakras. This is an area that can cause confusion because although you need to concentrate only on the first four chakras for emotional psychic development, all the chakras must be opened before you will work properly. In other words, although you may only practise energy control up to the heart level, it's essential that you open all seven in the first place, so that you can establish a proper flow of energy throughout your body. Once you are fully opened up, then you remain open during work, but focus specifically on the base, navel, solar plexus and heart. As you work your way through the book, this will become more clear. However, do remember that all chakras have equal strength of purpose and our task is to balance and distribute the energy in such a way that we facilitate whichever area we're concentrating on.

It will help you to return again to these Chakra Exercises and to study different aspects of them each time. After you have explored each chakra once, you can then use a certain technique to help you re-study those which you need. You may already know which areas you need to look into more than others and if so, then you can choose which to concentrate upon. If you aren't sure which you want to study, then you can use the following method to help you.

CHOOSING THE RIGHT CHAKRA

Go into your opening-up process, using your breathing and the white light to relax and energize you. Then, rather than trying to decide which chakra to choose, continue breathing comfortably, with your eyes closed. Decide that, this time, you'll ask your inner voice to guide you, so that you can benefit from looking at the chakra which is the most suitable for you at this time. Silently ask yourself which one you need to look at. Ask for help in making the right decision. Don't try to think too hard; don't push yourself in a panic that nothing will happen. Just keep breathing and relaxing. Something will happen when you are ready. It may take a few minutes, or it may happen quite quickly, but either way, that's not important. As you sit there waiting, eyes closed, you will slowly see a ball of light coming towards you out of the far distance. It may take a while before you can see it, because it's coming from such a long way away. It may take a while to approach you, or it may be move at speed. As it comes nearer, you will see the colour and know that this is the area you need to concentrate upon. Remember, you need to memorize the colours to acknowledge which is which:

Red – Base
Orange – Navel
Yellow – Solar Plexus
Green – Heart
Blue – Throat
Purple – Third Eye
White – Crown

It will stop in front of you. It may come close, or it may stop some distance away, but the colour will be clear to you. Often, it's not the colour you're expecting, which shows you are truly listening to your Inner Voice. Whatever the colour of the ball, thank your Inner Voice for guiding you, and ask that you will continue to receive help, when you ask for it. Now concentrate on the ball in front of you and go into your meditation on that chakra. Always remember to cleanse and renew your energies when you finish.

Now you are nearing the time when you can start working psychically, you need to create a special space in which to work. This is an important part of your development.

CHAPTER 6

CREATING YOUR OWN SPACE

Creating your own space doesn't just literally mean making a physical area for your work; it's also about creating enough physical time and emotional space, in which you can work comfortably.

Let's start by looking at time and how you relate to it. Do you feel there are never enough hours in each day? Or do days often drag by for you, each minute feeling like an hour? Or do you feel that each minute is important and that we should balance our needs so that we can effectively use time to work with us, not against us?

Time is an important issue within psychic development because we are all so used to working within the physical timescales that we have set up on earth, that we constantly limit ourselves. Man created seconds, minutes, hours, days, weeks, months and years and most of us have now come to believe that this is the only time that really exists. We base our time on movements in the solar system. A year is the amount of time it takes the Earth to orbit the sun. A day is the amount of time it takes the Earth to do one complete spin on its axis. Did you know that the earth is orbiting the sun at a rate of nearly nineteen miles per second? This means real time is not standing still. As you are sitting reading this book, you are actually moving at more than 67,000 miles per hour. It doesn't sound possible, does it?

Interestingly, other planets move at different speeds. The moon, for instance, takes 27 days and eight hours to revolve once on its axis. Therefore, a day on the moon would mean more than 27 of our days. Confused?

Do you know how long it takes a beam of sunlight to travel from its source, the sun, to our destination of Earth? Eight and a half minutes. The earth is 93 million miles from the sun. If we took a modern jet to the sun, the journey would take us nineteen years. Surely sunlight can't travel here so quickly?

Time is an area you can use for contemplation on many levels. Haven't you experienced occasions when you felt time was standing still, because it was going so slowly? Usually, when something exciting or worrying was imminent: Christmas Day or test results, for instance. Then you have images of time speeding by you although you long for it to slow down: during your holiday period, or when you have limited time with a loved one before you have to spend time apart. During those moments, you are experiencing time spontaneously. You are completely aware of time and how it really feels. On other occasions, your mind is being dictated to about how you should think about time. Try the following two experiments:

SAD TIME

Set a timer for three minutes. Close your eyes and immediately concentrate on a time in your life when you felt unhappy. It can be any incident, small or large, recent or far back in the past. Recall what happened and how you felt. Focus on your feelings and what it felt like. Try to keep your attention on the incident until the buzzer goes off. When it does, re-set the timer for three minutes again.

HAPPY TIME

As soon as you have re-set the timer, close your eyes and immediately focus on a happy time in your life. Recreate the time in your mind and feel the sensations of happiness washing over you. Remember just how good it felt. Let every part of you relive the joyful sensation of euphoria. Keep focused until the buzzer goes off. Cleanse and ground yourself again.

Did you discover that the sad time went much more slowly? Were you waiting for the buzzer to go off? Conversely, did the happy time fly by in a flash? This is most people's experience. That was you responding to time by feeling every moment as it comes along. This is something we very rarely do: appreciate each segment of time. We use time as a means of getting through the day: so many hours for work, so many hours for sleep, because we are stuck in a routine and we believe that is all we have. The reality is we can create time for anything we want. It's a question of how we recreate it.

Now try an experiment to see how you value time. Take a pen and paper and draw a large circle. This circle now represents your day. How do you divide up your time each day? Divide the circle into individual 'pie slices'. Obviously, some days are different from others, but take an average day and work out where you devote your energies. Be completely honest with yourself; if you spend twelve hours at work, put that down. If you watch television for three or four hours every night, write that down too. The more detailed you are, the more you'll be able to see exactly how you use your time. Instead of just breaking the twenty-four hour period into sleep, work, travel and socializing For example, put in the following:

— *how long you spend getting ready in the morning*

— *how much time you spend eating*

— *when you fit any physical exercise into your day*

— *what part of a day you spend reading and whether it's a newspaper, novel or factual book*

— *how much time you spend with family and friends*

— *when you find time for appreciation of nature*

— *how often you go shopping*

— *how much time is spent cleaning and cooking*

— *when you listen to music*

— *how many hours a day you devote to hobbies*

117

— *how often you spend on the telephone*

— *how much of your day is spent with other people*

— *how much time you take just for yourself for quiet reflection*

By the time you get to the last statement, your piece of paper will probably be looking a complete jumble and you'll wonder how you fit everything into each day already. No wonder you never take any time for yourself. The reason most people aren't good at this, is because they feel guilty. They associate time spent alone with being selfish and ungiving. You think you are a better person if you spend all your time rushing around sorting out other people. You don't need to concentrate on yourself because you're fine. Anyway, it would be selfish.

You need to understand that there is a difference between time alone, used for spiritual growth, and time alone spent eating chocolate, drinking coffee and watching television. This isn't to say the last three haven't got their own pleasures; most people enjoy those aspects of life from time to time. The crux of the matter is whether you also spend any time in stillness and silence, getting in touch with yourself. Most of us don't. The other reason for this is simply fear. We aren't sure what we may discover if we stop living our hectic lives and spend some time thinking. Most of us don't want to stop and think too much. Most of us have areas of our lives which we don't want to look at, because if we did, it might mean changes. Some of those changes might have to be major upheavals and might be upsetting. It feels safer to stay in whatever hole you're in now, rather than poke your head out and risk the outside world. Better to settle for what you've got.

If that truly is how you feel, you wouldn't be reading this now. You obviously know there is more going on out there and you are prepared for some of the changes that may happen along the path.

One of the changes you now need to make is a physical change. You need to find at least fifteen minutes each day that you can call your own, without interruption from outside forces. It would be better if you could find half an hour, but if that seems too daunting at this stage, then compromise with fifteen minutes. It needs to be fifteen minutes every day, not just once or twice a week, or when you feel like it. It should ideally be the same time every day, too. This is an important discipline for you; you have to train your mind to respond to new needs, as well as new ideas. You'll probably encounter a fair amount of resistance along the way. You're probably resisting even as you're reading this, wondering how you can manage even fifteen minutes. You can. Everyone can. It's a question of determination, coupled with a logical approach.

Look at the circle you have drawn on the paper. It's no doubt a mass of small 'pies' now, as you've tried to be specific about everything you do each day. Now really look at what takes up your time; really study everything you do. What isn't really necessary in your day? What perhaps hinders, rather than helps, your personal development and that you could decrease, or cut out, without harming anyone else? Do you need to spend so much time getting ready each day? Could you take a shower instead of having a bath? Do you need to do so much cleaning and shopping? If you have children, when could they be occupied doing something they really enjoy, while you have your own free time? Would your partner actually welcome fifteen minutes of their own free time when they could do their own thing? Do you really need to spend all that time at work? Do you stay late/arrive early when it really isn't required? (Look at how you arrange the work part of your day, if necessary.) Could you get up fifteen minutes earlier each day, or go to bed fifteen minutes later, without causing much hardship? If you keep looking and keep considering new possibilities, you really will see how you can find fifteen minutes a day. If you are dedicated enough, you may find half an hour. Try to find the same time each day. If you're a morning person, choose some time then. If you're a night owl, opt for evening time, but try not to make your free time just before you go to sleep. Meditation often makes the mind active and it's hard to shut off sometimes afterwards. Also, inspirational thoughts often occur after you've had some quiet time. Morning and afternoon are the best choices, if you can work your schedule that way.

Once you have found your fifteen minutes of free time, you need to be committed to it. Sometimes, during your meditations, you'll feel

119

discouraged and irritated. Your progress will seem slow and sometimes seem to take steps backwards. Continuing through all the setbacks is part of your discipline.

After you have found your time for yourself each day, don't try to set yourself goals about your speed of development. If you've worked in large companies, you'll probably be used to working in a framework where you set yourself specific goals, always using an ambitious timescale. Psychic work can't operate on this level. Apart from a commitment to fifteen minutes or half an hour each day, you can't further determine what you will accomplish within any period. You move forward when the time is right for you and you have to trust that this is the right way for it to be. Some of you may find the opening-up process to be an easy one, others will struggle with it; others will find once they have opened up that it takes them a while before they can tune in on the psychic level; others will tune in quickly but then be confused about the information they're receiving; some of you may sit there for weeks and not experience any sensation at all; others will open up and receive so much information so quickly that they aren't able to assimilate it all. So your progress will be individual to you and if you are working with a friend or partner, don't compare notes and set up an unconsciously competitive environment. This will only hinder both of you. If you want to discuss your separate experiences, make sure you do so in an encouraging and positive manner, supporting each other and never criticizing.

Now you have created your own quiet time, you need to consider further aspects of yourself to allow the best opportunities to develop psychically. Some of the following points may seem obvious to you, but, if you're honest, you probably don't always adhere to them. Try to incorporate them as much as you can, but be aware that you are also human and not perfect. You can do your best, but be kind to yourself when you slip up.

Firstly, consider how you look after yourself physically. You've already been looking at why physical exercise is important; do you exercise three times a week? It doesn't have to mean going to the gym or jogging for miles around the streets. Brisk walks are just as effective.

You could join an evening class in yoga, t'ai chi or chi gong. Biking, swimming, rowing, dancing, or any form of active sport: any of these can be enjoyable as well as health-giving. If you're going to share the activity, it also gives you the chance to spend some time with someone you love. Perhaps you may feel you haven't had enough time with your child recently; share an exercise together and enjoy two positive experiences at once.

At the other end of the spectrum from physical exercise, is the need for sleep. This is a personal affair, as we are all different. Some of us need at least eight to ten hours; others operate well on six. Many people have the wonderful ability to cat-nap for ten or fifteen minutes at a stretch and to wake up refreshed; if others try that, they wake up feeling disorientated and grumpy. Start listening to the needs of your body and learn what works best for you. Are you sleeping more than you need because you want to block out aspects of your life? Are you not getting enough because you think sleep is a nuisance that you have to fit in when you can? Sleep is essential for refreshing and renewing all aspects of your being. If you tune in to your own requirements, you really will feel the benefits. You'll have far more energy; every part of you reaps the rewards.

Now consider what you eat. You already understand that food has its own energy and you are actually consuming that energy when you eat. Therefore, different energy foods will help you in different ways. How the food is grown is important. We all know fruit and vegetables are good for us; they're a wonderful form of pure energy. However, acid rain, pesticides and environmental pollution are heavily diminishing much of food's natural energy. If you consume organic food, you are giving yourself the best chance of high-energy food. This isn't always possible, but it's an ideal towards which you can aim. Keeping food for too long will also work against you. Food's auric levels drop considerably when they are left to spoil. Also, over-cooking will burn off their energy; steamed vegetables will benefit you far more than heavily boiled ones. Steaming trays which fit inside any sized saucepan are now easily available and very inexpensive.

Whether or not you choose to eat meat is a personal decision that you must make for yourself. However, it's important for you to know that an animal which is slaughtered in terror will contain within its flesh the energy of that deep distress. By eating its body, you are then consuming the energy of that fear. This isn't to say that you should stop all meat-eating; you need to make up your own mind about what feels right for you.

This book isn't a nutritional guide, so you won't find details about the specific foods you should or shouldn't eat. You can use your own common sense. Heavily processed foods have little or no natural earth energy within them; any excess of any type of food will not benefit you. You no doubt realize that a diet high in fresh fruit and vegetables and whole grains will benefit you more than a diet of abattoir-slaughtered meat and convenience foods jammed with chemical additives and preservatives. Excessive consumption of stimulants such as alcohol, tea and coffee will damage your aura; filtered or spring water will nourish you.

Water is a particularly important part of our needs; we often overlook its power. Human beings are seventy per cent water. The brain is more than ninety per cent water; even our bones are sixty per cent water. We need to constantly renew our water system and most of us let ourselves become dehydrated without realizing it. Drink as much spring water and herbal teas throughout the day as you want. You're unlikely to over-dose on your needs.

If you are concerned about your diet, or want to know more, consult a nutritionalist who specializes in individual requirements. Any holisitic health centre will be able to guide you. Our make-up is unique, so we all have different needs. If you want to be certain you are eating what is best for you, someone who is well-trained in holistic health can advise on all your needs: those of your emotional, mental and spiritual being, as well as your physical body.

When you work psychically, there are a few dietary 'musts'. Alcohol and drugs never, ever mix with psychic work. Whatever your interest in either, you should not have consumed any at least six hours prior to working. An excess before that will also leave its effect on you. You simply can not tune in altered states of awareness when under outside influences. Whatever information you receive will be jumbled, inaccurate and frequently distressing, as you'll be tuning in to lower energy levels. Can you remember the Basement level in the Expanding Your Thoughts Exercise in the Introduction? You are likely to receive distorted information on that level. It's dangerous, imbalancing and highly upsetting. By all means, have a drink after psychic work to celebrate your progress; drinking before work means you won't have any progress to celebrate. Eating a heavy meal before you start work will also adversely affect you. Your body will be busy using its energy to digest the food and it will direct energy away from your psychic work. Of course, if you're feeling extremely hungry, this will also distract your attention. A light meal about four hours before you work, will best support you. This isn't always possible, depending on your day's activities, but it's the ideal when you can manage it.

How particular are you about physical hygiene? This is another area that affects our spiritual and psychic growth. Our skin is the means through which energy flows in and out. We need to keep that clean and unclogged. This doesn't just mean washing regularly, although of course that is important to cleanse away unwanted residues. Try to use natural, non-toxic soaps, moisturisers, make-up and shampoos. Do you clean your teeth thoroughly? Stale food left between the teeth is unhealthy energy. Floss your teeth to ensure they're really clean and use natural toothpastes whenever possible. Keeping your nails clean is also important. Once you appreciate how easily we can pick up unhealthy energies, it makes it less of an effort to be particular about hygiene. You can accept it as part of cleansing your aura and something that positively benefits all of you.

What sort of clothes do you wear? Are they natural fibres such as cotton, silk and wool? How many of your clothes are synthetic? Looking at the labels makes you realize how little clothing is made from natural fibres. This doesn't mean you need to change your whole wardrobe. It does mean it would help if you could choose mostly natural fibres to wear next to your skin: underwear, for instance. Cotton pants and vest and socks would be a good compromise. How tight is your clothing? Is it restricting your skin's ability to breathe? When you are practising psychic work, try to wear loose, comfortable clothing.

The less aware you are of your clothes, the more you can concentrate on your work. Particularly as a beginner, it's best if you practise without wearing footwear, apart from socks or tights. You need the soles of your feet to maintain direct contact with the ground, so that you are helped as much as possible with your grounding techniques. Shoes, especially high heels are not suitable. If you're working on your own, undo your belt or shirt collar or bra. Help yourself by relaxing as much as possible.

What sort of colours do you tend to wear? Colours and their influences are a fascinating subject, but they require a book on their own. Each colour has its own positive and negative vibrations and trying to list them all here isn't possible. Generally speaking, constantly wearing dark colours will tend to deplete your energy field. It makes it harder for you to release unwanted energy and for other energies to penetrate you. This doesn't mean that sometimes this isn't a good thing. Think about the tradition of wearing black when someone has died. That is usually a time when people feel very vulnerable and emotional; black can help protect them from others, it can make them feel protected and cocooned. Grieving is an intensely private process. However, if you constantly wear black, then you are always preventing yourself from opening up to others and receiving their energies back. How you use colours is a question of balance.

To find out what colours are right for you each day, simply open your wardrobe and look at your clothes. What do you feel drawn to? After you have done this for a week, you will be tuning in to your intuitional sense without trying. You unconsciously know what colours you need to nurture and renew your energies.

A clue to help you is to relate them to the chakras, although this is a basic level and it is more complex than that. Are you planning a sexy evening with your lover and wanting to enhance the energies? Try orange. Do you need to feel loving and giving in your work today? Choosing something green will increase the heart chakra's vibrations. If you feel your day will require inner strength and a sense of calm, try using some blue. When would purple seem appropriate as a choice? When might you use red?

Jewellery is another influencing factor. How often do you put on a piece of jewellery without considering whether its energy is compatible with your energy fields? Now you understand how every object carries its own energies, this becomes increasingly important. You can check for yourself whether a piece of jewellery is right for you. All you have to do is hold it in the palm of your hand and see what you feel. Is it warm or cold? Does its energy feel sharp and brittle or strong and comforting? Do you feel a sense of well-being sweep over you as you hold it? Have you started to feel uncomfortable or unbalanced? Unless the item feels rights for you, choose not to wear it. You can also hold it to the area where the item will be resting, to see if it feels right. Hold a necklace up to your throat. Is it compatible with your throat's vibrations? Experiments will guide you and, after a while, you will know by looking at a piece of jewellery whether it's right for you to wear that day. Your hand will be drawn to certain items without your stopping to question it. You may have often worn certain items without thinking about it and now realize it's because of their energies that you did so. You may also find out that items you have previously worn a lot and have grown fond of, are not naturally suited to you now. You can cleanse an object of its energies; details of how to do this can be found in Chapter 24 on psychic defence. You may need to do this with certain items eventually. There is no need for you to get rid of any object, unless you consciously choose to do so.

Now let's move on to look at the physical space you need to create. You know that every space has its own energy and that energy is created by the people and objects within it. You need to think about creating a space of your own in which to practise psychic development. The reason this is so important is because your growth is helped enormously by the environment in which you are working. By always being in one space, you are constantly charging the energy there with your own psychic work. The energy will therefore become stronger. It becomes your own haven of safety and comfort, where enlightenment can reach down and touch you, because you have created the positive energies for this to happen. If you shift from room to room, you don't allow the energy to strengthen. It will become dissipated by the various areas and none of those areas will resonate as powerfully as your own private space.

Creating a room of your own may be difficult for some people. It doesn't have to be large. If there isn't a whole room available to you, try sectioning off part of a room by using a tall screen or bookshelves. Make sure whatever you use as a room divider resonates with your own energies.

Once you have found a small area you can call your own, you need to start furnishing it in the way that feels right for you. This is a personal matter, but below are some ideas for you to consider.

You were reading that colours are important in the clothing you choose. They are also important in creating your own space. If you have the opportunity to colour the walls as you want, then do so. Again, dark colours are generally draining, so you're best to choose lighter shades. Be careful in your choice. Some pale, natural shades can give off a depressing hue to certain people. Spend some time in a paint shop, or acquire some paint cards and really study each colour. Does that mushroom beige make you feel very different from the lemon yellow? Is forget-me-not blue making you feel good, or do you prefer that rose pink? Is one colour making you feel sleepy? Is that colour making you feel slightly agitated? As your relationship with colours may still be in early development, don't rush the process. If you feel uncertain, you could try buying a small sampler first and testing a patch of wall. A wallpaper with any design on it will most likely prove distracting and jar with the energies you create. Keep the colour and design simple; let it enhance your vibrations without confusing them.

If re-painting your space is not a viable option, then try putting up some pictures. Artwork is a very powerful form of energy. Again, it's very personal. What resonates well with one person will completely unbalance somebody else. Look at the pictures you have hanging up in your house. Do you like them all? Do certain ones make you feel particularly good, or inspire you? Look at their shapes and colours and see what it is you like about them. Move them into your private space and see what they feel like then. Has the energy now changed within your room? You may not like it once you've moved the picture. It may have worked better in its original place. When you have time, visit art galleries and start looking more closely at pictures. You will find some artists instinctively appeal to you more than others. You don't necessarily have to understand why to appreciate your feelings. See if you can purchase posters of the paintings and put them up in your space. Of course, reproductions can never be the same as the originals. Understanding energies makes you appreciate why original work has a more vibrant power. It isn't simply that the colours don't copy as well; you are also being influenced by the painter's own aura. Spiritual awareness also affects art appreciation. You'll be amazed how much more a painting will mean to you once you have tuned in to its energies.

You need to consider your floor and ceiling space as well as the walls. The lighter the ceiling the better for your development. Floor covering is again a personal choice. Some people find bare floorboards purifying and energizing; others find them cold and uncomfortable. You may prefer a mixture: bare floorboards with a rug of your choice on top. If you have carpet already and don't like it but can't afford to replace it all, then you can purchase an inexpensive rag rug to cover most of it. The colour and texture of the rug needs to complement you, but it needn't be a costly item.

Now what furniture and objects do you wish to have within your own personal space? You need an upright chair with a padded seat for many of your exercises. You may want to lie down for others. You may need a table to hold books and a lamp. You may want to have some crystals around you (they're discussed in more detail in Chapter 17) or a music player for cassettes and CDs. You may like candlelight. Do you want some plants around you to increase the energy, or some metal? Animals aren't necessarily beneficial as they can be distracting. However, as it's your space, you can put into it whatever you want.

One word of warning. Creating a jumbled space will create a jumbled mind. An object should be there because it has a functional use and because it's an energy-balancer. If you fill your space with a variety of different objects and furniture, instead of it feeling comforting, you will find it claustrophobic and uninspiring. It's easy initially to confuse a chaotic, crammed space with cosiness. After a while, you will appreciate there is a big difference. If you do put too many things into your space, you will gradually want to take items out again.

If you are re-arranging a space that is already full of things, look at the items carefully. This means delving into drawers stuffed with oddments and perusing over-flowing bookcases. Do you really want that old birthday card? Do you need that newspaper cutting? That piece of ribbon taken from a cake, that cork from an old wine bottle, the old telephone directories, the shirt you haven't worn for five years: look at all those items and decide which you really want to keep. This isn't to say you should throw out sentimental momentos because you have to be clean and uncluttered. You can re-group items into contained areas so the energy is focused and not scattered. Where an object is placed in a room is as important as whether it's in there at all. Perhaps you have a number of items that bring back pleasant memories but they're spread into odd corners and drawers. Try putting them all together, perhaps on one shelf, or in a box. How does that feel now? Keep going through your space, re-arranging and clearing away what you know you don't want. This alone has an amazing effect on the energy in the room.

You know how you feel so much better after a good clear-out, whether it's the contents in your fridge or a whole attic? This isn't just because you have done something you meant to do for ages; it's also because you have changed the energies by doing so. Old, stagnant vibrations have been replaced by new, vibrant energy. Spaces have been cleared to allow it to move more freely around and through everything.

What you're reading about is discussed in much more detail in feng shui. Many of you will have heard of this: it's an ancient Chinese art of designing an harmonious environment. Feng shui is based on the concept that human energy needs to be balanced with earth energy and the way we accompish this is through attention to a number of details: the geographical location in which you live, the weather, the position of all doors and windows within your home, the flow of water around your home, the stars, animals, neighbours, and room design within your home. Its intent is to create a holistic environment in which you maximize the flow of healthy energy throughout your living space. Where location and design are not ideal but cannot feasibly be altered, mirrors are used to deflect negative energy and sound is used to rebalance areas. A good feng shui guide will be able to harmonize all the energies to best suit your home. However, it cannot harmonise you!

Although positive vibrations around you will enhance your own development, nothing can take the place of your commitment to working with your own personal energies.

Light is another consideration, both natural and artificial. Sunlight is a powerful energy-restorer and balancer. If possible, have natural light within your own space. If you have to resort to artifical light, avoid fluorescent illumination. It's not compatible with your aura; it actually strobes in a way that is discordant with human energies. Many problems with office workers' headaches have been linked to the ever-increasing use of this cheap form of lighting. However, it's not cheap if workers then have to spend both time and money correcting energy imbalances that have made them ill. Use soft lighting, if it has to be artificial. Choose soft-coloured light shades and pearl bulbs. Another helpful aid would be the soothing qualities of candlelight, provided you put candles in secure holders and ensure there is enough of the candle to last through whatever you are working on.

Using candles creates a special energy all of its own. Most of us associate candlelight with romantic scenes. The warm glow of a candle help ignite our own loving capacities. When you want to increase loving vibrations within your aura, try this visualisation technique using a candle:

THE CANDLE
Light a candle and place it on a table in front of you. Sit in your comfortable, upright chair, facing the candle. Focus your eyes upon the candle flame. You don't need to stare intently; it should be a soft, relaxed gaze. Remember to breathe deeply. If your eyes start to hurt, close them for a minute, then continuing looking at the flame.

After a few minutes, close your eyes. You should see the flame in front of you still. If it isn't there, or it disappears very quickly, open your eyes once more and focus on the light. Then try again. Once you can close your eyes and keep the flame in front of you, you can move on. See the flame in front of your closed eyes for a moment, and then imagine the flame moving from in front of you, to inside your chest, filling your heart with a warm, golden light. (If another light colour seems more appropriate, that is fine, but don't visualize a dark colour). With each breath, feel the warm light filling every part of you, making you feel more peaceful and loving all the time. Let the sensation of tranquillity and true unconditional love fill every part of you, until every cell of your body is vibrating with this wonderful, soft energy.

Stay in that state for several minutes, then slowly visualize the flame withdrawing from your chest and returning to your vision in front of you. Slowly open your eyes and focus on the candle flame in front of you. If you feel light-headed, remember to concentrate on your feet. Feel them flat against the ground and notice how heavy they feel as you balance yourself again.

If that worked as a powerful visualization for you, perhaps you should consider having a candle with you whilst you work. That exercise is very good at restoring your loving energy if you have had a disagreement with someone, or if you generally feel out of sorts with the world. It will soothe you, helping to restore balance after any anger or irritation.

Another good energy-balancer is sound. Sound has been used to centuries as a way of focusing the mind and also for healing techniques. Many religious groups use chanting as a way of increasing awareness; medicine healers of all cultures and countries have used it to balance unhealthy individuals.

There is a wide range of music available on the market and you need to experiment to discover what sound soothes, uplifts and inspires you. Classical music has been known to have positive effects on many people. Others prefer the New Age composers who use synthesisers, chimes, flutes and harps to create a very light, floating sensation. There are also tapes of 'natural sonds', such as flowing water, ocean waves, dolpin or whale sounds and birdsong. Once you start looking for yourself, you'll appreciate how much there is on offer. Your taste will be individual to you. What one person finds spiritually uplifting, another will describe as fingernails on a chalkboard! When you work with other people, or give a reading, music is not necessarily appropriate. During your own personal development, it is an essential part of your growth.

Different types of music have been shown to work well with different chakras. For example, drum beats are said to activate the base chakra, which connects us to our earthly roots. Popular and rock music is said to awaken our sexuality within our sacral chakra. Love songs awaken our heart centre, and pure harp music is said to benefit the higher chakras. If you experiment for yourself, you will tune in to what works best for you. If you live with others, you should consider using head-phones for these experiments. Remember, what you like may not necessarily be their choice and by inflicting it upon them, you're disturbing their own energy fields. That will adversely rebound on you.

Research has also been done into how sounds are directly related to nature. This is called Cymatics. The late Dr. Hans Jening conducted a series of experiments whereby he placed fine grains of sand onto a metal plate. He then sent a steady, unbroken stream of sound through the plate. The sands formed into a distinct pattern. When he changed the sound frequency, the pattern changed again. He returned to the first sound; the sand reformed into its first pattern. He found this to be a consistent phenomenon; every sound frequency had its own pattern of sand. When the sound was stopped completely, the grains of sand then returned to settle according to gravitational pull. Further work has been carried out by many other people since.

Of course, sound can also have very stressful effects upon us. Noise pollution has become a recognised problem, particularly in large cities. To avoid imbalancing your energies, try wherever possible to control the effect of noise pollution. Sleep in well-glazed rooms, use heavy drapes to help cut out noise, use ear plugs, close the doors in your home to help cut out other people's music and noise, and soundproof areas if you have that option open to you.

It can be particularly difficult if you have children who are passionate about certain types of music which you find stressful. Restricting their appreciation of music may only hinder their own individual growth. Instead of asking them to turn the sounds off, opt for purchasing an inexpensive set of headphones as a gift. Then you can all pursue your own level of needs.

Unless you dislike houseplants, you should try putting one or two into your own space. Their energy is different again, and offers a balance to our aura. What you choose depends on you. Some people are passionate about cacti; others find their shapes disturbing. Some like plants which gives off a scent, such as many of the geraniums; some of you may find that over-powering. Choose a size that seems right for your space. Too large a plant will make you feel suffocated; a small one may not increase the vibrations sufficiently for you to feel the effect. Also, ensure the plant has enough natural light; most will die without a moderate amount of sun. Fresh flowers are also an option. Many psychics always work with a posy next to them. If that suits you, make sure you get rid of the flowers when they die. Dead flowers leave another form of stagnant energy within a room, as well as an unpleasant smell.

Scent is another important aspect to consider. What smells do you find appealing? Fresh lemons? Cinnamon? Lavender? Or do musky scents, such as dry autumn leaves, resonate well with you? Perhaps you prefer the smell of pine needles. You need to develop this appreciation through experiments.

Most of you will have heard of aromatherapy: using scents as a form of therapy. It's now easy to purchase, on the market, aromatherapy oils taken from a wealth of substances. Some products are excellent: pure, distilled oils from natural substances, without any synthetic additives. Unfortunately, a growing number are now coming on the market that profess to be aromatherapy oils when they are no more than synthetic odours diluted into a cheap carrier oil. These will not assist your energy levels in any sense. In fact, they may clog your field by their very synthetic nature. When in doubt, question the shop as to the oil's ingredients. A good shop will soon clarify the issue for you. These oils can then be used in the bath, diluted and used as a massage oil, or vaporized into the air using a variety of methods available on the market. Even a few drops placed onto a ball of cottonwool and then left in front of you on your desk can have a wonderful effect. However, some of the pure oils can be expensive and you may not wish to spend the money. There are alternatives that are easier.

Do you like lemon oil? Buy half a dozen lemons and place them in a wooden bowl in your room. If pine smells terrific to you, take a walk in a pine forest and gather a small handful of needles. Place them in a small dish. If a friend grows lavender, ask them for a few cuttings which you can then tie and turn upside down to dry. The delicious smell of sweet lavender will fill your space for months. If geranium oil appeals to you, buy a small geranium plant whose leaves are scented. Then simply brush your hands gently along the leaves and its sweet perfume will be left on your hands. Appreciation of odour doesn't have to be a costly business. With a little imagination, you can create your own pleasant aromas for next to nothing.

You also need something pleasing to touch. (Have you realized that in creating your own space, you have been giving thought to four of your five senses? Taste isn't appropriate during actual work, as food and psychic study don't mix well.) What textures do you find comforting and enriching? For many people, it's something soft like silk or satin. Do you have a small cushion you could place on your seat which you could touch as you start work? Perhaps you just have a small square of fabric which you like. You could even take a trip into a fabrics and furnishings shop and look at different fabrics, including their colour. Buy a small length of whatever feels and looks right to you, and keep that on your chair. You will then charge it with your energy and can use it as a means of re-charging yourself quickly when you sit down to work.

Lastly, you need fresh air. If your space doesn't have its own window, make sure you can create a through draught where air can circulate freely. You should air your space every day. There are also air humidifiers you can purchase to improve air quality. Other methods such as smudging, crystals and auric brushing are included in Chapter Twenty-Four . Whatever you use, remember you need to keep the energy flowing. Imbuing everything in your space with your own energy doesn't mean leaving it all there to stagnant. All energies need to flow and circulate to keep them vibrant and healthy. Try moving objects around within your space. If you don't like the result, you can then put things back where they were. It's important your space grows and changes, reflecting and encouraging growth and change in you.

Now we're going to take a last look at meditation and relaxation exercises, before you start learning your tuning-in process that will enable you to work psychically.

CHAPTER 7

BREATHING AND RELAXATION

You probably realize why relaxation is such an important area in psychic development, but the key to becoming truly relaxed (and also the key to opening up in psychic work) is through your breathing.

Our breath is the means through which we can access higher awareness; the deeper and slower our breathing, the better we can work at higher levels. Most of us never make full use of our breath during our lifetime. If you have spent time studying yoga, you'll already understand how important it is, and know that deep breathing takes many years of practice before you can become proficient. This book is intended to point the way for you, but only your own time and dedication will make the difference.

It will help if you understand the physical process of breathing. If you look at the diagrams on pages 136 and 138, as you read through this, you'll see how it works.

We should breathe in air through our nose. It's important to use your nose and not your mouth, because your nose contains little hair follicles and mucous membranes that help filter out the impurities of the air. The nose also warms and moistens the air as it starts its route towards the lungs. Have you noticed if you're outside on a really cold day and you take a deep breath in through your mouth, that it hurts inside your chest? This is because the mouth hasn't warmed the air the way that the nasal passages do, and the cold going into your lungs is painful.

Once the air is drawn inside our nose, it then travels down the larynx and into the trachea. The trachea then divides into the two main

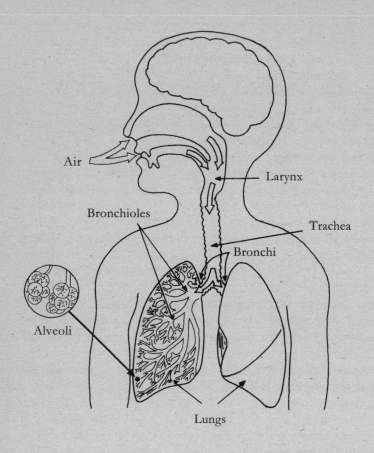

Breathing

bronchi, which in turn each lead into a lung. Once the bronchus gets into the lung itself, it then divides into smaller branches, called bronchiole. At the tip of each bronchiole, there are tiny balloon-like cavities, which are called alveoli. Each lung contains nearly half a billion of these tiny sacs. If your breathing is shallow, you never inflate all these tiny ballons and they will start to deteriorate. The lift-giving exchange of oxygen for carbon dioxide happens through minuscule blood vessels in these balloons' walls. (The pumping of the heart is then responsible for distributing the blood around every part of the body, via a complex web of blood vessels.) When we exhale, we release the carbon dioxide waste from our lungs.

These two lungs themselves are a powerful house of energy but we rarely use them to their full capacity. Most of us only fill about one third of our lungs. Although each lung can be sectioned into three areas-upper, middle and lower lobes – we have yet to learn how to make full use of them.

The muscle which is responsible for controlling the lung activity, is the diaphragm; see page 138. This is a large dome-shaped muscle that separates the chest cavity from the abdomen. It lies directly under the lungs and, as you can see from the diagrams, during inhalation, the muscle stretches out to allow air into the lungs. As you exhale, the diaphragm curves inwards and upwards to help force all the unwanted air out of your lungs. This diaphragm is one of the most under-used muscles in the human body. For successful psychic work you need to learn how to strengthen it. Most of us breathe in the upper part of our chest, rather than letting the diaphragm do its work properly. Here's an exercise for you to check whether you're using your diaphragm properly when breathing.

Please note, however, that all these exercises need to be done gently when you first start. If you have never breathed deeply before, you may quickly end up feeling dizzy. This means you have built up too much carbon dioxide in your body too quickly and your body is asking you to breathe faster to get rid of it. Build up to all breathing exercises with care. If at any time during them you start to feel slightly light-headed or dizzy, immediately revert to your normal breathing, until you feel

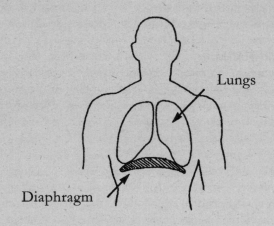

Lungs

Diaphragm

The Diaphragm when inhaling

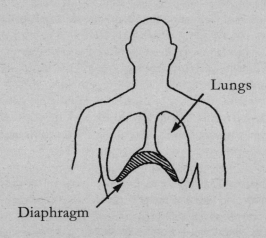

Lungs

Diaphragm

The Diaphragm when exhaling

grounded again. Wait a few minutes before you try again, and then breathe less deeply. Your body won't know what is going on if you rush the process. After all, it's got quite used to your shallow breathing over the years and it doesn't know what on earth you're doing to it now!

THE DIAPHRAGM

Position yourself in front of a full-length mirror (or a mirror that at least shows you the top half of your body, down to your waist). Stand up straight, with your legs shoulder-width apart and fix your eyes on your ribcage. Now place your hands gently over the base of your ribs, with your middle fingers barely touching each other. Try taking a comfortable breath in, but don't force it. Watch your ribcage as you do so. Is it expanding outwards, such that your fingertips are no longer touching each other? Exhale slowly. Do your fingertips meet again as you finish? Try again, gently, to see if you can move your fingertips apart. Then exhale again. Are your fingers moving at all? Now breathe in again, but this time look at your shoulders. Are they lifting upwards as you take in your deep breath?

For most peoeple, their shoulders lift but their fingertips barely move apart. This means that you are shallow-breathing, using your upper chest and not your full lung capacity. For psychic work, you need to learn how to use the diaphragm muscle and deepen your breathing. This will be a gradual process but you can accomplish it. Now continue the exercise but try this:

Let your arms hang loosely by your side. Imagine that your shoulders have weights attached to them. Notice how heavy your shoulders feel resting in their sockets. Make sure you don't slump any part of your body as you do this. Think of the weights as grounding you, helping you to connect with the earth energy, rather than forcing you into the ground. When your shoulders feel nice and heavy, then lift your arms and place your fingers over your lower ribcage once more. Keep concentrating on how heavy and relaxed your shoulders feel. Now consciously take in another deeper breath. This time imagine your breath is going right down into your lower ribcage. Visualize it filling every part of you, nourishing and rejuvenating you. Has your ribcage moved outwards and have your fingertips moved just a little now? Practise this technique every day and you will notice a difference.

If you observe someone sleeping, you will see that they are unconsciously breathing deeply. Their shoulders won't lift but their chest and lower ribcage will. It seems when we don't think about it and when we are truly relaxed, deep breathing becomes second nature to us. You may find it helpful to lie down sometimes and practise your diaphragm work. Lie flat on your back, placing a small pillow under your head, and a slightly thicker one under your lower back. (This helps open the ribcage.) Now practise your deep breathing, with your hands lightly over your ribcage. This may help relax you and expand your ribcage more easily. However, do make sure you also practice standing and sitting as, when you start to work with other people in the room, you can't lie down on the floor to get yourself prepared! You need to breathe deeply and be relaxed in a sitting or standing position. Practising your diaphragm development should be part of your every day fifteen-minute programme, even if it's only a couple of minutes each time.

Below are further exercises which you can use to aid your deep breathing. Always remember, start gently. Never try to force deep breathing: let it feel a natural part of you.

ARMS AND BREATH
Stand with your weight on both feet, legs shoulder-width apart. Let your arms hang loosely by your sides. Take a few comfortable, easy breaths. Now breathe a little more deeply and, as you do so, raise your arms slowly out in front of you. Finish with your arms directly above your head as you have completed the intake of breath. Hold the breath for a count of five. Now exhale through your mouth, letting your hands drop down by your sides again. Repeat this exercise several times more, but stop if you feel dizzy.

BODY AND BREATH
For this exercise, you can either stand up straight, sit on a padded, upright chair, or lie down with your back flat against the floor. Close

your eyes and concentrate on your breathing. Start off with gentle, comfortable breaths, gradually increasing their depth. As you breathe deeper, imagine the breath going deeper and deeper into your body. Start by imagining your lungs filled with warm, life-enriching air. Now imagine the breath is filling your shoulders, down both arms and into each hand, filling up each fingertip. As you breathe out, imagine the air filtering through your fingers. Now imagine the breath is going further into your body, filling your stomach with a warm sensation. Now imagine the air is going down into each leg, through each thigh and knee joint, down to each shin and down into each foot, right through to the tip of each toe. Then allow the breath to filter out through the toes. Now imagine each breath is filling every part of you, and let each exhalation filter out through your fingertips and toes. Let the sensation of your breath fill every part of you. Make sure you concentrate on each part thoroughly. When you think of your hands, imagine every part of your palm and joint of every finger. The more specific you are, the more powerful the exercise will feel. Remember to return to your normal breathing before you open your eyes. Wait a few minutes before you do anything else.

ENERGY AND BREATH

Sit comfortably on your padded, upright chair. If you prefer, lie with your back against the floor, knees bent if it's more comfortable. Close your eyes and breathe comfortably. Now place your hands gently over your solar plexus, fingertips lightly touching. (The solar plexus is just below your ribs.) As you continue breathing comfortably, imagine you are breathing in the pure white light of cosmic energy. Make the energy as pure and intense as you can. See it as a light so bright you couldn't open your eyes against it. Feel that vibrant white light come down into your body, right down into your solar plexus, below your hands. Exhale softly and repeat the image every time you breathe in. Feel the intensity increasing with every intake of breath, and become aware that the energy is transferring into the tips of your fingers, through your solar plexus. This recharges and revitalizes you. If you have a pain in another area of your body, you can transfer the energy via your fingers to help. Wait until you feel the power of the energy transferring into your fingers then, after a deep inhalation, hold your breath and move your fingers to the other part of your body that aches. Now exhale, feeling the energy of your fingers transferring deeply into the spot that hurts. Feel the energy disperse the pain. After you have exhaled completely, wait until you've returned your fingers to your solar plexus, before you inhale again. You can repeat that process until you feel the ache has subsided.

These last two exercises are particularly good for you, as you are learning to channel energy in a specific way. This is what psychic work is all about.

You can only channel your energy correctly when your own energy is balanced. You know you can balance your energy levels by maintaining a good flow through all your seven chakras. Now we're going to look at balancing energy in a slightly different light, together with a highly effective exercise that will really improve your psychic development.

Before reading this book, you may have thought of balance in the two-tiered form of positive-negative. It's also referred to as yin-yang, man-woman and sun-moon relationships. You can find that dual-power pull within the composition of the atom, in every cell, and in the polarity of the earth. This negative-positive power can also be described within our own body with the discovery of the nadis.

Nadis are thin electrical currents or very fine energy channels through which our energy flows. Exactly how many nadis we have depends upon which belief system you favour. General consensus is that there are at least 72,000 tiny, thin lines running around and through our body, criss-crossing in every direction. Others believe there may be as many as 350,000. Fortunately, to understand how we may balance the male and female parts of ourselves, we only need to look at three major energy channels. These are:

1. *The Sushumna – the main, earth nadi, which runs vertically through the spine, connecting all seven chakras.*

2. *The Ida – the female, negative nadi, which spirals up from the left of the*

base chakra, *winding itself round the Sushumna, to culminate in the left half of the brain.*

3. *The Pingala – the male, positive nadi, which spirals up from the right of the base chakra, winding itself around the Sushumna, to culminate in the right half of the brain.*

Looking at the diagram below will help clarify the image in your mind. Perhaps even more useful is a symbol used to personify this configuration of energy: the wand of Hermes. It's called the Caduceus and it's shown on page 144.

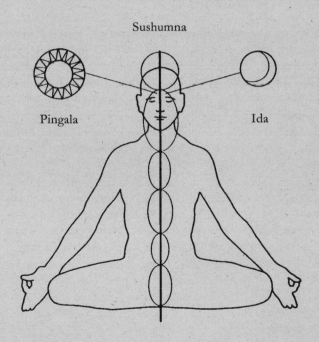

The Nadis

You'll notice that the principle of this energy is the same as that of any electrical current: the negative, positive and earth wires.

The Ida is often symbolized as the lunar system and referred to as the Ganges river; the Pingala is connected to the solar system and referred to as the Yamuna river.

Do you remember that three energy channels were mentioned within the third eye chakra? These are the three meridians and, when they're flowing freely, they're said to be able to awaken 'kundalini'. This is described as the all-powerful, pure cosmic energy that lies within each of us, waiting to be discovered. Its home is in the base or root chakra, where it lies dormant within all of us; it's depicted within the chakra as a coiled snake, waiting to release its energy.

The image of a snake may make many people uneasy; the symbol is very apt. It is such a powerful energy that it is discovered only under strict guidance of spiritual teachers who have a true understanding of this energy and will be able to teach others how to use it safely.

The Caduceus or Wand of Hermes

Although you won't be able to discover kundalini for yourself through this book, you can learn how to balance these three energies so that they may take you further along your path to enlightenment. The exercise below is a form of yoga and is extremely powerful when done properly. Initially, it feels odd and uncomfortable and it can be difficult to hold your breath for the seconds given. If this is so, then reduce the number of seconds for each section, and gradually increase the number when you become more proficient. Although the exercise is explained using your right hand, you can use your left, as it'll make no difference. You could try experimenting with first one and then the other, to see which is more comfortable for you. If you have sinus problems of any sort, you won't be able to follow this exercise. You need two clear nostrils to benefit from it.

BALANCING ENERGIES

Place your hand over your face, with your palm resting lightly over the lower portion of your face. Now place your thumb gently against your right nostril so that, in a moment, you'll be able to close off the air flow into that nostril. Now place your fourth (or ring) finger over your left nostril, ready to do the same. Place your index and third fingers so that they rest gently against the third eye chakra at your forehead. Now lightly close your right nostril and breathe in slowly through your left nostril only, for a count of four. Now also close your left nostril so that both nostrils are closed, and hold for a count of four. Release your right nostril only and breathe out through that nostril for a count of four. Without interrupting the flow, breathe in again through the right nostril only, for a count of four. Cover both nostrils, and hold for four seconds. Release your left nostril and breathe out again through that nostril only. Repeat this process five more times. Here's a quick run-down of the order:

1. *Breathe in through left nostril only for four seconds.*
2. *Keep both nostrils closed for four seconds.*
3. *Breathe out right nostril only for four seconds.*
4. *Without stopping, breathe in through right nostril for four seconds.*
5. *Keep both nostrils closed for four seconds.*
6. *Breathe our through left nostril only for four seconds.*

When you see it written down it looks confusing, but as soon as you have got into the rhythm yourself, it will be easy to maintain a smooth flow. Four seconds is a low count; gradually increase the seconds until you can manage at least ten seconds on each section. This won't be possible immediately as you will make yourself extremely dizzy unless you build up to it slowly over a few months. Again, this exercise should be done every day. When you have developed a regular flow of breathing and can do five or six sets of the exercise without pausing, you will really notice a difference afterwards. It's not a difference you can easily put into words but you will actually feel yourself regaining a sense of balance. Both halves of you will seem more equal in weight and size. It isn't until you finish the exercise, that you can appreciate how imbalanced you were before you started it!

Much of what you've been reading in this chapter is used in yoga. If you have the opportunity to take a yoga class, it can greatly increase your spiritual awareness and aid psychic development. There is an old yogic proverb:

Life is in the breath; therefore he who only half-breathes, half lives.

It's a known fact that we can live without food for weeks and we can survive without water and sleep for days. How long can we live without breathing? No more than a few minutes.

Most of us take this most wonderful of gifts completely for granted. Do you ever stop to think about your breathing and how it is essential for every part of you to function properly? Do you ever stop to appreciate the energy that we breathe into our system which totally nourishes us? Did you know that a small number of divine saints are known to have lived almost without food? Breathing in divine spiritual energy, or prana, was sufficient for them to be able to live on it and be nourished by its strength. Of course, this isn't to suggest you should ever try to do the same. What a saint has acquired through intense spiritual growth cannot be compared to how we generally lead our own lives. However, it's a means through which we can appreciate some of the untapped power of controlled breathing and awareness of energy.

Control of your breathing will lead you into states of relaxation that will also develop you psychically. Nerves are a major problem when you first start to work with other people. No matter how confident you may be in the safety of your own space, when others come into it and you feel obliged to offer them some concrete proof of your psychic abilities, it is extremely daunting. You won't fully appreciate how true this is until you sit in front of your first sitter and try to relax and open yourself up. The more often you do it, the easier the process becomes, but it always requires enormous discipline. You use your breathing to focus and calm yourself. Without control of your own breathing, you will feel lost and out of control.

You can practice using your breathing to relax you in dozens of ways throughout your day. Here are just a few suggestions:

> *1. Next time you get hiccups, just stop whatever you're doing for a moment, close your eyes and relax. Take a few deep breaths, and imagine your breath going down to the air-lock in your stomach and gently releasing it. Let your breath go to areas of your body where you're holding tension and feel the tension easing out of you with each exhalation. Within a few minutes, your hiccups should go.*

> *2. Next time you feel very nervous about a pending situation, take a few minutes to sit or stand quietly. Close your eyes, breathe slowly and concentrate on how heavy your feet feel on the ground. Let the solid contact with the earth both centre and comfort you. Remember, whatever happens, you will learn and grow from the experience. Ask your guides to help you. Your nervousness should decrease as you do so.*

> *3. When you feel anger building in you over a potentially volatile situation, stop for a minute. Back away from the confrontation while you centre yourself. You'll be amazed how much heavier you feel all of a sudden. As your energies settle again, take a few deep breaths and feel the tension easing in your body. Now return to the situation and try to deal with it rationally.*

There are many more instances when becoming conscious of your breathing will help you on a day-to-day basis, but they're discussed in more detail in a later chapter. You may often have been told in the past,

'Count to ten before you speak', but now, instead of simply counting to ten, use the time to concentrate on your breathing. The more you remember the power of breathing, the more it will help you in everything you do.

Here is one last relaxation exercise for you to try. This is to focus your attention on the effects of tension and the benefits of relaxation:

TENSING AND RELEASING

Lie flat on the floor with a pillow under your head. Close your eyes and breathe comfortably, but not too deeply. Now concentrate on both your feet. Scrunch up all the muscles so that they feel tense. Hold that tension for a few seconds and then release it. Do your feet feel more relaxed than before? Remember to keep breathing through all the stages. Now go through each part of your body, one by one, and repeat the process, tensing and releasing: legs, buttocks, abdomen, solar plexus, ribcage and chest, shoulders, arms, hands, fingers, throat, neck and head. Remember all the muscles contained within each section. The head has eyes, nose, mouth, jaw and tongue to consider. Notice when you tense one area, what other area is also affected. When you have isolated each area, then try tensing your whole body, holding for a few seconds more, and then finally releasing. How did you feel when you were tensing yourself? What sensations came over when you let go of the tension? Lie there for several minutes, enjoying the sensation of your body feeling competely relaxed. If you are still aware of tension, then let your breath go to the area this time and use your breath to caress away the stress. Finish by visualizing your breath going to each part of you, gently washing away the cares and troubles. When you feel really relaxed, let yourself lie in that state for several further minutes, enjoying the peace and comfort. When you feel ready, slowly open your eyes. Then wait a further two minutes at least before you get up.

Were you surprised by just how much tension you were holding in parts of your body? Most of us think we know when we're getting tense, but we rarely pay attention to all our muscles. When you know we have over six hundred and fifty muscles, it's perhaps understandable that we're not as tuned in to our body as we thought we were. Start becoming aware during the day when you think you are becoming stressed. Stop for a brief minute and concentrate on the area which is aching. Gently send a few deep, comfortable breaths to the area and feel the tension ease out of you. The more often you try doing this, the faster and better it will work for you.

If you feel you have now absorbed the content of these first seven chapters, particularly the summarized details of the chakras, then you are now ready to start experiencing the opening-up process.

CHAPTER 8

TUNING IN

Now you have developed an understanding of what you are dealing with in psychic development, and an appreciation of the respect and discipline it requires, you are ready to start the process of opening up. It will help you most if you read through this chapter several times, absorbing its contents, before you try putting the process into action.

Firstly, have you remembered certain physical points which will help you? Have you:

- *created your own special place in which you work, encorporating as many factors as possible from Chapter 6?*
- *made sure your space is secure and won't be interrupted by human or animal?*
- *put on loose, comfortable clothing in the colours you want?*
- *only eaten light quantities of food in the last few hours?*
- *not imbibed drink or drugs in any form for over six hours (longer if an excess was consumed)?*
- *got a suitable upright chair, with a padded seat or cushion, in your space?*

If you've done all the above, then you're ready to begin.

TUNING IN
Settle yourself in your chair, legs uncrossed, feet resting flat on the floor, and your hands resting loosely in your lap. Close your eyes. Feel how heavy your weight feels in the seat of your chair. Become aware of your breathing. Concentrate on each breath coming in and each breathing out, enjoying, as you do so, the sensation of each part of your body slowing down and relaxing. Feeling the

151

comforting rhythm of your heartbeat, gentle and constant. Start becoming aware of each part of your body. Start with your feet. Are they aching? Hot? Sore? Send your breath down to them, using each exhalation to release the ache. Work your way up your body, slowly releasing tension in each area.

Let your breath wash away any troubled thoughts you are having. Imagine, as you breathe out, that your thoughts or worries are being released into a balloon that flies up into the far distance and disappears. Do this several times if the thoughts return. Keep using your breath to release the images. If someone is troubling you, imagine them whole and well, being released in a large balloon into the sky. Let your mind become empty and clear as possible. More thoughts will probably crowd in, but gently release them as well.

When you have emptied your mind as much as possible, then concentrate on your ribcage. Feel it expanding as you breathe in and gradually deepen your breathing, letting it slow as you do so.

Now start to imagine the pure, white light coming down into the room from above. (If you still need to imagine the ceiling lifting off to do so, that's fine. After a while, it's no longer necessary, because you know that cosmic energy transcends all physical matter.) Let the intense, white light stream down endlessly into the room. Feel it firstly come down on you, then feel it circle all around you, placing you in a circle of love and protection. Feel its intensity and strength all around you now, nurturing and cushioning you from harm. Feel safe and secure in this warm, glowing circle of beautiful energy.

Now offer a silent prayer to whomever you wish, asking for their guidance and love during your work. Ask that you may help others without harm through all your work. If your spiritual intent is pure and clear, this will make the white light intensify in strength, feeling even more vibrant as it pulsates all around you.

When you feel ready, draw the white light in through your crown chakra. Remember that this is always open, so the energy will pour in gently through the chakra. Feel it slowly filter through to every cell in your body, cleansing and refreshing as it does so. Let it wash through every joint and muscle, releasing the day's tension with its spiritual strength and energy. Breathe as deeply as feels comfortable for you, pulling more of the white light into you each time. Let it wash out all your fingers and toes every time you exhale. Feel the tension drain away as this happens and feel the difference in your body and soul. Enjoy feeling refreshed and revitalised, ready for further work. Take as long as you like, drawing in the white light and experiencing its rejuvenating properties.

When you feel ready, take your concentration down to your feet on the floor. Feel the soles of your feet firmly resting against the ground. If they don't feel heavy, then see long roots coming from the soles of your feet, reaching deep into the ground, connecting firmly to the earth's energy. Now you're going to draw that energy up into your system, ready to increase your connection to everything physical and to further prepare you for psychic work. Feel the earth energy coming up into the soles of your feet. Imagine a soft pink or gold colour slowly washing up over your legs, your knees, your thighs, your hips, your abdomen, touching each vertebra on your spine, and then moving up to your shoulders and sweeping down through your arms and hands, before trickling out through your fingertips. Then draw the earth energy up through all of your neck, up into your head and feel it meeting the beautiful white light at the top. Repeat this process several times, enjoy the grounding sensation of the rich earth energy, making you feel connected to all the earth energies, making you feel ready to tune in to all earthly consciousness.

Once you are filled with cosmic and earth energies, feeling balanced and refreshed, you can open your chakras.

Each chakra is located a few inches from your physical body, so as you open each centre, you will probably feel something taking place just outside your body. This sensation is different for everyone . Some feel a tingle or a light tickle; some say it's as though a butterfly is brushing past; others say they feel a tingle or *a little rush of air or a change in vibrations; others feel as though something is twirling round. A few feel absolutely nothing, but their chakras have still opened. Once you experience the opening up process on a number of occasions, you will recognize your own sensation that will be personal to you.*

Everyone also uses slightly different techniques for opening their chakras. Firstly, you need to focus on the areas of the chakra that you're opening, and then use your own visualisation to see it happen. The image of a flower opening its petals can be powerful for some; you can use the thought of switching on a fan to make its propellers spin; try seeing a spinning top being set in motion; perhaps a drawbridge door is being pulled down or any sort of door is opening; see it as a parcel being unwrapped; create a spinning wheel and twirl it. There are so many images you can use but you will soon discover your own method that feels right for you. For your first time, a flower opening its petals is likely to be the easiest and most powerful. You've already been reading about the lotus flower and how each chakra is allocated a different number of petals.

You're going to start with the base or root chakra. It's at the base of your spine and it opens downwards to the ground. It's always open, like the crown chakra, but you need to increase its vibration for psychic work. Remember to keep your breathing deep and even, as you focus your attention on that part of your body. See the cone-like shape (as in the diagram on page 91) spinning at low frequency when you first visualize it. As its image becomes clearer to you, use your own technique to make it spin and open. See it happening and become aware of any sensation as you do so. If you feel nothing, that is fine. If you feel uncomfortable at any time during the opening process, always use the white light to cleanse and energize you. Do that as often as you feel necessary.

Once you feel the chakra has opened, visualize the colour red. Again, there are different techniques you can use. Imagine anything you can think of as being red. (If you have already done the Chakra Exercises earlier, this shouldn't be too difficult for you.)

See a red apple, a red pillar box, a red fire engine or a red poppy. You might prefer to see your red ball coming towards you. When the image of red is clear and vibrant, then draw it up through your base chakra. Fill yourself with the rich colour of red. Let it filter into every part of you so that you actually feel yourself become that colour. All of you is red. See yourself pulsating with it. Wait until you have experienced this fully before you move on to the next chakra.

This is the navel chakra. Remember that this opens both front and back so the feelings will be different here. You should have a sense of connection between the back and front of you as this chakra opens. Focus on the area just below your navel and see both centres, front and back. This chakra is not normally open, so it will be motionless when you first see it. Now use your visualisation technique to start moving. It may feel harder at first because the base chakra is always in motion and often easier to tap into when you start. Don't rush the process of making it spin. Let your thoughts create the movement. After a little while, it will happen. Try to make both front and back centres spin evenly; you may find one is naturally faster or easier to open than the other. Enjoy the sensation of both navel chakras and the base chakra all spinning together. Notice if the navel chakra feels different from the base.

Now you want to concentrate on the colour orange. See a juicy orange, or a carrot, or a bright orange goldfish. It could even be a favourite sweater that's orange. Use your orange ball if that is there for you. Now feel orange entering in through both the back and front navel chakra. Feel its warm, energizing colour filling into every part of your body. Instead of just seeing it happen, feel it. Feel that you and the colour orange are one. Every part of you is vibrating with rich orange. When you have experienced that sensation to the full, move up to the next chakra.

This is the solar plexus and it also opens both front and back. It's located just below your chest and slightly to the left. If it helps you to keep all the chakras in a straight line, then you can imagine this centre directly above your navel chakra. If you feel a sensation to the left, you'll know why, but at this stage it won't harm your development. Are you remembering to keep breathing deeply? Often as you concentrate on the centres, your breathing unconsciously becomes more shallow. Keep going back to your breath to check what you are doing. Imagine the solar plexus centres opening, front and back. These are also closed during normal activities, so they have to be started from a motionless position. See their cone-like shapes first and then slowly make them spin. You control how quickly they move and how much they open. Wait until you feel you are balanced before you move on. Notice what sensation you experience as they open up. (Sometimes, imagining centres along their back opening up, makes people feel vulnerable. This is why the white light is all around you in a complete circle. This is your protection.)

Now think about the colour yellow. See it as bright sunshine, or a field of yellow rapeseed. Imagine a Van Gogh painting filled with rich yellow. See a lemon or banana. A sunflower is also a good image. When the yellow is strong, bring it into both of your chakras, front and back, and feel the warmth of the sunshine yellow filling you up. Let it soak through into all of you, so that you're a pulsating body of pure yellow. Completely experience the moment and luxuriate in the rich yellow. When you know you have completely received the gift of the yellow, move upwards again.

Now you're at the heart chakra. This is where the vibrations start to change, start to become finer, lighter and brighter. It feels slightly different when you open the heart chakra but until you experience it for yourself, you won't quite understand it. When you do, you immediately recognise the difference. This chakra is in the middle of your chest and also opens front and back, so you have two centres to concentrate on. Again, this centre is usually closed so imagine it quite still at first and then use your own method to slowly start it working. Try to balance both front and back so that they spin evenly. See if you can feel any difference as you open these cones. If you feel the same, or nothing at all, you don't need to worry at all. Just keep breathing comfortably and continue.

The heart chakra is grass green. Imagine grass itself, or evergreen trees. You can use a green parrot or a lime or any green vegetable. Feel yourself being filled, front and back, with the loving colour of green. This is particularly important for compassion and empathy, two important characteristics of psychic work. Take as much time as you like with this chakra. Make sure the green is flowing into and through all of you. See yourself as a green body, pulsating vibrantly with love. Wait until you feel it, as well as see it, before going on.

Now you've reached the throat chakra. It's located at the hollow of your throat and opens front and back. This is also closed normally, so see both cones motionless and then gradually have them open. This is a lighter vibration yet again, so it may be harder to feel anything as they open. Or you may have a very slight sensation but it will be so faint, you'll be uncertain if you've imagined it. If it's harder to get a clear image of this centre, it doesn't matter. Know that it's there, and sense that both centres are spinning evenly, before you go further.

Create the colour blue. See a clear sky or a calm blue body of water. Use the image of a blue forget-me-not flower. You may have a scarf that shade of blue. Now feel blue entering into you, front and back, and washing through all of you. As you go higher, remember the lower half of you. Sweep blue into every toe and each part of your feet, as well as everywhere else. Know you have become the colour blue and feel the effect of its cooling, calming, purifying colour. Let it thoroughly fill every crevice in your body, and then move up again.

This is your third eye chakra, in the middle of your forehead. It also opens front and back. As this chakra vibrates at an even higher frequency, you will find it even more delicate, even more elusive. You may sense and feel nothing as you start these two centres moving. It doesn't matter. All you need to do this is to know that this chakra exists, although you can't yet feel it. By imagining the two centres opening and visualising them in motion, you are doing enough. If you feel the slightest sensation, know that it will become stronger in time. Keep that regular breathing rhythm in acton, try not to revert back to shallow breathing.

Now create the wonderfully spiritual colour of purple. You could focus on the image of a violet flower, or a purple plum. Create a piece of rich purple amethyst or see your beautiful purple ball coming towards you again. Now let that purple stream in through your third eye centres, back and front. Feel it sweep down and through all of your body. Feel yourself become purple. Feel yourself vibrating with that unique spiritual essence. Stay as long as you like with this colour. Feel its uplifting presence.

Now you have reached the seventh chakra, at your crown. This has only one opening, up to the sky. You know this chakra is always open, like your base, but you need to open it further, to speed up its vibrations. See the cone-like shape of its centre reaching outward from just above your head and imagine the cone opening further and twirling faster as it does so. You will probably feel nothing as this happens but it's not important. Create as powerful an image as you can and know that it's happening on a very fine , bright vibration.

When you feel the chakra has opened further, then let the beautiful, bright, white energy flood in through your crown chakra again and slowly feel it filter through every chakra; third eye, throat, heart, solar plexus, navel and base. Don't rush the experience.

After you have washed yourself through several times with the white light, you will probably feel very light headed; it's a sort of spaced-out, high feeling. As you have worked your way up through the chakras, you have connected with your higher vibrations, but forgotten your contact with the earth energy. You can't work psychically in this state because you're not grounded. You need to reconnect yourself to work properly.

So now concentrate on your feet again. Feel them anchored deep into the ground. (This doesn't mean your other chakras will close down; they will remain open until you consciously close them.)

Feel your energy drop down into your feet and let them become heavier and heavier. When you know your energies have dropped again, you can open your eyes. You are now ready to work.

HOWEVER, BEFORE YOU DO SO, YOU MUST NOW GO THROUGH THE CLEANSING AND CLOSING DOWN PROCESSES. THIS IS ESSENTIAL FOR YOUR OWN PROTECTION.

You already understand that you can pick up unwanted influences whilst you are open and working. This won't harm you in any way, **PROVIDED YOU KNOW AND HAVE THOROUGHLY PRACTICED THE CLEANSING AND CLOSING DOWN TECHNIQUES. DO NOT CONTINUE UNTIL YOU HAVE DONE THIS.**

If this is the first time you have practiced the opening up process, no matter how little you felt and how concerned you were that nothing was happening, your chakras have still been opening. This is the nature of psychic development. The progress may happen slowly and you won't always be aware of it, but there will be progress. The fact that you don't always realize what effect it is having, shows how doubly careful you should be.

If you open your eyes now, you will notice that everything seems a little brighter, a little sharper. Colours may seem stronger, textures more sensitive to your touch and you may really feel the energy in the room and how it is moving and vibrating. This shows how much you have opened up. Your awareness is now increasing and you are preparing yourself for psychic work. Now close your eyes and go straight on to the cleansing and closing down processes.

CLEANSING

This is extremely important, not just at the end of your work, before you close down, but at all times throughout your work. You will often pick up uncomfortable sensations and feelings as you work; most you will release without difficulty. Occasionally, some remain with you and these you need to shed as you go along. Therefore, you can cleanse a dozen times during your sessions and that is perfectly acceptable. You may want to cleanse fifty times if you have a particularly difficult sitting. The more you cleanse, the more you clear your aura to receive further information. It's like having a clean car engine; it makes the car run much more smoothly. Never under-estimate the power and importance of cleansing and, especially as a novice, do this repeatedly. You have already practiced some cleansing work during earlier exercises, but this explains the technique more thoroughly.

Visualise your bright, white light coming down into your crown chakra and draw it down into all of you, flooding your body with an infinite supply. Let it sweep out through the ends of your fingers and toes, releasing the unwanted sensations with it. You need to become aware of which parts of you are holding onto the uncomfortable aspects. In most people, it around the navel and solar plexus areas. This is where we store a great deal of energy and a lot of our own emotions. If you are dealing with someone who is feeling sad, your own empathy is likely to make you feel concerned for them. Therefore, you let your own emotions become affected. You can't work effectively on that level; to receive psychic information you have to be a clear, empty vessel. Use your white light to empty you.

Adding another image to the white light can be a wonderful help in the cleansing process. See the bright light as beautiful clear water coming from a holy source. Then feel the pure water actually coming down and cleansing you, inside as well as out. Further increase this visualization to make it more powerful. Create a perfect setting in which to enjoy this water. Perhaps it's a waterfall in a sweet-smelling forest. See and smell and feel what is around you. Make a powerful image for yourself that is uplifting, as well as cleansing. Make it as idyllic as possible. See it as so beautiful you know it can't be on this earth; it must exist on a higher level of consciousness. Or, if you prefer, create your own setting of a perfect bathroom and shower. Step inside that image every time you cleanse. Make sure you create the bathroom completely: feel the flooring, smell the scents around you, see the colours, taste the cool water on your face. Continually create it to make it more and more vivid so that you know this cleansing place as well as you know your own home. In fact, you know it even better because, every time you step into it, all your senses are alive and refreshed. It's your own special haven that belongs only to you; never share your cleansing place with anyone else. It cleanses and refreshes because only your energies are present, ready to be cleansed and rebalanced by the divine water.

Feel the water or light coming into you every time you inhale. On each exhale, let the residue filter out of your fingers and toes. Make sure you are releasing everything. You may take longer when you first work to release influences but the more you practice the faster the process becomes. Also, the clearer your image of your cleansing process, the faster it comes into focus. This can then become an invaluable tool for every part of your day-to-day life. You can create it at any time and use it to help you.

Make sure you have created a thorough image of your cleansing space before you try opening up for the first time. Once you have cleansed, you can close down. Make sure you don't do it the other way around.

CLOSING DOWN

This can also be done during the day at any time, even when you haven't consciously opened up. You will find certain chakras will open up of their own accord during the day, when you're involved in certain activities, and especially if you're discussing your psychic work with other people. This isn't dangerous, unless you forget to close yourself down afterwards. If you're in doubt about how much you have opened, close yourself down anyway. This closing down process shouldn't be confused with shutting yourself off from people. They are two different things. Closing down means shutting down chakras that need to be closed to allow normal protection. Shutting yourself off from people is an altogether different act of withdrawing your energies deep inside of you. Closing your chakras means guarding yourself from unwanted outside influences, whilst continuing to experience and connect *with energies all around you. Never feel that closing down is in any way a negative action; it's a positive process to nurture as well as protect yourself.*

During psychic work and other activities, your aura will expand. You know that it is constantly fluctuating and reacting to what is around you. As you work with your own energies during psychic development, so your aura expands to help you. Therefore, you need to be aware of how your aura has grown so that you can withdraw it again to its usual size. This is an awareness that you gradually develop, the more you concentrate upon it.

As you sit there with your eyes closed, visualise how large your aura has become. Where are its outer edges? This may be three, four, five or more feet away. It may feel even larger if the space in which you're working is big. Now you're going to draw it back towards you. Decide where its outer edges are and then, as you take a breath in, feel yourself drawing its edges closer towards you. As you exhale, feel your aura settle for a moment, readjusting its energies. Now take another deep breath and pull it in closer. Let it rest again as you exhale. Keep doing this until your aura feels comfortable again. Until you're more experienced, you may pull your aura in too tightly and feel restricted. If this happens, then reverse the process: breath in, feeling your aura spread outwards again. Rest as you exhale. Breathe in again and feel your energies puff out once more. Practice until you feel comfortable.

Now you need to close your chakras, one by one. The colours aren't used in the closing down process; they're used as an opening tool only.

Start with your base chakra. Focus on its centre and see it spinning. Now you need to slow it down, but not stop it completely, as this chakra always remains open. Try the reverse of your opening technique: see the petals of the flower closing, close the drawbridge, see the spinning top slowly stop, switch off the fan or re-wrap your parcel. You may choose another different image;

some people simply imagine a light touch of a finger which stops or closes the chakra. You'll have to experiment with all of the above, and perhaps some others as well, before you know which works for you. This is always a personal voyage of discovery. It may take you a while to control the chakra's movement, but make sure you don't move on until you are in control and you have slowed the base chakra's spinning. If you feel you just can't do it, this is only you refusing to take control. Psychic development is all about control, so you might as well start now. Use the focusing of your mind to make it happen. You will know instinctively how slowly the chakra should end up moving; everyone's speed is slightly different. When you have reached that level, psychically seal the chakra with protection: cover it with a cross and a circle of light. If you like, use an imaginery pen which contains light instead of ink, and then draw the circle and cross.

Now do the same with the next five chakras: navel, solar plexus, heart, throat and third eye. Remember, all these have two centres each, front and back, and you must completely close all of them. If one still continues to spin, don't move on until you have stopped it. Again, you are in control, no one else. As soon as each chakra is closed, cover both centres with the seal of protected light, drawing a circle and a cross. When they feel properly closed and protected, then take your attention to the crown chakra.

The crown is always open, so this time you just want to slow its vibrations and give it protection. Wait until the chakra is spinning at the right level, and then protect it with a circle of light and a cross.

Then, once more, draw the pure white light into your body and feel it refresh and cleanse you. Do this several times, using your waterfall image or white light, whichever you prefer.

You will probably still feel light-headed at this stage, so focus your attention again on your feet. Feel your feet being pulled into the ground by the force of gravity. Make them feel really heavy. You will feel all your energies settling down again, when you have done this properly.

Now you should feel very much back in your own body and ready to continue on your day. If you still feel 'high', use that waterfall or white light yet again, and then continue working on your feet. Create long, strong roots growing out of the soles of your feet and anchor them so deeply into the ground that you see the roots disappear into the centre of the earth. This should thoroughly centre you again.

Before you open your eyes, there is one last protective measure. You need to create a psychic cloak to cover and protect all of you. This is again an individual experience. Some use an image of pure, brilliant light. Others create a fabric to draw over them. Some use a white crystal in a dome or pyramid shape. Some actually see it as a transparent egg-shell. It doesn't matter what you use, provided the colour is light. Dark colours absorb energy and may leave you feeling drained, rather than refreshed. You may discover a soft, fluffy towel suits you best, or a cloak of soft velvet. Draw the cloak up over you and fasten it with a zip, or buttons. You can do whatever you like with your cloak; no one else will ever see it so it can be your own private creation. It might seem humorous to others but none of that matters, as long as it feels right for you.

When you have settled comfortably into your cloak of protection, then say a short, silent prayer to the source of higher conciousness. Give thanks for their guidance and love, ask for your growth to continue, and ask for their protection. You will want to use your own words and thoughts as you progress, which is quite right. When you have said all that feels necessary, sit quietly with your eyes closed for a minute. When you feel ready, open your eyes.

Did all that feel rather strange? For some of you, you'll have felt so little that you will wonder if you're not able to work on a psychic level. You'll be stuck in the 'Other people fall in love, not me' syndrome that was mentioned earlier. Rest assured that whatever you felt, whatever happened, it was right for you at this stage of development. Many successful psychics working today never actually feel their chakras opening; it's still happening, however, because they wouldn't be able to work otherwise. They also all have strong self-protection mechanisms that they can call upon the minute they need them.

This chapter is your blueprint for all future work in this book. You need to read and re-read this section, going over and over the Tuning In, Cleansing and Closing Down Exercises. Even after you've been working for a few months, continue to revise this chapter. You will probably remember something you'd forgotten or just stopped doing. The following chapters all refer to tuning-in but they don't repeat details of the process. It's now up to you to become really familiar with all the stages. You need to memorize the chakras' order and their colours so that it becomes automatic. You need to keep doing further private meditation on all the chakras to increase your awareness so that your psychic development can grow, instead of standing still. Cleansing needs to become second nature to you, so that it's as easy as blinking your eyelids. Closing down needs to feel a safe, controlled act that protects and nurtures you. You aren't ready to work with other people, offering your psychic development to them, until all this has happened.

To remind you, cleanse and close down at any time during the day or night, but never, ever, open up anywhere other than in your own safe space. As you read earlier, certain chakras will open without your realising it and you may end up going out into crowded areas without proper protection. This can be a distressing experience that is easily avoided. Just close down. If you're sitting on a train, feeling affected by those around you, consciously close your chakras, especially your navel and solar plexus centres, and draw your private cloak around you. No one will have a clue at to what you're doing, but it will protect and help you. Be especially aware if you are talking to others about psychic work. It will be a natural reaction to do so, especially when you start working and you start receiving results. It's very exciting and you'll want to share it all. Just remember after you've been discussing everything, to cleanse any tensions away and close the chakras again.

You can never cleanse and close down too often! When you're in the slightest doubt that you might have picked up something unpleasant or uncomfortable, cleanse it away immediately.

Now you have experienced opening up for the first time, let's move forward and look at some of the small experiments which you can carry out by yourself in your safe space. This will give you some confidence, as you work towards giving a sitting with someone for the first time.

CHAPTER 9

THE EARLY STAGES

Once you have practiced your opening up and closing down techniques, your next impulse will be to start trying out your new levels of awareness. You'll probably be thinking, 'The sooner, the better'. Unfortunately, the more you push to progress swiftly, the slower your progress will be. Psychic abilities come from the realms of the sixth and seventh senses of 'intuition' and 'knowing'. This takes longer to develop in some people than others, but generally those who are willing to let the process work slowly, are the ones who progress more quickly! If you enjoy each step along your path and accept where you are at each step, you will then be ready to move on again. You aren't ready to move forwards until you acknowledge where you are at present.

It can be likened to the process of grieving after someone has died. If you accept the pain and sadness you feel afterwards, you can then truly acknowledge where you are and how difficult it is. You then have the means, albeit slowly, to learn how to release some of that hurt, and to move on. If you have lost someone you love and refuse to accept that you are unhappy and distressed, you can't move forward. You keep the pain buried inside you, but it's always there, never released. You never learn to move past your pain, so you can't move forward in life and find peace and contentment again. (This isn't to relate suffering to psychic development – they're very different experiences! – but the process of moving forward is the same.)

Once you start to practise psychic development, you have to find someone on whom you can work. This person is called your 'sitter' and is discussed in detail in Chapter 11. Right now, you probably feel daunted by the thought of having a sitter in front of you, waiting for you to open up and then produce some psychic information for them. This chapter is about building your confidence so that you feel more ready for the experience.

Here's a simple experiment to start:

THE LETTER

Wait until a letter comes through in the post which you don't recognise. This means either the hand-writing or postmark (no cheating!). Take it into your private space and place it near you. Now sit down, close your eyes, and go through the tuning-in process. Do go slowly and work your way through each section without hurrying.

When you feel tuned in and ready, open your eyes. Pick up the letter and hold it in your hands. What sensations do you feel? Hot? Cold? Does this letter belong to an expressive or controlled person? Are they a calm soul, or do they have a lot of pent-up energy within them?

Now see what images, if any, come in front of your eyes. Whatever they are, don't immediately dismiss them as irrelevant. Try to remember what they are, especially if they don't make sense at the time. If you're sitting there feeling rather silly, thinking it's all impossible, then remember what you now know about energies and the Hologram Theory. Remember how you felt your own energy in your hands and saw the earth energy as you looked at the sky.

Then go back to your letter and concentrate again. Does holding the letter make you feel happy or sad? Does the image of a friend or relative suddenly come into your head? You may think you see the pen with which it was written; you may smell a perfume; you may taste apple because they were eating one as they wrote the letter. There are a myriad of possibilities that may present themselves to you. See yourself as an open vessel and let the images and sensations come in. If there are any that are unpleasant or distressing, immediately clear them through your cleansing technique.

When you feel ready, go through the complete cleansing and closing down process before you open your eyes. Make sure you are well grounded. Before you open the letter, write down the images and sensations you had. Try to remember them all, even if they seem silly or non-sensical. Once you have written down everything, then open the letter.

Can you connect any of the images with the person who wrote the letter? This will be easier if you know the person; more difficult if it's a casual acquaintance. If you have the confidence, contact them and ask if they'd be willing to clarify some things for you. Most people are intrigued if you start discussing psychic matters with them; very few are completely dismissive. At this stage, you don't need to go into your experiences too thoroughly. If you pick up something uncomfortable, you may not want to discuss it with them. Remember always to be careful how you phrase things; try to be tactful and sensitive. If very little fits, don't try to make it fit. It doesn't matter. It's also possible that you may pick up energies left on the letter by the postman who delivered it. Depending on how well you know your postman, you may be able to sort some of the images out. If you can't, just let them go. This was an experiment for you to learn, not for you to dazzle people with your skills.

If your success rate was nil with this first experiment, don't feel discouraged. Often imagination will come into play when you first start working. This is because you won't trust your instinct; you usually panic when you begin, because you are so anxious to feel or see something, anything, that you let your mind take over. Psychic awareness is about letting your mind and imagination go to sleep for a while; it's not easy to do. That's why these experiments on your own are important. You can make mistakes, be totally inaccurate, learn to know the difference between imagination and awareness, work on separating the two, and then begin to fully use your psychic gifts.

There is another way of putting the above which is more blunt but very accurate: leave your ego out of psychic work. This is hard to do but it's a big part of your growth, spiritually and psychically. When you looked at the benefits of psychic work during Chapter 1, did you notice that 'making yourself look good' was not one of them? It's part of human nature to want to look good and have people like, admire and respect us. Spiritual and psychic growth doesn't work when you get caught up in the 'looking good' syndrome.

Most of us have fairly large egos and the more we immerse ourself in the material, physical sphere, the bigger that ego grows. Ego is part of the 'wanting more' sickness that has come upon us: that faster car, larger house, better job, newer clothes or latest space-age appliance. This isn't to say that ambition is always negative and destructive; it's to say that we could benefit from looking at the reasons why we want certain things. Do you want that latest computer because you need it for your personal progress, or is it because you feel good knowing you have the newest on the market? Have you bought that new car because you need it, or because you want other people to look at you and envy your success? Is a bigger house necessary because you love your family and they need the space, or is it a status symbol that says you're wealthy and powerful? Are you working on psychic development because you want to impress people with your abilities?

For most people, there's a 'yes' somewhere within the answer to that last question. It may not be a conscious 'yes' but it's probably hidden underneath. You might know that you want to develop your psychic skills because you love people, you want to help them, you want to learn more about yourself and you want to learn about spiritual consciousness. However, do you fear 'looking bad' if you give an inaccurate reading?

Everyone worries about this, but the truth is that your ego is getting in the way. Of course, you might respond that wanting to give people helpful information all the time, only means you care about their welfare. Therefore it's nothing to do with your ego, because you're being unselfish. That's only partly true.

If you truly want to help others, then you don't care what you look like in the process. If you are willing to sound silly and have people laugh at you, then you're on the right path. If you know that making mistakes is sometimes good and everyone can learn lessons from that, then you'll move forward. If you always ask for guidance before you start a reading, and accept whatever form of guidance that follows, you'll be growing and learning. You'll also be letting go of your own ego.

Don't most of us hate to be proved wrong over something? We always want to be 'right'. In psychic work, you can't be right all the time. It isn't possible. You have to learn to be wrong and not be upset by it.

Then there will be occasions when you'll be absolutely right, but your sitter won't want to acknowledge it, because they don't like what you're saying. They will keep saying 'no' to everything, as you become more and more panicky, convinced that you're useless and talentless. Giving in to the insecurity will only put you further into a spiral of anxiety. You have to learn to cleanse and renew your energies and then really tap into what is going on. Are you on the wrong path, or are they not willing to listen to you? Are you phrasing things badly and making them shut off? You have to tune in to their needs, access the situation and learn how to deal with it after that. More of this is explained in Chapter Eleven.

Letting go of ego is a huge part of psychic development and most of us struggle with this for a long time. Let's try looking at this from another angle.

You read earlier in the Letter Exercise that you should think of yourself as an empty vessel. This is a big clue to understanding how ego gets in the way. During psychic work, you need to become an instrument through which energies can flow. If your own energies are perfectly balanced with the cosmic and earth energies, you become a powerful instrument, which resonates in perfect harmony, and which then becomes a good transmitter of information.

To make yourself the best instrument you can possibly be, you need to work on yourself outside of psychic work. You need to look at every aspect of your life and try to balance it so that others' needs are met as well as your own. This balancing act is a lifetime's work in itself. It's very hard to achieve. The more balance you can create, the better you become as a psychic tool. So you need to work on yourself when you're alone, when psychic development is not in your thoughts, when you're looking at how you relate to everything and everyone around you. You need to look at the areas of your life which aren't working, and why. You need to be willing to delve into the bits of you which make you feel uncomfortable, and learn why. You have to learn how to release pent-up, destructive emotions and clear blocks. You are then learning how to make your own energies flow harmoniously. You never stop learning about how to do this.

However, and this is a big however, when you then come to opening up for psychic work, you have to leave every bit of that behind. You can't be thinking about your child's progress at school, or your partner's problems at work, or your mother's recent illness. You can't be thinking about how tired you feel, or how angry you are after an argument. You also can't be priding yourself on how much you're improving, and how accurate your readings are, and how much you are enjoying yourself. Why can't you do this? It's because all the above restricts and imbalances your energy flow. True psychic work is when you utterly leave every earthly part of you behind and trust implicitly in your inner self and higher consciousness. This is your goal. When you can truly leave your own ego behind, then you will really become powerful in your work. When you can have a wonderfully rewarding sitting and a very difficult, unproductive sitting, and treat both as equally good experiences, then you will be on your way.

You won't create this state immediately. Depending on how large an ego you have, it will be a gradual process. Try to remember this concept of being an empty vessel as you try further experiments. Remember, empty doesn't mean without energy. Empty means clear of earthly thoughts and problems, vibrating with pure energy and completely connecting and interrelating with the cosmic and earth energies. If you feel you understand what has been said in the last few pages, you could go on to try this exercise below.

CONNECTING WITH ANOTHER PERSON
Choose someone you care about, with whom it is easy to talk and share things. Make it someone you know you will be able to speak to within a day or two. Ask them if they would mind being in your

experiment. Explain that you would like to spend ten minutes or so one day thinking about them and tuning in to them. Do explain that you're trying to develop more awareness. Don't give them a specific time, but let them know the day. They can then make more of an effort to remember what they're doing. Make sure they are a willing guinea pig before you proceed. If they feel uncomfortable about it, it won't help you.

Provided it's all been settled, retreat to your special space, and note down the time on a piece of paper. Now open up as usual. When you feel ready to work, concentrate on the person you have chosen. Think about them. Really think about them. See how special and unique they are, inside and out. See their image in front of you. What are they wearing today? What are the colours? How do they look? Cheerful? Tired? See their features clearly and smell their scent. What else can you smell? Are they near flowers? Is it a smokey atmosphere? Are they in a stuffy office or an open park? Can you taste gum in your mouth? What flavour? Do you taste beer or coffee? Take your time over the different sensations. If it takes five minutes before you feel anything, that is fine. No one is judging you.

Now think about their physical body. Is it aching anywhere? Are they feeling tense? Or are they quite relaxed? Concentrate on their face. Is it smiling or serious? Are they talking to someone? Can you widen your image to see who it might be? Or are they alone? Perhaps they're involved in some task. Are they writing or typing? Perhaps they're reading a paper. Or are they watching television? Keep focusing and see what is happening. You may find yourself going into what is happening on a deeper level, depending upon how close you are to the person involved.

When you feel ready, thoroughly cleanse yourself and close down again. Don't rush this process. Then open your eyes, check the time, and write down everything you can remember.

It's extremely important that you have asked permission before you do this exercise. Never just focus in on people. It can be intrusive and inappropriate. Although the other person might not know what is happening, they might suddenly feel uncomfortable and uneasy. You must ask them first. It's not a good idea to give them the exact time you'll be concentrating upon them, although if you want to narrow it down to morning or afternoon or evening, that's fine. If you give an exact time, they can be nervous or try to actually project an image to you. This isn't about telepathy, it's about tapping into someone's energies to understand them better. It's a subtle difference, but it's there. You must always ask permission before you 'tap'.

When you speak to them, be clear about your images and don't try to make them fit into what was happening to them. There's no point in deluding yourself about the experience, because it won't help your progress. Was there an area you did get right? It may just be one thing. For instance, perhaps they were chewing gum. This may mean you tuned in to the smell or taste. Can you remember which? This could prove to be the strongest form of psychic awareness for you. Perhaps smelling and tasting are both very important in your life and you have a well developed sense of them. Or perhaps you saw a colour correctly, but it was a sweater they wore, not a shirt. You may be sympathetic to colours and their significance and you may see other vivid colours during your work. Perhaps you could hear their voice as you were tuning in; some people hear music and songs as they work and then learn to interpret their meaning. You may have been surprised by how much you did get right. Everyone who does this exercise will have a very different experience.

Discuss time with the person in your experiment. You may find that they somehow knew when you were concentrating on them. You may also find odd things have happened with time. For instance, a fair amount of the information you received may have been accurate, but it may have taken place the day before. It's possible that they did a certain thing an hour before you tuned into it.

If you only got one area of information right, such as how they were feeling, or where they were, your first temptation will be to think that it was only a coincidence. Our old habits always jump into place: critical and cynical feels safer than staying open to other possibilities. Whatever you got right during the exercise, happened because you were tuning in properly. You probably won't feel comfortable with that idea, but if you keep repeating it to yourself, it will eventually start to feel natural. Breaking out of our sceptical barriers isn't easy.

To help you believe in yourself, try doing the following:

THE INTUITION BOOK

Acquire a small notebook. Now start making a note of every time you feel or sense something that turns out to be accurate. You can begin with the information from the first two exercises that you were able to verify was correct. This doesn't mean you have to tune in and open up every time before you feel these things; these moments can happen at any time during the day or night. Be sensible with yourself about what you put down. If your partner returns home at 6.30pm every evening, don't write that you sensed they'd turn up at 6.30 and they did! However, if you suddenly feel one evening that they are going to be late (when they haven't told you they will be) and they don't come home until 7pm, then make a note of it. If you feel someone is about to call you, and they do, write it down. If you feel someone is unhappy and you contact them to find out it's true, write it down. If you think a friend is going to get a job after they went for an interview, and they do, write it down. If something happens and you have that sensation of knowing it was about to before it actually did, jot it in the book. If you think your child did well at a test at school and he comes home to tell you he got an excellent mark, write it down.

Dreams are also an interesting source of information. Interpreting dreams would require a large volume on its own, but if you dream about someone and they contact you the following day, put it in the book. If you dream something is going to happen and then it does, make a note of it. Do this for a month and then look back through your book. How many entries have you made? Ten? Twenty? Perhaps there will be even more. The longer you keep using your 'Intuition' book, the more you will find it easy to fill.

Keeping this journal can be a powerful affirmation for you. It's a process whereby you can start using your intuitional sense and validating it, rather than constantly dismissing your feelings. The more you see that it works, the more confidence it gives you, the more you will trust it and the more you will tune in to all the energies around you.

You see, your intuition wasn't pure chance, it was you tuning in to other energies. You might wonder whether some of the above comes into the realms of fortune-telling, after being told earlier in this book that psychic work wasn't a fortune-telling tool. What you are then forgetting is your own free will. We may have the possibility of something open to us, but our own free will dictates if we choose to take the opportunity or not. Therefore, we can't be certain of what we think we see in the future.

Let's look at the case of a friend getting a job. Your friend tells you they've had a job interview and they really want the job. You tune in, and see them getting the job. Are you seeing into the future? Not necessarily. You may be connecting with the energies of the people who have decided they want your friend for the job. If the energy is already created, whereby your friend is about to be offered the job, it's quite feasible you should tap into that field. Or, you may be connecting with your friend's energies. They want the job so much that they have created, within their own aura, the image of them having got the job. Then what you are seeing is what they want, not necessarily what will happen. Another possibility is that your friend may be offered the job but then suddenly be given a better job elsewhere. So they turn the first job down! That is why predicting the future is so hazardous. Nothing is ever decreed as absolute. Our energies are changing and fluctuating all the time. We respond to what is around us, but how we respond is up to us as individuals.

As psychic work is so much about connection with your inner self and establishing a relationship together, it's important you find a means of strengthening this bond. Below is a meditation to help your awareness:

YOUR INNER SELF

Settle yourself comfortably in your space and close your eyes. Open up in your own time, without rushing any of the process. Wait until you feel relaxed and ready to work. Keep your eyes closed throughout this exercise.

You discover you are walking in a garden. It's your garden, but it's the garden of your dreams. Everything is perfect within it; it's exactly what you want it to be. Walk slowly down the garden, admiring everything you love; it could be flowers, trees, shrubs, a pond, a lake, ducks, squirrels, birds. Every single thing that you cherish about a garden is here. Hear the birdsong, feel the warm sun on your head. If you prefer warm rain, feel that gently caressing your head. Create what makes you feel best.

As you walk along, you see a gate in front of you. It's a wonderful gate that looks inviting. You open it up and walk through. In front of you, you see a building. It's your image of a perfect place to be. As you approach, you see a key in the door. You turn the key. The door opens and you step inside. The interior is decorated exactly as you want it to be. It's comfortable and welcoming, furnished with everything you love most. The colours are perfect for you. The smell and light and space feel exactly right.

You sit down in the middle of your wonderful abode and close your eyes. Very soon, you hear a voice calling you. It sounds soft, gentle, welcoming. This is your inner self. Acknowledge its presence and ask for its help. Explain you want to get to know it better. Ask advice on how you may do this. Hear how loving and wise the voice is as it replies. Feel nurtured and safe as it speaks. Ask any questions you feel are important. If the time is not right for you to hear the answer, the voice will tell gently tell you this.

When it is time, the voice tells you that you must return. It also lets you know that you can return again when you wish to do so. You thank the voice for its guidance and wisdom. Then, you slowly get up and make your way to the door.

As you turn around for one last look at your private sanctuary, you see there is a gift for you in the centre of the room. This is personal to you. This gift is for you to meditate upon; it's related to the discussion you have just been having with your inner self. Take the gift with you.

As you leave, close the door behind you and turn the key in the lock. Walk back to the gate and go through into the garden, closing the gate behind you. Walk back through your heavenly garden, holding your gift in your hands, until you return back to where you started.

Now you are back in your seat again, with your eyes closed. Think about what your inner self told you and why your gift was important. Then use the waterfall or light to cleanse through all your thoughts. Make yourself feel empty and clean again. Go through the closing down process thoroughly and ground yourself with the earth energy. Concentrate on your feet for several minutes before you open your eyes again.

This is a meditation you can return to when you feel the need. This is a good way to get in touch with your inner self. After a while, you may not need to go through your garden and into your sanctuary to make contact, but it will help you to do so initially. Were you surprised by some of the things you were told? Or did you feel that part of you knew them already? Trust your inner voice. Listen to it whenever you can. Always ask for its help. It's part of the higher you and is meant to be used. Trust it. Believe in it.

The early stages in psychic development are all about building up your confidence. It's about learning that it's alright to fail. Some of you may spend months feeling nothing. Sometimes this happens because you're not using your energies as effectively as possible. The next chapter deals with further exercises that will increase your psychic energies, preparing you for eventual work with other people.

CHAPTER 10

EXPANDING EVERYTHING

Once you have tried the Letter and Connecting With Another Person Exercises, some of you will be feeling pleased that you have had some positive results; others will be feeling discouraged about their seeming inability to work psychically. Whatever you are personally feeling, you need to expand more to work well with other people in the room with you. These exercises are all ways to do this. They're important, because as soon as others encroach upon your safe space, you will unconsciously close up, revert to your old shallow breathing and have a few minutes of panic. This chapter acknowledges that this is what happens to everyone, and suggests practical ways in which you can control your fear and then move past it.

When you do your first sitting with someone, the first thing that usually happens is that you forget all your grounding techniques. Do you know how you start to feel light-headed when you are nervous? There's an unreal sense of not quite being yourself, without knowing why. This happens because you forget your connection to the earth's energy and you start shallow-breathing. This first exercise is all about re-connecting again.

EARTHING YOURSELF – SITTING
Sit on your chair and close your eyes. Take a few deep breaths, remembering not to lift your shoulders. Feel your ribcage expanding outwards. Be aware that your feet are flat on the floor and feel the force of gravity pulling your feet. Be careful not to slump your shoulders or let your head drop forward.

Now think about your buttocks resting on the chair seat. Really concentrate on them. Is the weight distributed evenly between both buttocks? (It almost never is in anyone). Decide which buttock feels heavier or lighter than the other. You now need to balance them both to be properly grounded. You use your breath to do this, but you can do it in one of two ways. You can either let some of the air out of your heavier buttock, or you can breathe air into the lighter one. You need to decide which feels better. Unless you are feeling depressed, it's probably more appropriate to breathe air into the lighter one to make it feel heavier. Take a comfortable breath in and then, as you breathe out, feel your breath moving down into the lighter buttock and filling it with air. Fill it with as much air as you think necessary. Repeat this process several times until you feel balanced. Sometimes it's helpful to think of your two buttocks as two balloons which you are blowing up or releasing as you wish. It's not uncommon to find that it takes a while to balance both halves. You don't realize how unbalanced you are, until you really concentrate on yourself.

Once your weight feels evenly distributed on the chair, feel how every part of you is responding now to the earth's gravity. Again, this doesn't mean you should let your shoulders droop or your head fall forward. To help you with this, try imagining that you have a string running from the base of your spine, from your base chakra, all the way up to the top of your head, to the crown chakra. Now pull this string so that it is just straight but not pulled taut. Imagine someone is gently holding the string above your head, as if you're a puppet that is relaxed, but upright, ready to move when necessary. Once you have accomplished the sensation of earthing your body, whilst being comfortably upright, you will be better able to work. You can then further continue to ground yourself by imagining your feet with roots going into the ground. You can also repeat your alternate nostril breathing as described on page 151, if you still feel the need to balance yourself.

This technique becomes easier and quicker to do, the more you practise it. Initially, you may have trouble assessing how your buttocks are feeling! This can be a physical area that we don't like to concentrate upon, for a variety of reasons, but it's important to move past your embarrassment. Your buttocks and feet are the only parts of you that are taking your weight when you sit down and therefore they're your means of earthing yourself. This exercise can be practised anywhere, anytime. If you're sitting on the train or bus, check whether you're balanced by closing your eyes briefly and tuning in to yourself. Then breathe the air in and out until you feel better. Relax; no one knows what you're doing! You can be sitting at your desk at work; you can be balancing your baby on your knees at meal time; you may be sitting in the cinema watching a film; perhaps you're waiting nervously in the dentist's or doctor's surgery; you might be half-way through a long and tiring business meeting. You needn't even close your eyes, once your powers of concentration are strong enough; simply sit quietly, and use your breath to balance yourself.

You can also do this exercise whilst standing.

EARTHING YOURSELF – STANDING

Don't close your eyes for this one; it may knock you off-balance. Stand with your feet about shoulder width apart and try to have your feet pointing straight in front of you. Have your arms resting loosely at your sides. Feel that your weight is distributed evenly over both feet. Sway slightly from side to side to check this is so. Make sure your knees are not locked tight; your legs should be straight but your knee joints should feel soft and relaxed. Bend your knees a few times to check you're not holding them tensely. Take a few comfortable breaths.

Again, use your string technique to hold yourself upright without being stiff. Feel the string running from your base to crown chakra and see it coming out of the top of your head. Imagine someone is gently holding the string, keeping you upright but in a relaxed fashion.

Keeping that image in your mind, now feel how heavy your body is, as the earth's gravity pulls your feet into the ground. Feel the strength of gravity, almost as though your body is sinking into the ground, but remember that your string is holding you upright. Keep your eyes open. Feel the comfortable weight of your shoulders as they obey the law of gravity. This helps release tension in them,

181

too. Feel as though your fingers are reaching down into the ground, feeling connected to the earth's energy. If you concentrate enough, they'll start to tingle and pulsate with energy. Spend a few minutes focusing on your feet, shoulders and hands. When you move, do so slowly. Don't suddenly rush off to continue your day's tasks.

Again, this exercise can be used at all times during the day. It's not only good for focusing and earthing, it really helps to relax and release tension. Next time you're standing in a long queue, or waiting to go onto a platform to make a speech, or standing in a crowded train, or even pausing during a walk, use the technique to re-focus yourself. The more you do this, the faster you will achieve positive results each time.

Once you have focused and grounded yourself (and this won't take long once you've practised it for a while), then you have to open up in front of your sitter. This is daunting, because you're aware that they're sitting there, watching you expectantly. Initially, you can't speed up this process and they need to have patience. That's why who you choose to work with in the early stages is so important. You need to develop the confidence to sit there quietly, aware of someone else in the room, but still able to concentrate fully on the opening up and tuning in processes. Once you have grounded yourself, this makes the task easier. Always ask for help from your inner self as you start. Never rush the opening-up exercise. Once you have opened, it will help you to consciously expand your aura. Your nervousness will make it contract more than unusual, so try to take a minute or two to do the following:

EXPANDING YOUR AURA

Once you have opened up, keep your eyes closed and concentrate on your own energy. Can you feel it pulsating around you? The more you focus on this, the more vibrantly you'll feel the energy around you.

Now decide that you will spread that energy outwards a little, to expand your awareness and help you work more effectively. Decide how far you want to spread yourself. If it's a small room, you may want to fill most of it. If it's a large area, you may choose just to create a large circle around both you and your sitter. When you know how much you want to spread yourself, focus on your breathing. By now it should be quite deep and regular in rhythm. As you breathe in, feel your aura puff itself out, gently but firmly. Actually visualize your energy fanning outwards. See it as streamers, or a fluffy cloud, or a filmy vapour. You could even imagine yourself puffing up like a blow-up doll. Whatever works for you is fine. You never have to tell anyone else what image you use. As you breathe out, feel the edges of your aura settle where they are. Is that big enough now? You won't know, until you start the process, what feels right. Don't feel you ever have to stretch yourself to any limits. This isn't about biggest being best. This is about you discovering your own level of expansion. Never strain or push during this exercise.

When the size of your aura feels right, stop, and take several deep breaths. Is that comfortable now? You should feel open and relaxed and it should be easy to breathe deeply. If it isn't, retract your aura as you do during the closing-down process; as you breathe in, feel your aura being sucked back towards you. Let it settle before you start working. The feeling of it settling is rather like having a big billowing cape all around you, that slowly settles on the ground. Wait until the energy movement has stopped billowing before you continue.

Again, this should be practised on your own, before you work with anyone else. Don't do this when you're out in public; by expanding your aura, you're likely to pick up all sorts of unwanted energies. By all means, use your process of closing down and retracting whenever you like. This may help you if you're in crowded places, feeling claustrophobic. You actually feel as though you need less space when your aura shrinks a little. You can expand again when you are in a cushioned environment that isn't susceptible to everyone else's energies.

Another way you can help yourself prepare for your first sitter, is to ensure you are surrounded by a few objects that will inspire your senses. This is like a psychic security blanket for you; something you need when you first start work. These objects can be small and needn't be on prominent display, unless you wish them to be.

For your sight, you could choose something that you especially love looking at: a small picture or a beautifully shaped piece of wood. It may be a photo of a loved one. Whatever it is, it should lift your spirits when you focus your eyes on it.

For your smell, you could choose a favourite oil to burn, or a scented candle. Fresh flowers might be another welcome choice. You should always check that your sitter doesn't dislike the smell first; some people react strongly to certain odours.

For your taste, although eating doesn't combine well with psychic development, you could choose to have a bowl of apples nearby, or another fruit whose smell you find appealing. This gives you a combination of two-in-one: a pleasant aroma as well as a taste memory. A word of warning though: this may be counter-productive if you're hungry as you'll be distracted. If you tend to be a comfort-eater, you're better off avoiding the taste sense.

The sense of hearing can be complemented by light music in the background. Again, you need to check on your sitter's preferences. Or you may find that the chatter of birds is soothing, in which case you could place breadcrumbs on a nearby windowsill and enjoy the benefits. What else comforts you? A ticking clock? You may favour windchimes, placed outside, near your window. All these are personal choices, of course. One person may find a ticking clock to be as soothing as fingernails on a blackboard; another may find it deeply therapeutic.

The sense of touch is important, too. Wear a fabric that feels good against your skin; have a soft piece of material by your chair. Your sitter needn't know why it's important to you.

Remember to nurture yourself during your early stages of psychic work. It doesn't matter if your 'security blankets' would be laughable to other people because you're only pleasing yourself in this respect. Make sure you choose objects that are uplifting without being distracting for you.

Last, but certainly not least, you now have to start raising and lowering energy through your chakras. This is essential for all psychic work. Until you have full control of energy once you take it into your body, you won't be able to pick up a great deal psychically. This control is a skill that you need to learn. The more skilled you become at lifting and lowering energies, the more you will pick up and the faster you will receive information. As soon as you forget to use your energies correctly, the psychic abilities are depleted and the information becomes vague and weak. After a while, you learn to recognize the signs and you gradually train yourself to use the energies almost automatically. It's similar to when you're driving a car. After you've been driving for several months, you don't consciously think every time your foot moves from brake to accelerator, but you still do it, knowing you want the car to run smoothly. The following is an exercise you have to fully understand and to practise constantly.

LIFTING AND LOWERING ENERGY THROUGH THE CHAKRAS

You need to open up fully and be ready to work, with your energies well settled back at the base chakra. Make sure you are well grounded.

It would help if you now think of your chakras as different levels in a lift. The base chakra is your ground floor. This is where your energies are at the start of all psychic work and it's where they return when you let them drop at any time. Your navel is the first floor, your solar plexus is the second and so on, up to your third eye which is the fifth level. (You don't need to take the energies up to your crown during psychic work; you simpy raise them as far as the third eye chakra.) You need to practise whooshing your energy quickly up and down through these chakra levels. It sounds difficult to begin with, and it's the thought that it ought to be difficult that hinders you. Once you let your visualization take over, lifting and lowering energies can feel as natural as lifting and lowerng your hand to your mouth while you eat. You may not even physically feel the energy moving up and down inside you; you may only think the process in your mind. That's fine. The thought alone will make it happen.

Start by seeing your energy resting at your base chakra. Now imagine that energy is moving up in a lift to your navel chakra. It needs to be a fairly swift movement; the slower your energy moves, the slower and more sluggish your psychic information will be. Visualize it as a fast-moving lift and feel the energy surge suddenly from base to navel. You may take a few minutes to create that sensation.

Then, as soon as you do manage that, and the energy reaches the navel area, it will quickly plummet back down to the base! This is the skill you need to acquire: to lift the energy swiftly to the level you need, and then hold it there. Discipline yourself so that the energy is kept at a certain level. It will eventually sink down again and you then have to renew it by using your psychic lift. You don't need to concentrate furiously as you do this; the more you try to force the energy movement, the more it will resist. This is an easy, fluid experience, once you have the confidence to know that it's possible. An experienced medium will open up and lift their energies to the third eye within a matter of seconds. This isn't because they're particularly gifted; it's because they're well trained and have been practising it for years.

Your opening-up process may take you ten minutes and you may need another five before your energies are working as you would like them to. That's fine. The important thing is your belief in yourself and in a psychic development system that can yield results. They just won't be immediate.

Once you have practised lifting the energies from the base to navel, then work on lifting them from the base to the solar plexus. Lastly, take the energy from the base all the way up to the heart. You needn't go any further than that, because all the emotional levels of psychic work function between the base and heart chakras. If you try to take the energies higher at this stage, you may well succeed in taking the energy up to your third eye, but it will then either shoot up through your crown chakra, or it will plunge again immediately to your base.

This discipline of lifting and lowering energies is not easily acquired. You may find, as you try to lift from your base to your heart, for example, that the energy shoots right up to your throat. It is very frustrating initially as you try to control the action, because you feel so often as if you can't control it. The truth is that you can. Not only that, but it's imperative that you do because, otherwise, your information will be garbled and inaccurate. Just keep practising with your psychic lift. Every time you start working with the energy levels, remember that you are in control. You alone operate the lift buttons and any time your energy shoots off into unwanted levels, it's because you aren't being firm enough with yourself. After a few sessions, you should at least be able to lift the energy to the level you require. Learning to keep it there is another skill.

Sometimes people think as long as they don't breathe, the energy will stay at the same level! You need to maintain deep breathing at all times during psychic work, so try not to hold your breath as you concentrate. The trick is to visualize your energy being maintained at a certain level. If you have lifted your energy to the solar plexus, for example, see it staying there in your mind. Let your thought process control it. Remember always to keep renewing your energy and to continually draw it up again to the solar plexus chakra, but each time you do so, see it staying there, ready for you to work. Every time you open up, you need to practise lifting and lowering your energies, even if it's only quickly: base to navel, base to solar plexus, base to heart. Make sure you hold each level for a few moments and let the energy subside to the base between each movement and the next.

There isn't a quick method of learning how to use your psychic lift. Some of you will find it much easier than others: usually the more self-discipline you possess, the easier it is for you. Those whose self-control is not the greatest will find it a challenge. Don't be discouraged if your progress seems slow; you will learn to master the technique provided you refuse to give up. It helps if you remember that the more you can control this energy, the more powerful your work will be.

Once you have become reasonably adept at lifting and lowering your energies, and once you feel thoroughly familiar and confident with the tuning-in, cleansing and closing-down processes, you are ready to think about practising with someone else.

CHAPTER 11

YOUR SITTER

Your sitter is the person upon whom you're going to practise. There is so much you need to take into account when choosing a suitable sitter, especially for your very first attempts.

You'll probably be tempted to choose someone you know quite well, as they will give you confidence and be supportive. The difficulty with this is that it's counter-productive for psychic work. If you do a sitting with a close friend and you receive certain information, you can't be sure that what you're receiving is from the psychic level, or from the knowledge that you already have of them. For instance, you may pick up on a difficulty with a personal relationship. However, you already know about this from having talked to them about it. You'll find it confusing, not being sure if you're speaking from what you know already, or from pure psychic ability.

Therefore, the less you know the person upon whom you're working, the more you can be sure of your results. Perhaps you could choose a friend of a friend, or a relative with whom you're not in constant contact. This first person upon whom you're going to work is important for you, so there's no need to rush the process. As your first few sittings will be hard for you, you need the person who will benefit you the most.

Here are some of the qualities that will help you. Someone who is:

— *receptive to the possibility of psychic phenomena, without being frightened*

— *known to you through another person, i.e. not a complete stranger, but about whose personal life you don't have many details*

- *happy to give some time to you, without putting themselves under pressure*

- *not going to want to talk constantly all the way through your sitting*

- *relaxed about sitting in a room with just you and no one else*

- *patient!*

This last trait is a very necessary one, because you really can't be rushed during the early stages. It may take you ten minutes to open up and your sitter needs to be someone who is happy to quietly sit there and relax, whilst you prepare yourself.

Some people are most uncomfortable about sitting alone in a room with someone they don't know very well, particularly if the space is a small one, and it'll make matters difficult for you if they're not relaxed. Any fear on their part will contract their aura and they will put up defence barriers that, as a beginner, you will find almost impossible to penetrate. Likewise, if they are rushed and don't really want to be there, because they have so many other places they ought to be, that distracted behaviour will also hinder you.

If they hold deeply cynical views about anything to do with spiritualism and psychic activity, you should also choose someone else. When you are more experienced, it can be a good challenge for you to deal with people who are staunch non-believers because it's beneficial to deal with all levels of energy and to learn from them. Right now, however, you need to be kind to yourself.

So, your first task is to start talking to a few friends and family. You'll soon find many people are interested and those close to you may be anxious to help. You'll have to find sensitive ways of rejecting them, but you can use it as good practice for your future work: paying attention to how you phrase things and how to treat others with tact and diplomacy. Provided you explain yourself clearly, letting them know that you need to work on people about whom you know very little, you're unlikely to offend others.

When those around you start suggesting someone else, make sure they don't give you too many details about the person they're proposing. It really affects your chances of working well. Our brains are so quick to pick up possibilities and to make stories around people; none of this belongs in psychic development. If you hear that someone happens to be a nursery teacher, for example, you'll be expecting to pick up details of young children. You can then create that yourself via your imagination. You might think you won't but unfortunately it usually happens in the early stages. The less you know about them on every level, the better it will be for you.

In case you are tempted to choose a complete stranger, a word of warning. You might think you'd be better off putting an advertisement in the newsagent's window and, by phrasing it carefully, find the right person that way. Please don't. You have no idea what sort of individual you'll be inviting into your home by doing this and you may not be able to handle their energies. It's a sad fact that psychic work can also attract some very lost and unbalanced souls. Whilst they may not be danger-ous, these people can be difficult to handle, even when you're experienced. You really need to stick to a personal recommendation from someone, never a complete stranger. Don't ever break that rule.

Wait until you find someone who fits the criteria well. It doesn't matter if it takes a few months before the right person comes along; you can be practising by yourself in the meantime, working on your meditations and exercises. It's never wasted time to do this, and if the right person doesn't come along straight away, perhaps it's because you aren't quite ready yet.

When you do get hold of the right person, you should know it. Your intuitional sense should come to the fore. If someone makes you feel uncomfortable in any way, they aren't right at this stage. Trust your instinct and don't veer from it. Once you have found the right person, you need to be honest with them.

Explain openly that you're a beginner and don't promise them any positive results. If you delude them in any way, they'll end up feeling cheated and used. However, be careful not to belittle yourself, or psychic work, when you do this. You don't need to apologize for the fact that you're a novice. We all are in everything we do initially. Don't keep saying to them that probably nothing will happen because you aren't good enough at it. Any negativity you utter will only fuel your own subconscious, make you feel inadequate and encourage a lack of results. If you enrol people into your work with honesty but enthusiasm, they'll be more willing to help. You have one advantage from the start, in that most people are curious about psychic development.

Also, one important point. Never, ever charge a fee during your early development. It's morally wrong and karmically detrimental to do so. Some people believe that you should never charge for psychic work, whatever your degree of experience, because spirituality doesn't come into the realms of material greed. Everyone is entitled to their own thoughts on this subject and you can eventually make up your own mind about what feels right for you. However, as a beginner you shouldn't ever get caught up in exchanging money. Your role is to treat your sitters with the utmost respect and appreciation and to ensure you have the time to do this work without finances entering into it. Once you have trained for several years (and that doesn't mean just studying this book, it means attending other courses and expanding your horizons), then you can re-think. Until that time, always offer your services free of charge.

So, you have now found the right person and explained honestly about your novice status. Next, you need to explain briefly what happens during psychic work. The chances are they really won't have a clue and that sense of not knowing will make them nervous. This doesn't mean that you need to give them a detailed version of what is contained within the first ten chapters of this book. It does mean you need to find a simple, concise way of explaining psychic ability so that, instead of alienating them, you make them feel reassured and interested. Here is a suggestion as to what you might say. After a while, you will create your own style and wording to suit you.

> *Psychic work isn't about voodoo or black magic. Basically, it's about tapping into energy. We all know that humans give off energy and all I'm doing is training myself to learn how to read that energy. You probably know we only*

use a tiny portion of our brains. Psychic work is about learning to use that little bit more. So I'm not dealing with spirits or ghosts; I'm looking at what is here now and around you today. The energy you give off is like a video that contains a lot of information about you. So I'm trying to play that video by using some extra bits of my brain.'

You may find a shorter way of putting it, or want to choose another analogy, but do make sure you say something that takes the mysticism out of it, and try to use words that make them feel comfortable. The word 'aura' often makes people shut off, but as soon as you talk about 'energies', you're using a word which they can relate to and which makes them feel safe.

It's important for you to mention the fact that you won't be making any contact with deceased people during your sitting. Most people only connect the word 'psychic' with fortune telling and messages from dear, departed ones. You need to explain that what you are doing works on a different level. You don't need to go into the emotional and mental spheres, or mention the chakras, as most of that is likely to make people's eyes glaze over. Just explain that you are picking up information about them as a person and what is happening in their own life; it might help if you let them know that this is the level at which all psychics need to start.

Ask them if they would please keep their comments to a minimum during the reading itself. Reassure them that when you have finished you can have a good discussion about everything and clarify any further points. You need to create your own energy flow during work and if your sitter constantly interrupts you, you will keep losing your rhythm and have to keep renewing your energies. This continual interruption will make information more fragmented and indistinct. You needn't say all this, because it's also likely to confuse your sitter; simply say it's better to chat at the end. You can explain that if they give too much away, you're then losing the opportunity to pick up the information for yourself. If they do start to say things like, 'Oh, yes, that makes sense because I've just started a new relationship,' or 'That's because my job is doing so-and-so', don't be afraid to stop them and refuse further details. They'll respect you for your earnest desire to get the facts for yourself, psychically.

Always remember to thank them for their time, when they arrive and when they leave. You need to learn to treat all sitters with deep respect and concern, so you might as well start straight away. Really let them know you appreciate their help and that you don't take it for granted. If they feel good about being there, they're more likely to want to continue coming to see you.

As soon as they arrive check that they are comfortable. Let them know where the toilet is, offer them a non-alcoholic drink and ask them if they're warm or cool enough. Make sure the chair is comfortable for them and that they approve of any scent or sounds you have within your space. Be clear about how much time they have to spare and make sure you stick to that time span. The more they feel looked after, the more they will relax, and the more you will be able to pick up information from them.

Now you have to look at one of your biggest responsibilities in psychic work: how you phrase the information you receive. This is an area where even trained mediums can fall down; how you say something is just as important as the content of what you're saying. Most of us don't really stop to think before we speak. How often have you said something and then regretted it? It can either be because it was the wrong time, or the wrong way to say it, or because it was true but hurtful. Developing your psychic abilities is also a chance for you to restructure what you say and how you say it: in all aspects of your life, not just during psychic work.

We're going to look at a number of examples, discussing what you might pick up psychically, how you might express that, and the effects of what you say. As you read through them, you'll probably be thinking that you would never, ever be so inconsiderate or tactless. You haven't yet experienced the excitement of picking up psychic details and then having to relay them. Before you have this chance, please look thoroughly at what is below.

The first thing you have to consider is what you might see or sense that could cause alarm or distress to your sitter. This list is potentially a long one, but here are a few examples:

— *threatening objects such as a knife, gun, rope or sword*

— *heavy colours such as grey, brown or black*

— *items associated with death such as a coffin, grave, wreath or cross*

— *sensations such as a pain in the stomach or a headache*

— *feelings of depression or loss*

— *worry about a relative or friend who has been unwell*

— *travel in a car, plane, train, boat or bus*

— *images such as gargoyles or masks*

— *a large mass of water*

— *dark tunnels*

This isn't to imply that you shouldn't see any of the above during your work. You almost definitely will see most of them at some time, and more besides. It's not the fact that you see or sense potentially disturbing situations: it's more about how to interpret what you see and when not to mention things that might cause concern or confusion, especially if you're not certain as to their meaning. Let's look at some of these situations in more detail.

Items such as guns and knives are always very difficult for beginners to deal with. If you're sitting waiting for something to come through to you and, after a few minutes, you finally see something and it's a gun, you're going to want to mention it. If you just say 'I see a gun' and leave it at that, can you imagine what their thoughts might be? Rather as we are conditioned towards cynicism and self-doubt, so most of us are ready to think the worst. To most people, a gun means an ugly situation. They will either fear that they're going to be shot, that they're going to be involved in a hold-up of some sort (or that someone close to them will be) or that they need to get a gun for self-protection.

Knives prompt a similar response; rope often makes people think of suicide; swords usually bring up images of conflict.

Of course, these items needn't mean something negative or worrying. A gun could mean your sitter shoots clay-pigeons or works for the police; a knive could mean they're a chef or butcher or that your sitter feels as though someone is metaphorically stabbing them because of a particular situation they're in at present; a rope might indicate that they are being pulled in different directions, or in a specific direction for a good reason, or that they are a tight-rope walker; a sword could show that your sitter is a survivor and fighter, who refuses to give in when the going is tough, or that they collect antique swords and have a case full of them at home. The possibilities are endless.

However, when you first start, you're unlikely to understand what you're seeing. If you're sure what you see or sense won't cause concern, then report what you see without trying to embroider upon it or letting your imagination come into play. However, with any potentially threatening object, it's better to say nothing, unless you immediately understand what it means. If, for instance, you see a gun and see it amongst a collection under a locked cabinet, and it's not accompanied by any sensation of fear or anxiety, then you might mention something along the lines of: 'I'm seeing a gun in a collection. This doesn't make me feel upset or worried in any way, I sense no threat here, but I wonder if you have a collection of guns or know someone who does?' You still run the risk of your sitter saying they don't know anyone who keeps guns and then having them go away and worry about the possible implications.

If they do respond in the negative to some image like that, make sure you repeat yourself at the end of the sitting and assure them that your sensation with the gun was not one of fear or threat. Make sure they hear what you say; learn to really watch their body language and know that their minds are left at rest. Never, ever just say 'I see a gun' (or knife or whatever) and leave it at that. When you're in the slightest doubt, don't mention it at all. This doesn't make you an untruthful person; it's you protecting and nurturing your sitter whilst you experience your early development. When you are experienced, you can deal with everything on a deeper level. For now, your sitter's well-being is of paramount importance.

People also react strongly to colour, with everyone having their own interpretations. Generally speaking, dark colours such as grey, brown and black are considered by most to be negative images. They make people think of depression or bad news or death. They aren't necessarily. Brown can be about someone's connection to the earth energy and their relationship to nature. Black can be about someone conserving their own energy and centring themselves. Grey or silver can be about communication and speeding up vibrations. Of course, those colours can also relate to depression and confusion. Until you develop your own special relationship with colours and learn to interpret them, it's best if you avoid mentioning those which might make people worry. If you see brown in front of your closed eyes, quietly ask further what this means. Does it make you feel calm, nurtured? Do you think of rich, dark soil and its goodness? Or are you feeling sadness and pain, aware that you're holding on to emotions that are hindering you? In the first few sessions, you aren't likely to be able to work that quickly and get the answers you want. That happens with time and practice. People tend to feel less threatened by other colours, so if you see any of the chakra colours or soft pinks and golds, you're unlikely to worry people with those shades. They may be able to identify with them for their own personal reasons.

Any symbol that can be connected directly to death is traumatic for people. Most people have a great fear of dying and although you may not personally feel that way, you won't be in a position to convince your sitter otherwise during a sitting. Nor should you try to do so. Remember they're entitled to their own views and it's not your place to try to influence their beliefs, even if you feel strongly that you're right and they're wrong. A coffin isn't an uncommon image for a psychic to pick up, but it doesn't have to mean that someone has died or is about to die. It can indicate an area of your sitter's life that has gone, be it a divorce, job loss, or even a fear or problem that they have released. A grave might also symbolize this, or a floral wreath. You might mistake the floral wreath for a Christmas event that is relevant, although nothing to do with death. A cross needn't relate only to the crucifixion, it can just mean your sitter has religious convictions or even that they feel as though they have a cross to bear at this time in their life. Never mention an object immediately associated with death, unless you make it very clear that you are not seeing or predicting anyone's demise. Even then, it can be such an emotive and worrying subject, that you can leave your sitter worried for a long time after your meeting. If you see items connected with death, check first if you can understand their significance. If you can, mention what you sense but not the object itself.

For instance, if you see a coffin and then get or see the word 'divorce' with it, you could say 'I feel you have been divorced recently and are now making an effort to bury that part of your past and move on'. Don't say 'I see a coffin and I'm thinking of divorce'. The way most people's minds work, they may accept what you say at the time, and then later when they think over all the information they received, they will start to worry about that coffin and wonder if you perhaps got it wrong. Perhaps they're going to die soon. They may be fretting needlessly about it without you even being aware of the impact you've had. Our imaginations are such fertile mechanisms and it takes very little for us to fly off into a worrying scenario which we have totally fabricated through someone else's lack of consideration.

Mentioning physical pains or twinges is another difficult area. Again, most people's minds work straight onto negative patterns. If you say 'I feel a pain here in my stomach' or 'I've got the sensation of a headache', you can guarantee your sitter's immediate thoughts will be that they've got stomach cancer or a brain tumour. They won't necessarily say that to you at the sitting, but they'll go away and panic over it. You might have picked up on a little indigestion or a metaphoric headache that someone else is giving your sitter at that time. You might be getting stomach pains because your sitter is nervous about being there with you and they have that butterflies-in-their-stomach sensation. Never just say you have a pain in any area. Ask your inner self what that pain relates to and if it's easily explainable, then mention it, but not as a pain. Say 'I feel wobbly in the stomach, as though you're slightly anxious about being here.' Or 'My head feels tight, as though you're under pressure in a particular area of your life right now.' If you can name the area, so much the better. If you're in doubt, don't mention it.

Also, during your early stages, don't be tempted to offer any sort of diagnosis or theory about what is happening physically to anybody. If you are meant to work later in a healing field related to psychic development, this will happen gradually over a period of years. No one can start psychic work and immediately be able to diagnose illnesses. It would be dangerous and misleading for you to do so. You need to spend considerable time studying physical anatomy and energies before you could possibly be ready for this level of work. If at any time you receive any worrying information about someone's health, do not offer advice at this stage. You aren't qualified or capable and whatever you say is likely to be inaccurate. Cleanse any of these unwanted sensations, using your cleansing techniques, before you continue.

Talking about feelings of depression or emotions of loss is also problematical, unless you can deal with it in a positive manner. Your sitters aren't giving you their time in order to feel depressed by your reading. Whenever possible, try to see something positive about what is coming through to you. For instance, you may feel a sensation of sadness or see a sad symbol such as tears, when you start a reading. Before you say anything, see where this leads. Are those images remaining steadfastly in front of you, or is the picture changing to something else? Is there sunshine or blue sky or a smiling face coming through? Is this is about to happen or is it happening now? You may be tapping into something that has already happened. Wait until you understand what is going on, and never offer negative feedback.

Of course, it's good for everyone to have some 'down' moments and to learn from them, but would you find it helpful if you were feeling low and someone said all they could sense was darkness and a sad feeling? You want to know something better is out there, not be repeatedly confronted by depression. This is where your own spiritual presence comes into play, and the more you are in touch with your own spirituality, the more you will be in a position to offer loving support. This is not to say that you are to fabricate positive outcomes or to create good scenarios that aren't there. However, your inner self has the knowledge and ability to guide you and to encourage people into a more positive environment. This is tricky, because it must come from your higher self, not from you deciding what you think is best for someone else. There is a vast difference between your own thoughts and higher guidance. You will learn the difference as you work. In the beginning, if you're worried, leave out the negative images, until you can find the positive encouragement to go with it. The more you practice getting in touch with your inner self, the more quickly the guidance will come to you.

For example, you may start a sitting and feel an immediate sense of loss. This is a specific sensation and one you may come to recognize. Initially, you just feel sad and don't know what else to say. You know it's not helpful just to say 'You feel sad. You've lost someone you love.' However, if you are in communication with your inner self, you will be given help as to what you can say that will offer comfort and peace. It may be something further, such as, 'Through your loss, you have grown enormously. I can feel you coming out of a long tunnel. There is sunshine and warmth ahead of you. You've learnt from your sadness and become richer from it.' Of course, you can only say that if you know that is what has happened. It would be pointless to offer some sentiment like that if your sitter is still feeling deeply distressed, as though they were stuck in a muddy pond. You need to say something that is appropriate to their present condition and this will only happen once you and your inner self are working in tandem together.

Be careful in your sittings about mentioning people who are unwell. Again, this sets people worrying about situations that may not arise. You might say something in all innocence, such as 'I see you tending your father who is lying in a bed.' You mention the scene and then pass on, because it doesn't seem particularly significant. Perhaps their father did have a cold and was confined to bed, so they administered some nursing for a while. Provided this is all made clear and can then be left, that's fine. Don't just say you saw their father unwell in bed and not give further details. Make sure the image you described is recognisable and understood. Then clear up any negative emotions surrounding it before you move on. You might want to say 'I can feel you and your father are very close and you were instrumental in helping his full recovery.' Or 'Nursing him through his brief illness has given you two valuable time together and is good for both of you.' This is only applicable if you really get the information this way. Don't make it up, but search for the helpful and constructive in everything you say.

Another area that can cause upsets is travel. For the usual reasons, if you mention someone travelling in a plane or car, in particular, people start to assume you mean an accident is pending. Instead of taking it as a positive symbol of perhaps going on holiday or exploring new pastures somewhere, they relate it to a danger. There's no reason why you shouldn't mention any form of transport if it comes up, but make sure you prefix it with a statement such as 'This doesn't mean you're about to have an accident' or 'This isn't saying you have to be careful about it'. Always be clear about not alarming your sitter. Always think about how they might feel threatened by what you say.

People also react strongly against symbols such as gargoyles and masks; it's the sense of the unknown or fear of a threatening presence. If you see hooded figures or unpleasant images, clear them immediately. Don't try to stop and analyse them or encourage them. Let them go as negativity that won't assist you or your sitter. By washing them away, they cease to have power.

Water often comes up as an image in psychic work. Unfortunately, many people have a great fear of water, particularly the sea. Be specific about whatever body of water you see. If it's a trickling little brook, say so. If it's a large expanse of calm lake, explain that to your sitter. If you see an ocean, let them know if it's pounding surf or lapping, gentle waves. Always mention that seeing water is not about drowning or death. Explain it's usually to do with their love or hate of water and also their emotions. Most often, the state of the water reflects their present condition. A rapidly swirling stream could mean that everything in their life is happening so quickly that they fear being swept along by somebody else's wishes. A still river or lake with fresh water symbolizes a sense of peace. If it's muddy or stagnant, they have emotional issues they've yet to confront. Don't say they need to confront certain things. You might want to phrase it as 'There seem to be some emotional areas in your life that you are looking at right now. You want to sort them out and be able to move on'. Then see if your inner self can offer comfort in this area. If not, you've still said nothing negative or worrying.

Psychics often have tunnels amongst their images. This can make many people feel claustrophobic, although you don't intend it that way. Tunnels can be about people retreating for a while to restore energies; it can be about them looking at deeper areas of their psyche; it can be unknown paths they are taking in their life; or it can mean they are well-connected to the earth energy. If you want to mention a tunnel, then be clear about its meaning and try to discover where the tunnel is leading so that you can give a specific reading. If you see a look of panic cross their face, reassure them the image is symbolic and not literal in any way, i.e. it doesn't mean they're about to be buried alive. Let them embrace the image as a positive statement.

Are you now beginning to desperately wonder what on earth is safe to say? Are you thinking that everything seems fraught with dangers and responsiblities and there is nothing you can think or feel or see that is not going to have a negative implication? It's quite healthy for you to feel that at this stage. It means you are really acknowledging your commitment to your sitters and just how important that is.

You can never be too careful or too concerned or too tactful in your comments. Everyone is sensitive underneath, whether they choose to show it to you or not. You have enormous responsiblity for their welfare whilst they are with you. Never abuse it, use it lovingly and carefully at all times, and whenever you are in doubt, constantly ask for advice from your inner self.

What happens if you receive unpleasant images or hear distressing words or feel horrible sensations? It will happen to you during your work; it happens to every psychic. Remember to cleanse them away as soon as they appear. It's part of your discipline. You are in control, no one else. You can rid yourself of any unwanted influence at any time, provided you are firm and clear in your intention. You may have to cleanse several times, but you can cleanse it away. There are unpleasant and well as pleasant forces; you experienced that during your brief visit to the Basement level in the Expanding Your Thoughts Exercise. These unhappy forces may try to disguise themselves as positive messengers; they may even try to convince you that your higher self is speaking to you, but you must remember that all negative images and sensations come from lower sources. That's why you need to wash them away as quickly as possible. They soon get the message that you aren't about to play with them and the unpleasant sensations will cease. Until you show you are in control, they will keep trying. Practise your firm control from the very first time you open up and refuse to let any unwanted influences affect you. You have the power, not they. Higher consciousness is always about positive, spiritual growth.

A last word about how you treat your sitters. Always ensure that you finish your sitting with a positive and loving statement. Hopefully, you will have achieved this through most of your reading already, but, whatever has happened during it, always finish with something that will leave your sitter feeling refreshed and uplifted. What you say last of all is the final image that stays with them and what they remember later on. Make sure it is something they will want to hear.

Also, always, always check that they have not ended up confused or worried by anything you said. People will probably be hesitant to tell you or criticise you, especially as they'll know you're just learning, so it's up to you to make the environment as safe and open as possible. Ask them for feedback. Explain you can't learn unless you understand where you sometimes get it wrong. Really encourage them to be specific and you'll learn from it. You might have thought you had explained some image or sensation quite clearly, but they will have interpreted it in a completely different way. Go over any image that you think they might be left feeling worried about and check they really are feeling fine. Remember to thank them and to ask if they would be willing to sit for you again.

To check that you have properly absorbed the contents of this chapter and the previous one, below are a few situations that might arise during a reading. Practise the way you would phrase your comments. Do this aloud if you can, to give yourself confidence.

Your sitter tells you that they feel nervous, because they've never had a sitting with a psychic before. How can you make them feel at ease?

You open up and tune in, but after a few minutes you still aren't getting anything. What can you do to help the situation?

You tune in and pick up a sensation of panic. What should you do?

You see a grave in front of you and a person putting flowers on it. Should you mention it?

You see your sitter driving a car through pleasant countryside. How should you phrase what you see?

You feel a pain in your solar plexus area. What should you say?

You sense that someone your sitter loves is in hospital and they are concerned for their welfare. Should you discuss it?

You feel the colour grey around your sitter, which is then followed by streamers of green and blue. Is it acceptable to mention all this?

You see your sitter floating on their back in a smooth lake. The sun is shining. What would you get from this scene?

Once you develop your own style of working, you will learn what different symbols and sensations mean for you. The process gradually becomes very individual and personal as you learn to trust your own intuitional and knowing senses.

Now you have successfully completed your groundwork, you are ready to enter the second part of the book: where you actually begin to practise your psychic development. Chapter 12 explains that an Auric Reading is an excellent starting point.

CHAPTER 12

GIVING AN AURIC READING

This is a good starting point for psychic development work. Auric reading basically means using your energies to tap into your sitter's auric field and then receive information about them. What can you remember about the human aura and its seven different levels? It may help you to turn back to Chapter 4 and read through what can be found within the aura. It's hard to remember everything from one reading. You don't need to remember what information is contained within each individual level because you aren't going to consciously tap into every level separately during an auric reading. What is important is that you acquaint yourself again with just how much detail is within that energy field and the potential that is there for you to delve into. To begin with, you are only likely to receive information which is within the first three levels.

To help clarify the auric layers, you can group them together into just three sections: the physical, astral and spiritual planes. The aura is often described in this way to simplify matters, although seven distinct layers have been seen and recognized.

The physical plane refers to the first three levels and is described as representing the etheric body (first layer), the emotional body (second layer) and the mental body (third layer). In other words, these first three levels are all about how we operate within our earth body. This also balances with our base chakra being very physical, our navel being very much about our emotions and our solar plexus relating to our mental attitudes towards everything.

The astral plane is described as the fourth level, which is connected to our heart chakra. Do you remember reading that our heart chakra is like a hinge, linking our physical and spiritual beings together? This astral body is our bridge between two separate worlds.

The spiritual plane refers to the fifth, sixth and seventh levels and is said to emulate our physical plane. In other words, level five is a template for our first layer, but in perfect, spiritual form, so that the fifth layer is the ultimate version of our first layer. The sixth level is the perfect template for our second layer. The seventh level is the perfect version of our third level. You might have to re-read that a few times before it makes sense.

The level at which you will hopefully learn to work, is that of tapping energies within the first three layers of the aura – the physical, emotional and mental – that are often grouped under the collective heading of the physical plane. This isn't to say that it's impossible for you to tap into someone's spiritual nature and higher consciousness. It just takes more dedication and practice.

Also, some people are easier to 'read' than others. You will understand this fully when you practise on different people. Some are more in touch with their spirituality than others. The more their energies vibrate within a certain level, the more likely you are to be able to tap into it. Whilst there is a great deal you can learn from someone from their first three auric levels (or their physical plane), you should always be aware that there is more to each person. Every human has these seven layers of energy whether they're aware of them or not.

If you have time before your sitter arrives, it would help you to spend some time concentrating on the human aura. Think about its many layers of information, remember the sensitivity of certain areas, and consider how you will phrase delicate information. Go over the technique for expanding your own aura and be prepared to increase your own auric field for this work.

When your sitter arrives, it's particularly important that you put them at their ease as much as possible. In this reading, you are relying on the information within their aura and, as you now know, if you have someone who is nervous or frightened, their aura will contract and make your work more difficult. Spend some time with them explaining what you're doing in a practical way, and make every effort to relax them. If it takes ten or fifteen minutes before you feel ready to start, that's fine. Try not to ask personal questions during this time and if they offer details themselves, gently ask them to refrain from doing so until the end. If you're uncomfortable about making conversation, stick to the areas which concern their well-being. Is the scent in the room all right? Do they mind your lighting a candle? Would they like some gentle music or do they prefer silence? Is that chair the right height or would a cushion make it more comfortable? Would they like the window opened a little?

When you have helped them to relax as much as possible, explain that you'll take a few minutes to open up. Your sitter may feel awkward just sitting there as you do this, so you could encourage them to close their own eyes and rest. If your sitter leads a hectic life, they may be more than glad to sit quietly anyway. Make sure you let them know that they don't have to do anything to help you, that they don't have to concentrate or try to project any image. The more relaxed they are, the less they try to do anything, the more it helps you. It's important you explain this clearly; people immediately feel better when you do so. Any responsibility is being taken from their shoulders and that's a comforting feeling.

Now you're ready to follow the technique below:

AURIC READING

Close your eyes and go through your opening-up process. Take a moment to expand your own aura so that it feels more open, more receptive. Ask for guidance from your inner self, that you may give a helpful reading to your sitter. When you feel open, balanced, and relaxed, then continue.

You are now going to pull some of your sitter's aura into your own aura, so that you can read and interpret information about them. You don't have to keep your eyes closed to do this, but it often helps your concentration. Using your psychic lift, raise your energies up as high as your solar plexus chakra. Take a deep, comfortable breath and ensure that your energies are staying at the solar plexus level. As you breathe out, feel your aura expand and reach out into your sitter's auric field. Then, as you breathe in again, feel their aura being pulled back towards you. Breathe out again and reach out with your aura again. Breathe in and feel their aura coming into you again. Do this several more times.

By doing this, you're creating a spiral of constant energy. It's egg-like in shape, reaching out to your sitter in an arc and then returning towards you in a second arc. You need to keep this cycle of energy in a continual flow, to keep receiving information. You can use different visualization techniques to help you in this process. You could imagine your aura has a large arm: that it reaches out, scoops up your sitter's aura in a large receptacle and then returns it to you. Or you might prefer to imagine that your solar plexus has a lot of tentacles which reach out and then pull back information. Other people use streams of brilliant, beautiful light which they see streaming out from them towards their sitter, mixing together with their sitter's aura, and then returning back to their solar plexus. You may create another image which works better for you.

As soon as you receive some information and speak, your energy will drop again to your base chakra. You then have to lift your energies again, hold them at the solar plexus chakra, and continue the cycle of energy.

During your reading it's likely you will pick up some uncomfortable sensations. Most people have aspects of themselves with which they're not contented. Whenever you feel something unpleasant, stop the circle of energy flow, and pull the white light down through your head chakra, using it to cleanse and release anything unwelcome. You may even pick up a physical twinge somewhere, because you have pulled some of that sensation into your own aura. This won't harm you, but you must remember to cleanse it away as it happens. Wait until it has gone, before you renew your energies and continue with the reading.

The more you practise auric work, the easier it is to keep the auric egg of energy spiralling back and forth. Every time you speak, lift the energies up to the solar plexus again.

Once you feel you have received enough information or that you have worked at a deep enough level (always being aware of how your sitter is feeling and how they're reacting to what you're telling them), then let your energies settle back at your base. Cleanse thoroughly, several times, before you close down. Remember to retract your aura. Then cleanse again and check you're well earthed, before you open your eyes again. Now you can discuss with your sitter the information you received.

You may find the first time you try this that nothing happens. You may feel as though you are creating the egg of energy, but no information is coming through to you. This is quite common. Until you experience your first piece of information that is accurate, you hesitate to say anything at all. Also, images may come and go so quickly that you can't recognize them. This is particularly frustrating; it happens because you haven't learned yet to balance and control your energy flow. You have to be in control of the energy and, in the case of auric reading, keep the energy resting at the solar plexus. You also have to believe it is possible before it happens; you need to truly know that the human aura is a treasure chest of information. This is why spending some time studying the human energy levels and their power can be beneficial. The more you understand the concept of how it works, the easier it will be for you to work.

Often you will receive information or images but think they are so silly or inconsequential that you couldn't possibly mention them. This is your ego getting in the way again; you're worried about looking foolish. Whatever you see, (unless it could be misconstrued in a distressing way), no matter how odd it seems, say it.

Your initial auric readings are likely to contain much of their physical, daily existence. This is the densest area of their aura, and the easiest for you to first read. For instance, you may see a boiled egg. On its own, that seems peculiar. It seems highly improbable that it's significant in any way. Your first thought will be that you made it up and that you mustn't talk about something so trifling. However, if you had mentioned it, you might have discovered they ate a boiled egg for lunch that day. Knowing you got an accurate fact, would have given you confidence and renewed energy for your work. Food is a common image for new psychics to see, because it's such a necessary, basic part of our physical survival. Or you might see a pile of paperclips and again hestitate to mention such a mundane item. You might have seen them because they have a container of them on their desk and that item is in front of them for eight hours a day. Naturally, it would be part of their aura. These every-day objects are exactly the sort of thing you will pick up initially and you have to learn to overcome your embarrassment and insecurity and just say what you see.

If you see colours, at this stage they may simply refer to colours which surround your sitter, or colours which they like. You may just see the colour green and nothing further. They may have a favourite shirt in a shade of green. You may keep getting a shade of pale blue in front of you and not know what it means. Perhaps it's the colour of their office, or a room in their house. You may see rich hues of yellow and orange; it may be because they have several Van Gogh prints hanging in their living room.

Symbols are more difficult to interpret, and some people only have psychic experiences relayed in symbolic images. There are no hard and fast rules if this happens to you. You can only learn to interpret these through time and practice. If you start to see various symbols and patterns but they mean nothing to you, try to remember their shapes and colours, and write them down. Refer to them again when you do other readings and see if certain ones crop up often. Can you connect aspects of those two people in any way? You may also come across symbols in different books and gain an understanding of what they mean that way. Be wary of other people telling you what they look like or what they must mean. Do show them to your sitter when you've finished a reading, and ask them if they mean anything to them. They may have an understanding of them which you couldn't possibly guess yourself. However, showing them to someone quite unrelated to your sitter, may set off your imagination, rather than your intuitional awareness. You could spend some time meditating on different symbols if they occur frequently for you. Or you may choose to draw them and then have them around you during the day in some capacity. Perhaps pin them near the kettle, or by your desk, so that your eyes fall upon them and your subconscious can do some work on their meaning. This is an area where you have to do quite a bit of work by yourself because you're discovering your own individual way of working that may not conform to that of others. That's why it's difficult if you show a symbol to other people. They may say it looks like a flower or a helmet or a snake and set your mind working in areas away from your knowing sense. Trust your own instinct and let it guide you, gradually but surely.

You will encounter people who are very closed at times. If you have them during your early readings, this is going to be very hard on you. If you are getting absolutely nothing through at all, except you can sense your sitter is very uncomfortable or nervous, then you will have to work at a deeper level to understand them. You may be working with the first layer, the etheric level, when you need to go into the second and third levels, the emotional and mental, to understand them better.

Here the sensations are more subtle. You have to be tuned in to people and their emotional energies to do this. Are you aware of other people on a day-to-day basis and do you notice how they're feeling? Can you immediately tell if someone is upset, even if they don't show obvious signs of it? If you're not aware of other people's emotional vibrations, your work will be harder. Make a conscious effort to observe other people's feelings and notice their effect upon you.

Ask your inner self for help as you delve into the emotional and mental layers. You need to keep the flow of energy going, pulling their aura back into yours, but the work becomes deeper and more controlled at this level. Until you have experienced auric readings on different levels, it will be hard to grasp the difference, but when you do pick up some of your sitter's emotions and attitudes, the energy is finer and much more subtle. You have to work harder to receive information at this level. There are different ways in which you may experience it, too. Some people feel their sitter's emotions for themselves. Some see their sitter in front of them showing their emotion in an obvious way, being angry or sad or depressed. Some psychics sense emotion through colour. Again this becomes personal to each person, but red might show vitality or anger, and dirty, smudged colours often show blocks of energy manifesting themselves as jealousy or bitterness. You may have none of the above happen to you; you might just 'know' and not need to question further.

Whatever you see in their emotional and mental levels, you need special care before you comment. If we see that someone is distressed in some way, we usually want to comfort them and take away their hurt. Sometimes, people have to acknowledge their emotional pain and live with it for a while, before they can move on. If you receive information that can guide or nurture from your inner self, then pass it on in the most appropriate way possible. Always let them know it is all right to be upset and that being emotional about an issue, shows an opportunity to face something and move on. Let people know that wherever they are in a situation it's right for them, even if it's painful. Never offer advice such as, 'I can see you're quite a closed person, emotionally. You should open up more. It would help you.' Wait until you can phrase something positively before you speak.

Also, if people are closed in certain areas, there may be good reasons for this and you may not realize them initially. It might be because your sitter isn't ready yet to look at parts of themselves, or it may be that their day-to-day life requires a certain level of self-protection and they get so used to creating those necessary barriers that they forget to relax them later. Many professions require good self-defence mechanisms: police work and jobs within mental institutions, for example. There are others. If you're a teacher working within a 'problem' school, you won't help yourself by always being open and vulnerable during your day. Any field of nursing also requires a degree of detachment. These walls of protection are not just helpful, they're essential for people's well-being. That's why you should never tell people to 'open up more' or 'let their hair down'. You may realize it could help them to do so during social hours or in a protected environment, but most people can't open up and close down at will. It's a technique they need to work at; you run the danger of encouraging them to open up more, and then have them not close down when they need to for a work environment. Use your inner self to guide you into understanding more about the person you're reading.

You will also encounter people who are the opposite: open in every way. They go around continually soaking everything up like a sponge. Every emotion and feeling goes into their aura, good and bad. Psychics may see them as an open receptacle, pulling everything towards them like a magnet. These people are easy to read but it can be distressing. They often end up in situations as victims, unable to distinguish between a positive or negative influence. Bullies are attracted like radar to someone who is too open or vulnerable. If people learn to close down and get in touch with their inner self for guidance, they can move into a healthier existence. Again, it's not your duty to tell them this directly, unless you receive information which you can impart in a positive way.

Auric readings are one of the most powerful ways to learn about how unique every human being truly is. No two auric readings will ever be the same for you. It's impossible, just as everyone's fingerprint is unique and no two snowflakes ever consist of the same pattern.

From every person you read aurically, you have the chance to learn yourself. It's said that everyone in life attracts to them what is most necessary for them to learn (part of our karmic path). It's therefore quite possible that the people for whom you give sittings are also people from whom you could learn a great deal. You shouldn't be pondering this possibility during your sitting, as it will affect your concentration. However, provided you can find the time afterwards, sit quietly and think over what happened during your reading.

What did you pick up in your sitter that relates to you and your personality? If you saw a way forward to improve your sitter's life, how could this also affect your life? Or could you see areas of your sitter's life that were an inspiration for you? What could you adopt yourself? Or were there aspects of your sitter that were completely opposite from yours? Which provides the fuller life? Were there qualities in your sitter which irritated you or bothered you? What exactly were they? Why did they have that effect on you? How does this compare with your own ways? It's another fascinating concept that what we find annoying in others is a reflection of what we are ourselves. We hate it in others because we possess those traits ourselves and don't want to acknowledge them. The more you embrace this as a possibility, the more this belief crops up to confront you. It may be upsetting at times, but it's also a great opportunity for spiritual growth.

Try to use every auric reading as a valuable learning experience. The more you work, the deeper you will be able to delve. Remember that, in the beginning, you may only pick up a few physical items surrounding your sitter. That is how most people start. As you practise more, you will find yourself going more into their emotional levels and gaining further insight from that. Don't try to jump straight into a deeply emotional reading when you start. Not only will you not be ready for it, but your sitter almost certainly won't be either! Always start off your reading with a few lighter comments before you delve deeper.

Don't worry if there are a fair number of comments which your sitter doesn't find relevant. This will happen, especially in the early stages. It doesn't necessarily mean you are being inaccurate, unless you're still panicking and letting your imagination take over. The imagination won't be psychic information, so it's doubtful that your sitter will relate to any of it. If you feel you are relaxed and that the information you received was genuine, ask your sitter to go away and think about it.

So often your sitter won't connect something at the time, but later, when they're more relaxed and contemplating what you've said, they may suddenly realize the importance of what you've said. This happens a great deal, so don't be discouraged if you receive quite a few blank looks during your reading. You may find that, next time they come for a sitting, some of it has clicked into place.

Also, influences may come into your sitter's aura without your sitter being aware of them. For instance, you may see a vase full of carnation flowers in their aura. Your sitter may shake their head, saying they aren't particularly interested in flowers and they don't have any at home or work. You'll therefore think you've 'got it wrong'. However, it's equally possible that earlier in the day your sitter was sitting at their doctor's, waiting to be seen, and at their elbow on a nearby table, was a large display of carnations. They may not have consciously noticed them because they aren't overtly fond of flowers. However, the vibrational frequencies of the flowers don't know that! They had someone's energies touching theirs and they instinctively blended and inter-connected with them. If you ask your sitter whether they were sitting near to some flowers that day, they might be able to pull the memory from their subconscious. Most people need that sort of prodding before they remember.

This isn't to say that you have to try to make everything fit into place. Sometimes, no matter how experienced you are, some pieces will not fit anywhere into the puzzle. If this does happen, ask yourself what it felt like when you received that bit of information. Was the feeling different? Had you lost concentration for a minute because of something that had happened? Did you let imagination creep in or your own thoughts interfere briefly?

If you analyse closely enough, you may be able to identify what happens when you misread information. It may be a particular sensation that doesn't feel quite right and when you have that sensation again, you'll recognize it and be able to dismiss what is happening. This will become personal to you; others will have different warning signals that they come to obey.

If you are naturally insecure about your development, it may give you confidence to keep a book. You can use your Intuitional Book and add to it, or start a new one if it feels right. Write down who you saw and the date. Then make brief notes about what information you received and how much of it your sitter could understand. Be honest and don't make it sound better than it was. You won't learn much that way.

Then refer back to your book from time to time. The chances are that you will have been more accurate over the sittings that you expected. Your mind will be quick to criticize you, rather than acknowledge your growth. Your book becomes proof of your gradual growth. Use it on the days when you feel discouraged, to remind yourself how well you are progressing.

CHAPTER 13

PSYCHOMETRY

Psychometry is a fascinating subject and well deserving of a whole book on its own. It's more complex than some other areas of psychic work; many sensitives work solely in this field and attain a high degree of proficiency. We'll look at some of the basic levels that you can study and how you can start to develop this area yourself.

What is psychometry? This is when a medium uses an object to tap into the energies, not just of the object itself, but of the energies which have been placed upon it by others. You'll remember from discussion about human energy that all inanimate objects are affected by the energy which surrounds them. Remember the Letter Exercise in Chapter 9? That was a form of psychometry. So you can practise on your own, but when you work with your sitter as well as an object, the energies often intensify and make the reading easier.

Psychometry can also be confusing, because any object can be subject to a variety of energies and you have to learn to focus and really concentrate to pick up coherent information. This is true of auric reading, of course, except that you are dealing with just one person and their own individual energy. With psychometry you could pick up any variety of energies, from different people and different areas into which that object has been placed. A human aura can filter and release energies in a variety of ways. An object absorbs any strong influence.

'Strong' is an important word here, because the stronger the vibrations of someone, the more those will imprint themselves onto an object. For instance, a watch has belonged for several years to a very introverted person who is not adept at charging their own energies and who lives in a very secluded environment, away from others. They may work on their own in an office, perhaps, and go home every evening to a place without anyone else around. The previous owner of the watch (from several years back) was a very expressive, energetic person who had a varied, hectic social and work life. They were forever active, constantly using their energies and recharging them, always interacting with a wealth of other people. Which energies do you think will have most impressed themselves onto the watch? You probably won't have this information before you start the reading, of course. You simply see a shy person sitting in front of you. You tune in to the watch and pick up a high buzz of energy, with a lot of activity and various different scenarios shooting past in front of your eyes. Of course, this won't make sense to you. You can't relate it to your sitter and yet you know you are not imagining the images you're getting. So what can you do in a situation such as this? The information you're receiving is from a previous person, because they were the more dominant personality. This doesn't mean the other energies of your sitter aren't also there; it simply means they're more subtle, less pervasive. You can learn to tap into them but it takes greater focus to do so.

People often wear antique jewellery and this can also cause difficulties, even if they have owned the object for thirty or forty years. If you tune in to an ancient ring that, for example, was worn by a knight in the Crusades, it's quite feasible that you'll have images of destruction and war; an enormous vortex of energy is created by events such as the Crusades. You have to learn to cleanse those images from your mind and tap again into the object's energies.

To make life easier for yourself when you start, choose an object that won't have too many outside influences on it. A piece of modern jewellery that has been worn only by one person is a good choice. Some people wear chains, bracelets or rings that are never taken off their body; obviously they are then well imbued with that person and no one else. If your sitter has been given a pen that no one else ever uses, that would also be suitable. Perhaps they have a scarf or small item of clothing that no one else wears. They may have an object that sits on their desk or somewhere in their house that you can practise upon. (You will also be able to pick up influences of other people who come into that space, of course, but it will probably be limited if people dont ever touch the object.) They may wear glasses and it's unlikely they would lend those to others. Don't be afraid to ask your sitter about an object before they hand it to you. Check how old the object is, how long they have owned it and who may have had it before.

Certain objects are definitely not a good idea. Stones and crystals have a strong energy of their own and you're better off avoiding them until you're more experienced. There's a good example to demonstrate this. A psychic held a lump of rock that was from a previously active volcano. As they tuned in they were overcome by a sensation of burning heat and suffocation. It was overwhelming in its intensity and it took considerable control to release the image and cleanse it away. A less experienced person could have ended up traumatized for a period of time. Avoid coins and keys because of their metallic content and their tendency to be handled by so many people. Anything antique will also make your work harder. When you have practised on different objects, you'll gain a better understanding of how psychometry works for you and you will gradually be able to focus more and take on more challenging objects.

Another word of warning. People often think of psychometry as a means of contacting people who have died. You may find someone turning up with their mother's wedding ring or their grandfather's spectacle case. You won't be able to work at this level yet and, if you try, you'll only end up with disappointing results that may cause further distress to your sitter. Consistent, controlled communication with spirit can only happen after years of practice; whatever you might achieve before then would be spasmodic and most likely inaccurate. Don't ever offer false hopes to your sitters because it will leave them in a more vulnerable and unhappy situation than ever. They will appreciate your honesty and concern if you explain the position from the beginning. You may find you will proceed one day to the level of communication with spirit and you may be able to help them then.

As psychometry is so much about the sensation of touch and also about focusing your mind in a more disciplined way, there are several exercises you can do to increase your sensitivity before you even practise psychometry. Try what is suggested in the next few pages and see how you progress.

HAND BRUSHING

There are chakras in the palms of the hand and in the tips of the fingers. These need to be activiated to heighten psychometric experiences. You can do this in a very simple way by just rubbing your hands together briskly, palm to palm. It can be done lightly, rather than with force, but move your hands quite quickly as this has more of an effect than working slowly. Continue this brushing sensation for about thirty seconds.

Now you are going to activate your finger tips. Put the tips of your left fingers against your right finger tips and rub them briskly but lightly together. You can do this for a minute or so. As there are a wealth of meridians or energy lines at the tips of your fingers, it creates a general sense of well-being as you do this. Notice what other areas of your body feel better for this experience.

After this short exercise, you will have energized and sensitized your touching abilities. If you want to be sure that this has happened, you can do the following:

Go back to page 71 and briefly work through the Hand Energy Exercise. Pay close attention to how much energy you feel being moved back and forth between your hands. Now go through this Hand Brushing Exercise and then try playing with the ball of energy again. Is there a noticeable difference now?

That is such a quick exercise that you can do this as you're talking to your sitter before you start. You could even explain to them what you're doing, but make sure you use accessible words that don't alienate them. If you tell them you're opening your palm and fingertip chakras to heighten psychic consciousness, you'll probably find their eyes glazing over. Try explaining it in a more basic way, by telling them you're warming your hands ready for work, just like an athlete warms his body before working.

Below is another physical exercise that increases sensitivity. It again is beneficial in a wider sense. You may already have heard of reflexology: the concept that the whole of our body can be found within pressure points (or lines of energy) within certain parts of our body. The feet are often used in this way, and the hands can likewise be related to this. Therefore, by doing the exercise below, you are gently massaging more than just your hands.

HAND MASSAGE

You can do this with someone else and practise on each other, but you can also do it just as effectively on yourself. Massage one hand first and then reverse the process. Choose whichever hand feels appropriate to work on first.

Start with the palm and work from the wrist up and out towards the fingers. Your pressure shouldn't make you feel discomfort. Experiment until it feels firm but comfortable.

With your thumb, slowly work your way up each part of the palm, pushing against the skin, and always working from the wrist towards the fingers. Use your other four fingers to rest lightly on the back of your hand to balance this. Go slowly and work your way along every muscle and bit of bone. Some areas may be more sensitive than others. You may find some feel quite tense and you may want to linger a while over those areas to ease the knotted muscles. When you feel you have released the energy within your palm, work your way along each finger. Again, do this slowly and really feel each joint of each finger. Spend an extra moment massaging the tip of each finger, where there is a wealth of energy points.

When you feel you have properly massaged every bit of the hand, then lightly pass your whole hand over and around the hand you were massaging and feel any extra tension being released out in the sweeping movement. Do this a few times if it feels necessary.

Repeat the whole process on your other hand. Do both hands feel very different? Are you storing tension in different parts? Be sensitive to the different needs of each hand and notice how the energy differs. If you do this exercise properly, it can easily take up to five or ten minutes for each hand.

Do this exercise whenever you can find the time. If you're sitting in a traffic jam or waiting in a queue, you can quietly massage your hands to while away the time. People are unlikely to pay much attention to you and, if they do, smile and say you're massaging your hands to release the tension in them. It might prompt them to try doing the same thing!

Another point which may sound obvious but which is important: always keep your hands and nails clean and in good condition. How often do you massage a pH-balanced hand cream into them? Do you trim your nails regularly and keep them clean? It's easy to forget when you're leading a busy life. Stop reading this for a moment and look at your own hands. Notice if they need attention in any way and give them that care before the end of your day. Before any reading involving psychometry, always wash your own hands thoroughly and dry them well. This is to cleanse you of energies that you will have picked up from other objects. Also, always cleanse after a psychometry reading.

Now let's look at ways in which you can help focus your thoughts. This is to help you deal with the increased demands of psychometry and the need to focus on certain areas of energy at any time. This first exercise sounds incredibly simple when you first read it through but when you try it yourself, you soon realize it isn't.

NUMBERS

Close your eyes. Relax and balance yourself, but don't consciously go through your opening-up process; that isn't necessary. When you feel comfortable, think of the number one. See it in front of your eyes and focus on it. Don't concentrate on anything else. If other thoughts of any sort come into your mind, you're not concentrating hard enough. If you're thinking this exercise is quite easy, you're not making the exercise work for you. Your only thought should be of the number one. When you know you have attained that level of concentration, erase the number one and write instead the number two in front of you. Again, think only of that number. The number one should no longer be anywhere in your mind and you shouldn't be thinking forward to number three. Number two is all that exists in your universe. If you find your thoughts wandering again, go back to number one and start all over again. Keep repeating the whole process until you can get to number nine without once losing concentration.

If you are really honest with yourself, you probably won't get to number nine until quite a few attempts have passed. Certain numbers will prompt different responses. Two often makes one think of a partnership, three often makes one think of the expression 'and baby makes three'. Four could make you leap into thoughts of four-leaf clovers, and so on. Or you may find yourself wondering if you remembered to put bread down on the shopping list, or if you closed the car window properly. Very few of us ever discipline our brain to concentrate on one thing only, to the exclusion of all other influences. It's incredibly difficult to do this but, the more you practise it, the further you wil get each time before your mind wanders.

When you have mastered the numbers up to nine, try using the same procedure to go through the alphabet, through all twenty-six letters. This is even more challenging; how many letters immediately mean something to you? Don't worry if you can't master either of these exercises completely. This isn't about being perfect: it's about increasing the discipline you already have. Some of you will have poorer powers of concentrating and focusing, but be better at visualising hand energies and activating them. Others will never sense any energies or powers, but be able to focus from one to nine without letting their minds wander. Work out for yourself through practice which are your weaker points and spend some extra time on them.

There are also some basic visual aids that you can use to focus and expand your thoughts. Have a look at the diagrams on page 225. What happens when you try to rationalize your thoughts to put them into two recognizable shapes? These are irrational figures in that they can only exist on paper; you couldn't make them into three-dimensional shapes because it's impossible. When your brain looks at them and tries to 'rationalize' them, it has to bring into action its further perceptions of reality and possibility.

To explain this further, let's take a brief look at the human brain. It can be sectioned into two. The left controls the logical, analytical part of the human being. It deals with everything rationally, mathematically, and systematically. The right controls our intuitive, instinctive feelings and emotions. In most humans, the left side of the brain is better developed that the right section. What psychics needs to do is to activate more of the right-hand section to increase psychic awareness. The exercises you have been following up to now all have that purpose. If you spend a little time looking at the irrational diagrams, you are facilitating your right-hand brain into doing some work.

Now look at the optical illusion on page 227. What can you decipher? After looking for a while, you will see two separate images: the skull and then the twins with the puppy dog. Can you see both illusions together? It's virtually impossible because our brains can only connect with one image at a time. Go back and forth between the two images, first the skull, and then the twins and puppy. By doing this, you are making your brain work twice as hard, establishing two different sets of reality. This helps balance the brain's two hemispheres.

Once you have tried these exercises above, you could progress to your first experiment with psychometry. Although you can do this on your own in your space, using any object, it would help you to start by using an object belonging to your sitter, and to have them sitting with you as you work. Their energies will increase the vibrations and make your work easier. Ask your sitter to bring a suitable item with them, explaining what does and doesn't make a good item for psychometry. Ask them not to let others touch the item before they see you. When they arrive, ask them to hold onto it while you relax and open up.

PSYCHOMETRY
Close your eyes and go through your usual opening-up process. Before you open your eyes again, spend a minute or so thinking about your hands. Feel them pulsing with energy, tingling. Be aware of how sensitive they are and how they will help you during

Triangle Illusion

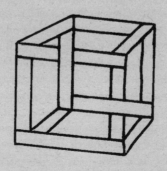

Square Illusion

your work. Ask for guidance from above, that you may be useful in what you say to your sitter.

Now start your psychic lift of energies. Take a deep, comfortable breath and feel your energy lifting as high as your solar plexus. Take a few deep breaths and ensure the energy is resting at that area and not dropping again. Wait until you feel confident and relaxed. Then open your eyes and ask your sitter to hand you the object.

You may want to cup the object between both hands. You may prefer to hold it in just one hand. Try one and then the other to work out which is more responsive. Some people like to start by looking thoroughly at the object and then describing it out loud. This isn't strictly necessary, but it can help to speed up the energies and provide a smoother flow of information. You may find this works for you, or you may find it hinders your process. Again, try both to see what works for you. Your first few sessions are all about experimenting, so you can't expect to be perfect in your first attempt.

Start by feeling the texture of the object in your hand. If it's a ring, does it have jagged edges at all? What might that say about your sitter? If it's a watch, is the strap a heavy leather or smooth metal? How does that make you feel? Does the object feel warm or cold? What does that mean to you? Does it fizz with energy, or do you feel a sudden slump in your energy as you're holding it? Do you feel calm or agitated? Say what comes into your mind as soon as it happens, unless it's negative or inappropriate.

Remember that, as you speak, your energies will drop to your base chakra. You have to lift them again to get more information. If anything is unpleasant or upsetting, cleanse it from you before you continue. Cleanse continuously if the vibrations are unnerving.

If you feel the link with energy weakening, try moving the object into your other hand. Some people like to hold the object against their solar plexus as they find that increases the energy flow. Try that and see if it makes a difference for you.

Optical Illusion

What is the first emotion that comes into you as you hold the object? Peace? Or do you feel worried? Take the first emotion you receive and work on it. Why are they feeling good? What is worrying them? Start with a basic emotion or feeling and then work at a deeper level.

If you are receiving a mish-mash of crossed wires and can't distinguish any one feeling or image, then cleanse everything away and start again. Ask your higher self to help you tune in to that which is relevant and which will best benefit your sitter. Never be afraid to ask for help and guidance. That's why your guides are there: to help your process.

Keep renewing your energies as you work. When you have said everything you need to say, you should feel your energy slowly settle back at your base chakra.

Hand the object back to your sitter and ask them to relax while you close down. Remember to cleanse thoroughly, then close and protect yourself. When you feel well-grounded again, open your eyes and ask your sitter for feed-back.

The most basic problem you may have with psychometry is that you may have picked up other people's energies as you were working. If your sitter can take very little or nothing of what you have imparted to them, check again if they alone have had possession of the item. Ask if they have spent a considerable amount of time recently with someone who is very close to them, and whether what you have been saying relates to them in any way. This isn't about making everything sound good and accurate: it's about you learning about energies and how to tap into them. If, for instance, they gave you their wedding ring to read, were you tapping into their spouse's energies? Or if the necklace was given to them by a friend, did what you say make sense about them? It's always useful to know if anyone owned the object before your sitter did, irrespective of how long ago that might have been.

As always, remember your responsibility to your sitter, phrasing everything carefully. Many people find psychometry a more powerful tool than auric reading, possibly because the physical touch of a solid object gives them added confidence. That extra confidence makes tham relax more and the information starts flowing freely as a result. If you find the sensations and images are even stronger with psychometry, then you need to double your determination to handle your sitter well. The more information flows out, the more quickly you'll want to speak, and the less you'll consider your phraseology. This is why it's better for you to start on a more gradual note with auric reading, until you have developed your own style of working.

After you have practised psychometry on a number of different objects, you will soon learn if it's a useful tool for your psychic development. If you feel a good connection with objects, you could try a further experiment one day, when you misplace an object and want to find it.

Most of us lose things at various times and it can be annoying and inconvenient. If you need to find something in a rush, you may find psychometry unsuccessful. However, if you want to try an exercise and further use your psychic abilities, try the following sometime:

FINDING AN OBJECT

The most effective way to start the process of finding a lost object is to have a photograph of the item. This may not be feasible; if you've lost a watch, it's unlikely you'll have a photo of it.

However, have you the case in which it often rests? Or was it placed on a mat by your bedside table? Did it often sit next to a particular object? Which wrist did you usually wear the watch on? Go to an area where the watch often rested and see what is around that may have picked up its energies. If you wore the watch often enough, just imagine it is resting on your wrist and lightly close your hands over the area. Can you 'feel' it resting there, and sense its energies? If not, choose an item which is near where the watch lay for lengthy periods of time.

Now go through your usual tuning-in process and lift your energies up to the solar plexus. Hold them there, remembering to breathe deeply and regularly. When you feel ready, either put your hand over your wrist or pick up the object which was near the watch.

Now imagine the watch. See it, see every shape and curve of its contours, see its colour and size clearly in front of you. How is it lying now? Is it tightly scrunched up somewhere in a small space, or is it spread out? Is it dark or is light shining onto it? Outdoors or indoors? Take your time in picking up the vibrations.

What does it smell like? Does it have a leather strap with its distinctive odour? Does it smell of your perfume or body scent from having been on your wrist much of the time? What does it smell like where it is now? Is it musty because it's in the back of a drawer? Is it lying near a vase of flowers or by a bowl of fruit or near a soap dish? Is it outside somewhere?

Now feel the texture of the watch in your mind. Feel the smooth clock face, run your fingers over the strap. When you finish touching the strap, what do your fingers touch then? Is it a newspaper? Is it a piece of fabric? Is it tarmac? Concentrate on what you're feeling to work out what it is.

Can you hear anything? You have touched, smelt and seen your watch. Now what sounds are around? Can you hear the noise of cars near it? Is there a clock ticking nearby? Birdsong? Or is it deeply still and quiet around your watch?

You may find by now that you know where your watch is. Always remember to cleanse and close down before you dash off anywhere. If you still feel uncertain or confused, try working at a deeper level.

Ask your inner voice simple questions. Try to use questions with 'yes' or 'no' answers, such as 'Is my watch in the house?' or 'Did I drop it outside?' Don't rush the question and answer process. Let your body and mind relax as much as possible. Once you have started receiving a response, then start to ask more specific questions. Gradually, become more and more precise, until you feel you know where the object is. This is a valuable exercise for increasing your relationship with your inner self.

This level of finding things is often extended amongst highly trained psychics into the realm of finding lost people or animals. It also goes into the world of police work, when psychics are asked to help trace escaped criminals or to describe murderers. This latter level of psychic work has been used more often than the public are probably aware, but for obvious reasons its use is kept fairly quiet. There are only a small number of psychics who are suitable for this degree of work; it can be particularly distressing at times and they need a high level of self-protection to deal with such energies. From your knowledge of energies and how they vibrate, you'll be able to understand why an article of clothing found at a murder scene could offer a great deal of information about what happened. However, it's not easy for a sensitive to be able to release those images afterwards and unless they have strong reserves of energy themselves, they're likely to find the experience very difficult. Most psychics will only agree to a small, limited amount of assistance in crime-related fields.

Once you have held a few sittings with auric readings and psychometry, you will start to become aware of certain specific needs of your sitters. Generally, these needs can be broken down into three areas: love, health and money/work. These are the elements of life in which most people have the greatest worries and interest. Of course, you may not necessarily be picking up much information in these areas, especially if you are working on the physical level, giving them information about objects and colours which surround them. So you would benefit from learning how to channel more specific information about certain areas of people's lives. This is another form of discipline which you can learn. It requires a more focused, concentrated approach but, with practice, you can learn to give more specific information.

For example, you understand from your sitter that they are anxious to know about their work and financial situation. In the beginning, they may be expecting a fortune-telling approach (most people are) so you have to explain your process will not predict anything for their future. However, by working a little more deeply and using your higher self for guidance, you can offer some insight into their present situation. This does require good contact with your inner self and you may not be able to work at this level initially. Wait until you feel more confident before you offer this to a sitter and always prefix it by explaining you are still in the early stages, so the information you receive may be limited.

FOCUSING ON SPECIFICS
Be clear about what your sitter is asking you; it will generally fall into the category of love, work or health. Make sure you are properly open, well-balanced and relaxed. Keeping your eyes closed, think of the area about which you would like more information. Say, for example, they are concerned about their present relationship with someone. Concentrate on the importance of a loving relationship and the learning processes that

stem from that experience. Ask your inner self for guidance and wisdom so that you may help your sitter in the most suitable way. Wait until you feel in good contact with your inner self before you move on.

Now take the object they have given you, but continue to concentrate on love and relationships as you do so. Whatever information you receive, immediately see how it relates to your sitter's concerns. If the object feels cold and unyielding, how does this relate to their situation? Is one partner being immovable over a situation? Is one of them holding back, emotionally? Why? If you feel a sudden surge of energy, what is that surge telling you? Is it an outpouring of love? Is it full of tension? Is it a reciprocal feeling or is it coming from just one party? Continually question each piece of information you receive, always relating it to area uppermost in your mind. Keeping asking your inner self for clarification and assistance.

If you see flashes of colour, ask yourself how that colour relates to the relationship they're in. Ask what that colour means. Ask yourself who is related to that colour and why it is significant for them.

Let the emotions of the object wash over you. What is the strongest emotion you feel? Is it sadness? Elation? Hope? Panic? Connect it to the relationship and see where that fits in. Keep asking your inner self to help you.

If you keep feeling confused or keep getting very little information, check if you are balanced and relaxed. Let the energies drop back to your base and wash through with your white light. Concentrate on your breathing again and re-focus your thoughts on the relationship. Lift your energies again to the solar plexus. Are you still receiving nothing? Turn to your inner self. Ask why you are receiving so little. Your inner self may explain that your sitter is not yet ready to hear what is happening, or that your sitter needs to discover the situation for themselves, without your intervention. Listen closely to what your inner self is saying. Take in the *information and then relay it in the most suitable and helpful way to your sitter. Always be honest, but make sure you are positive in your manner. Assure them that what is happening to them is right for them at this time and they will move forward again in the relationship when they are ready. Don't offer false hopes or say something because you know it is what they want to hear. Be loving but fair.*

When your energies drop, you will know you have finished what you have to say. Cleanse thoroughly, close down and protect yourself. Thank your inner self for the guidance you have received. Make sure you are well grounded before you continue with your sitter.

You may find this exercise powerful for your development. Focusing on one specific area can sometimes help you. It makes you feel more in control, because every piece of information you receive is being levelled at just one area. Being so specific can also help the energy to flow sometimes. If there is just one area you are targeting, you can sometimes release a clear stream of energy that is concentrated and fluid in movement. After you have held several auric reading and psychometry sessions, try this technique of being more specific at some point during every sitting. You will increase your relationship with your inner self every time you do so, learning to always listen to its wisdom. It also makes your sitter feel more rewarded, if they can gain insight into an area of their life which is causing them concern or distress.

Now you are ready to move on to a lesser-known but equally wonderful aspect of psychic development, which deals very much with people's spirituality: flower reading.

CHAPTER 14

FLOWER READING

Flower reading is a particularly spiritual experience and, although it doesn't suit all psychics, everyone should try it at least once or twice before deciding whether they can work with its energies in a productive way. People often assume that they need to have a close affiliation with flowers, plants and gardens before they can work successfully with flower reading but it needn't necessarily be the case. Using a flower to help 'read' someone is simply using an earth energy to speed up the already-existing vibrations of your sitter.

To clarify this, let's look at how flower reading works. Your sitter chooses a fresh flower which they then hold for a minute or two. They pass the flower to you, and by holding it and working your way along the stem, up to the flower head, you can receive information about your sitter. This is simply another form of psychometry, of course, but the flower's energies add another dimension. They speed up and intensify your sitter's energies. The combination of the energies can also provide information at a much deeper, more spiritual level so that you can tap into the very 'core' of your sitter, understanding them in a more complete, holistic manner.

You raise your energies up to the heart chakra, to assist this deeper process of work. As this is the first time you have worked at this level, you will have to practise your psychic lift work before you start flower reading. Your system will be so used now to lifting energy up as high as the solar plexus, that you will find that extra floor takes a while to reach. You will either find the energy sluggish to begin with, or you will find the energy shooting past your heart up to the higher levels of your throat or third eye. They will then plunge down again, infuriatingly quickly! Practise this level of control on your own, before you start this new form of psychic expression.

Do you remember that your heart chakra and the fourth level of the human aura is also called the astral plane; the link between the physical and spiritual? This is relevant for flower reading. You are now moving into a slighter different dimension. The vibrations will change; they will feel faster, lighter, less tangibly 'there'. This is when your intuitive and knowing senses will sharpen further. You pass from the realms of purely 'I feel', 'I think', 'I sense' into 'I know'. It's a big step forward but it will only happen gradually. You'll have flashes of working at this higher level and then you may slide back again for a while. This is all a natural form of progression and everyone experiences it as they learn. Once you have your first insight into the realm of 'I know' (and it often comes during a flower reading as opposed to other psychic work), you will always know the difference after that. You may not always be able to reach that level, until you are more experienced, but you will always know the difference between the two. It can be very exciting when this first happens.

However, let's back-track a little to some more basics. The type of flower that is chosen is important. Whenever possible, let your sitter make that choice themselves. If they have their own garden and can pick a flower from there, that is the ideal. Choosing one from a friend or relative's garden would also be beneficial. If none of that is possible, then ask them to buy just one bloom from a florist. The only stipulations are that:

— *the flower must be fresh, not dried or artificial*

— *it should ideally be the flower of your sitter's choice, not someone else's*

— *it should be handled only by your sitter, not by other people*

— *the stem of the flower is at least two inches long.*

Explain these facts to your sitter before you attempt a flower-reading and encourage them to bring whatever flower feels right for them.

What they choose in the way of size, species and colour, is all relevant to what is going on in their lives and available for you to interpret.

You will get varying responses when you tell your sitters you'd like to do a flower reading. Those who love flowers and whose energies resonate well with the earth energies, will probably react favourably and enjoy the prospect. Those who have little interest in plants and aren't very connected to the earth and its energies, may balk at your suggestion. Assure them that this new experiment is purely that: an experiment. Explain that whatever they feel about flowers will not affect your ability to do the flower reading. In fact, their actual response is a good indication of what is happening with them. Are they feeling guilty because they haven't found the time they feel they should for appreciation of nature? Does the suggestion of choosing a flower from their garden remind them what a mess their garden is in and how they ought to sort it out? Do they associate flowers with funerals, the only time they buy them? You won't understand the answers until you do the flower reading, but their initial response can be revealing.

Remember how they react when you first suggest a flower reading, and then compare it to their attitude when you have completed the sitting.

So, you have got them to agree to bring a flower the next time they come. Between that point and their return visit, ensure you practice with your psychic lift, raising the energies to the heart chakra. Do this every day during your quiet time and make sure you feel confident with the new level. Remember to ask your inner self for guidance with this new, heightened state of consciousness.

It would also help you to start noticing flowers more: when you walk past gardens, when you pass a florists shop or stall. What flowers are you immediately drawn towards? Why? Is it colour, texture, shape or size that attracts you? Or do you like the fragrance? What flowers do you dislike, if any? Why? Is there a colour you favour amongst flowers? What does that colour say about you? What shape of flower do you find particularly appealing? If you can, spend some time wandering around a garden, noticing the different flowers and plants.

Look at a herb garden, if possible, smelling the different scents and observing the different textures of the plants. Decide which herbs you feel most drawn to and try to incorporate some of them into your life. If you haven't got a garden, many herbs will respond well if kept on a sunny windowsill. If you have a friend or relative who keeps herbs, ask if you could have some small cuttings. Certain herbs such as mint, rosemary and lavender are particularly prolific and your friends will probably be delighted to off-load some your way. Use the herbs in simple ways in cooking. Pop some mint into your potatoes as you're cooking them; chop parsley and sprinkle over cooked vegetables; a sprig of rosemary greatly complements a rice dish. Herbal energies in your garden or home will enhance your appreciation of plants; the smell and taste will also increase your awareness.

You could also try the meditation below, which will increase your awareness of flowers and their special place within our universe:

THE FLOWER

Sit down in your space and close your eyes. Spend a few minutes relaxing yourself, using your favourite breathing techniques. You needn't consciously open up your chakras for this exercise unless you decide you want to do so. Wait until you feel balanced and comfortable before you continue; keep your eyes closed throughout.

When you feel ready, become aware that you are holding something in the palm of your hand. It feels tiny and light. You open your palm and discover that a very small seed is lying there. You look at that tiny speck and wonder what it would become if it were planted. As you are contemplating the seed, you slowly realize that you are now standing in your beautiful garden. It's a wonderfully warm, sunny day. Your favourite birds, animals and plants are all around you. The grass feels soft and comforting under your feet.

You look down and see a small patch of freshly dug soil by your feet; you know that the earth is asking you to plant your seed. Gently, you place the tiny seed an inch or so under the soil. There is a watering can nearby and you lightly water the soil.

You then sit back in the grass or on a nearby seat and enjoy the warmth of the sun. You look around at your garden, appreciating each plant, bush, tree and blade of grass. You think about how many seeds it took for each to grow and where they all came from. You see a bird pecking seeds from the ground and watch it fly off into the distance with a full beak. Then you notice a bee landing on a flower and slowly sucking the nectar into its mouth. A ladybird lands on another flower and pulls off some aphids; a butterfly hovers over a bush. A few seeds fall beside you and you look up, where you can see another bird flying overhead, intent on reaching another destination.

When you look back at the patch of soil, you see that a tiny green shoot is coming through. You watch, mesmerized, as the shoot very slowly grows and thickens. A gentle rain comes and goes, but you remain dry and comfortable. The shoot gradually fans out into a plant with buds. As you continue watching, the buds burst forth into beautiful blossom. You move closer to the plant to smell its fragrance. You drink in the colour and shape and marvel at the perfect beauty that has grown from that tiny seed. You think of all the occasions in life when the presence of the flowers offers peace, comfort, joy and enlightenment.

You are still in the midst of appreciating their qualities when you become aware that a wind is whipping up. The wind becomes stronger and as it does so, the blossoms slowly start to wither and then gradually crumple completely. Their faded blooms are whisked away by the winds. You feel sad as you watch the flower stripped of its glory. You feel the winds slowly die away, but your sense of loss remains at the flower's demise.

Then you realize something has landed in your hand. You look down and see another tiny seed is resting in your palm; it has blown off the plant. As you gaze at its tiny perfection, you realize that the spirit core of the flower hasn't died. It is waiting to be reborn when you plant that next seed. The flower is all part of the cycle of life and re-birth. You acknowledge that you are part of that chain, too. The sun bursts through the clouds again, filling you with *warmth and comfort. You close your hand gently over the seed and bless its presence.*

As you do so, gently withdraw yourself from the meditation. Become aware of your weight the chair and your feet on the ground. Use your grounding techniques to reorientate yourself before opening your eyes.

Did the seed become the flower you expected it to become? Often, when you follow this meditation, you are surprised at what bursts into blossom. Think of the flower you were expecting and what actually appeared in front of you. How do they differ? What does that say about you? What benefits can you draw from it?

Continue your conscious awareness of flowers and what they mean to you, right up to your next sitting. When your sitter arrives, ensure they have followed your instructions about their flower. Obviously, they can't help the fact that a florist may have handled the flower before them, but apart from that, it shouldn't have been left in anyone else's hands. When they sit down, ask them just to run their hands lightly up and down the flower stem and around the flower heads. Explain to them that they needn't try to transfer any thoughts onto the flower; they just need to relax and do nothing. Ask if they could please refrain from commenting on anything you say, until you have finished. This is particularly helpful with flower reading because the vibrations are faster in this work, and the information thus tends to come with greater speed. If your flow is interrupted, it's harder for you to resume, especially during your first flower readings. If flower reading is a powerful expression of psychic work for you, then you won't need to hear your sitter agreeing or acknowledging what you say, because your knowing sense will keep you going. You don't need reassurance or confirmation when your intuition and knowing is guiding you. Ask your sitter to hold onto the flower while you relax and open up. Again, repeat to them that they don't have to do anything: they can just sit and relax.

FLOWER READING
Close your eyes and go through your usual opening-up and tuning-in processes. As always, take your time and make sure your

breathing is assisting you, not hindering you. Balance yourself. Ground yourself again properly. Now lift your energies up to your heart. Practise lifting and lowering the energies between the base and heart chakras several times, to ensure you are properly in control. Wait until you're ready before you open your eyes.

Now take the flower from your sitter. Start off by looking at it thoroughly. Is it a long, smooth stem or is it short and twisted? Does it have thorns? If it does, how many? What does that say about your sitter? Is the flower strong or wispy? Is it large or small? Are there any blossoms? How many? Do they look healthy or rather sorry for themselves? What about leaves? Are they any nobbly sections of the stem? Smell the flower, not just the blossoms, if any, but also the stem and leaves. Is it a sharp, acrid smell or is it warm and sweet? Is it fresh or musty? What colour has your sitter chosen? What does that say about them? Feel the texture of the stem and flower. Is it soft or does it feel sinewy? Does it look tough but feel surprisingly soft to the touch?

You may find it helps you to vocalize as you're looking at the flower. You may want to say, for instance, 'I can see this is a very sturdy white carnation with several healthy blooms open and several more in tight bud. As I look at this, it makes me feel as though you are very robust and healthy; the strong stem shows that you are forthright in manner. The profusion of buds tells me that you have many facets to your life. You are always busy and putting your energy into different areas. However, the pure white would indicate a certain purity within you that you don't necessarily show to everyone.' Only speak if you know that what you are saying feels right. Don't fabricate something because you feel you should be speaking. If nothing feels right until the next stage, that is fine.

Now hold the flower at its base and close your eyes. Hold it quite gently and lightly; you don't need to grasp it firmly to receive information. The base of the flower represents your sitter's babyhood and as you work your way up the stem, so you are going through the stages of their life. The head of the flower represents their spiritual self, their inner path of growth. Try to keep your

241

movement up the stem gradual but constantly fluid, as this will help your reading. Don't consciously linger too long over any area and if you feel nothing during a stretch, just slowly continue inching your way up the stem. The flow is all-important here. Remember, any time you receive any unpleasant sensation, to use your waterfall of pure light to cleanse and refresh yourself.

As you start at the base, what is the first emotion that washes over you? Do you feel joyful or sad? Do you feel a sense of peace or agitation? Trust your first sensation and work with it. Don't stop to question or doubt yourself. You may see images of a child's toys or clothes or a cot in a bedroom. You might suddenly feel small and helpless. Perhaps you'll hear a baby's contented gurgles or anxious cries. Say exactly what comes to you without embroidery.

As you speak, inch your way further up the stem. When is there a change of feeling? Notice if the stem suddenly feels hot or cold, or if a smooth stem suddenly becomes gnarled and rough for a stretch. If you hit a leaf, what does that mean about that stage in their life? Sensations may come and go quite quickly now; you need to be well-focused to pick up on them all and interpret them.

You might come upon a stretch when you feel nothing at all, rather as if that section of the flower is dead. This usually symbolises an area of their life that your sitter doesn't want to look at. Either they have blocked it out because it's too difficult or distressing, or they simply aren't ready yet to look at the lessons they could learn from that period of their life. Be careful not to judge or criticize if this happens to you. Unless you can say something constructive, pass on to the next section. You're not under pressure to report on every year of their life, so don't feel you're failing if you leave out certain periods.

As you near the head of the flower, you may feel the vibrations quicken even more, rather like a film that is going at fast-forward speed. Everything feels lighter and headier at this level. Very gently, cup your hands over the head of the flower. What sensations and images come to you? Don't question them, just *speak as they appear, although you still have to consider your phraseology and responsibilities. You may find yourself speaking without realizing it; your words may feel as though they are being spoken by someone else. You won't know how or why you know certain things. All you know is that you 'know', and that knowing will be all-encompassing. You may have the ability to see deep into your sitter's core and see them for exactly what they are: a unique soul, encased in a physical body. Your realm of consciousness may expand onto another level so that words and images and feelings flow harmoniously, effortlessly.*

When you have said enough, your energies will drop suddenly back to your base chakra. Sometimes, it can feel quite a shock; it's a bit like the feeling you can get when you pull yourself out of a body of water in which you've been swimming for a while. Your whole body suddenly feels heavy and unco-ordinated. Use that pure white waterfall to cleanse and rejuvenate yourself. Make sure it filters through every pore and washes away any unhealthy residue. Then close down and protect yourself before you open your eyes and ask your sitter for feedback.

If flower reading has worked well for you, your sitter may be surprised by what you have told them. This form of psychic work can be unerringly accurate. You may be able to pick up on very personal experiences and emotions that your sitter thought nobody knew about or understood. This can also leave them feeling quite vulnerable, so it's doubly important during a flower reading that you are sensitive to your sitter's reactions and needs. You may be able to tell them things that they didn't quite know themselves. Hopefully, your phraseology will have been so constructive and so positive that they will also find the whole reading uplifting and encouraging.

You may also notice that much more of your reading was based on emotions and spirituality than was the case with physical images and conditions. This is quite common with flower reading because you are tapping into a person's higher self, which is not concerned with physical states. You may see their capacity for holistic love and compassion in a much stronger light and see their potential in a way that previous readings couldn't do. You may find generally that your comments are very much geared towards loving concepts and how they relate to their family and friends and to the universe as a whole.

A small proportion of you may find flower reading very uninspiring. This doesn't mean that there is something wrong with you or that you lack spirituality. You may find your talents lie in using another tool such as the Tarot cards or dowsing. You can't be proficient at every form of psychic expression, it simply isn't possible. Whilst a great many psychics find flower reading to be very powerful, the majority of them will also find many other areas uninspiring. You may start working with auragraphs, for instance, and then discover a new world for yourself. You need to experiment with everything, to find your own path, and discover your eventual way of working which will be different from others.

If you feel you do want to work more with flower reading but find your first few sessions to be lacking in results, it may be because your sitter has an aversion to flowers. Try a flower reading with someone else to see if you fare better. It might also be that you haven't yet fully explored your own understanding and appreciation of flowers.

Flowers are often considered to be a gift from God, or from the highest state of consciousness. Many gods and goddesses through mythology have been associated with different flowers. Floral fragrances have varying abilities to produce different psychological states. They are also considered to have enormous healing properties and have been used by psychics, healers and metaphysicians for centuries. There is a variety of books you can get on this subject which will expand your knowledge and awareness. However, it is only by experiencing the different flowers and fragrances for yourself that you can develop your own personal relationship. Your experience may differ from other people's but that is not to say you're wrong. You're simply experiencing the flower's energies in a different way. For instance, certain flowers have become associated with different aspects of life. Here's a small sample below:

Buttercup – new horizons, greater understanding, healing abilities

Carnation – self-love, appreciation and understanding of life, physical energy

Daffodil – connecting with the higher mind and inner beauty

Honeysuckle – youthful memories and confidence

Jasmine – self-esteem, transforming areas of life

Rose – healing with the heart, beauty and love

Tulip – trust in a higher consciousness, success

Violet – simplicity and humility

There is a wealth of other flowers and other associations as well. However, next time you find yourself near one of the flowers listed above, try holding your hand gently over the flower head and see what sensations you pick up. This can be in a park or garden, or even in a vase of flowers. You needn't open up fully or make a great effort to concentrate. Simply let your intuition guide you and see what sensations you pick up. Then refer back to the list above and see if it can be related to any of your feelings. It isn't important if it doesn't. It just means you are already developing your own style and relationship to flowers.

If you want to develop your awareness about flower energies, you could benefit a great deal from studying the Bach flower remedies. Dr. Edward Bach was a Harley Street Specialist, Physician and Homeopath who, in 1936, after years of intensive study and research, perfected a technique for distilling the life-force (or energy) of 38 non-poisonous wildflowers into individual remedies. These remedies are all related to specific, negative states of mind, personality, mood and temperament; imbibing the appropriate remedy is intended to re-establish an equilibrium between the inner self, mind and body.

Whether you choose to study the remedies and prescribe any for yourself is a personal choice. The states described are all highly specific and anyone who has a reasonable understanding of themselves would easily be able to identify their own characteristics. The remedies are all benign in their action and can be taken by people of all ages with absolute impunity. They are also very inexpensive. Whether you wish to use them or not, studying the characteristics that each flower was found to have, according to Dr. Bach, makes fascinating reading, and can certainly enhance your relationship to flowers.

For instance, if you look at the purpose of his honeysuckle remedy, you will see that Dr. Bach prescribes it for those people who tend to live in the past, constantly dwelling on nostalgic memories and suffering from home-sickness. It's interesting to note that honeysuckle in a flower reading is said to relate to youthful memories.

If you find you are sensitive to flowers and their energies, you might particularly benefit from keeping a phial of Bach Rescue Remedy in your cabinet. This is a combination of five of the flowers (Cherry Plum, Clematis, Impatiens, Rock Rose and Star of Bethlehem) and it's very much an all-purpose emergency potion that can be used in a variety of distressing conditions: any form of shock, distress or panic. It's often used by performers for stage fright and can be beneficial after any accident or for nervousness about an upcoming event of any sort. It can also be applied externally to burns, bites and sprains. The more you respond to flower energies, the more helpful you may find the remedy. The mixture will keep indefinitely in a cool, dark place.

Looking at floral remedies and their healing properties, it seems appropriate that you will next be looking at another very powerful and much used area of psychic and spiritual development: healing.

CHAPTER 15

SELF-HEALING

Healing is a complex subject that covers more than one facet of psychic development. We'll look at three aspects of it: self-healing, absent healing and hands-on healing.

Self-healing is probably the most obvious and much of what you've read so far regarding your own spiritual development has been to do with self-healing. Do you remember earlier details about the Hologram Theory? Self-healing is about treating all of yourself with the respect and love that you deserve.

Chapter 6 offered detailed ways in which you could give yourself the best possible treatment physically, by certain dietary considerations, physical exercise, healthy hygiene and some attention to your living space. Various meditations throughout have paid attention to your emotional and mental well-being and have encouraged your spiritual growth. This is all part of your own healing process, which basically means putting all the parts of you together in a way that resonates with pure harmony. It's back to the hologram of yourself again.

By now you may feel as though much of you is vibrating with an energy you hadn't used before. The more you have followed the exercises throughout, the greater the benefits you will be receiving from them. You may feel you still have quite a way to go before achieving perfect health, and feeling that way is a good sign. It shows you are truly acknowledging how complex and amazing humans are and how sorting out all our energies and making maximum use of them is not a simple task. However, it can be a constantly expanding and ever enjoyable one.

There are more areas you can explore in your self-healing process and we're going to look at some now. Start with this extremely simple exercise:

MIRROR NO. 1

Without thinking or preparing yourself in any way, go to the nearest mirror. Look into your eyes. Don't just glance at yourself and then quickly turn away. Really look, deep into your own reflection. What do your eyes tell you about yourself? The more you look, the deeper you gaze, the more you will see. The eyes are often described as the gateway to the soul. Now say out loud, 'I love you. I accept all of you exactly as you are.'

Did you find that very uncomfortable? Almost everyone does the first time they do it. Many people have a strong reaction against saying they love themselves. They confuse loving themselves with being a selfish act, thinking that it shuts out others and accomplishes very little. In fact, loving yourself is the first step to healing yourself and others. If you don't love yourself, your own energies won't flow freely and, if your own energies aren't flowing freely, you can't truly love and help others. If you don't love yourself and accept yourself exactly as you are, you are blocking your own energies.

This means loving all of yourself, even the elements which you don't like: your quick temper, your negativity, your inhibitions, your nose or chin or chest or hair, your cellulite, your wrinkles. We all have areas of ourselves with which we don't feel comfortable. The difficulty is that most of us get stuck into the thought pattern that if only we were younger, slimmer, nicer, taller, shorter, brighter, we would then love ourselves. The truth is, if you love yourself, all those things don't matter. When you love yourself and those traits no longer become important to you, then people start to see you in a different way. You learn to accept and love your height or size or personality, and suddenly everyone else starts to find you attractive as well. All that is happening is that you are releasing some of the energy blocks within your own aura. You are beginning to use more of your energies and you are vibrating in a way that makes people want to be near you.

So how can you release some more of that energy? How can you learn to make the most of the whole you, without blocking yourself? What follows is a very condensed version of self-healing. There is a wealth of books available now on the market which deal with healing yourself in much more detail; you may feel after reading this chapter, that you want to explore more.

If the starting point is learning to love yourself, how can you do this, if you are stuck in the belief that there is so much wrong with you? You have to learn to change your negative thought patterns. Go back to your mirror again:

MIRROR NO. 2

Now look at your whole face in the mirror, not just your eyes. Look at your hair, the shape of your face, your nose and mouth, your neck. Study your complexion and its texture and colour. Look at your ears. Most humans are programmed to only see the negative side of themselves. You will probably only be able to see what you consider the unattractive elements. You have to learn to look a bit deeper.

What are the parts of your face that you like? You may have good cheekbones or nice eyebrows. Your skin may be good or your eyes may be a wonderful colour. What part of your face is appealing to you? Touch your skin, your hair. How do they feel? Notice how various parts of the face feel really different. Enjoy this new discovery of the wonderful aspects of yourself. This is really hard for most people. They feel safer criticizing, rather than complimenting themselves. It takes a while to learn this new process. However, the more you look, willing yourself to look for the good, the more your brain will start to re-programme itself. Whatever you have managed to find that's positive, even if it's only one or two points, thank your inner self for the experience.

Now continue looking at your reflection and send yourself some love. You will have different ways of doing this. You may like to visualize green streamers floating towards the mirror and blending into it. You might like to use rainbow colours. You may just feel your loving energy cascading from you to the mirror. You may want to just think it. It doesn't matter which method you use. It won't be easy at first. You'll be busy trying to knock yourself down. You'll tell yourself that you feel silly or that you're not worth it. Just keep persevering. Give thanks for your negative thoughts. Don't feel angry about them. It's only by acknowledging your negativity, that you have a barometer against which you can measure change. Be grateful you have those negative traits so that you can learn from them. Feel yourself relax more and more as you send yourself waves of love. Only stop the exercise when you have enjoyed the warmth and benefitted from the sensation of self-love.

Some of you may not be able to do this exercise initially. You may have to try on more than one occasion. Perhaps you will eventually find one positive point but struggle for any more. Keep returning to your mirror at other times and really open yourself to see the good parts of yourself. The more you do this, the more you start to see yourself in a new light. If you persevere, you will reach the point where you can look at yourself in the mirror and immediately see all the lovely qualities you possess. You really will be seeing yourself in a new light and you will have changed the energies around you by doing so.

After you have grown comfortable with your own face, you can repeat this whole exercise by standing naked in front of a full length mirror and learning to love your whole body. This takes another level of courage and it's better not to try it until you've spent some time studying just your face. Move onto the rest of your body when you feel ready. It doesn't matter how long it takes.

You'll reach blocks in this process, of course. No matter how often you tell yourself that parts of you are good, you will have trouble accepting it. You may reach the stage when you can accept yourself physically, but then you will encounter further difficulties. You'll start to worry about your personality and your emotional and mental behaviour. No doubt you will find plenty to criticize there, too.

You may already have found some of the earlier meditations helpful for shifting awareness within you: the Karma, Chakra Awareness and Inner

Self Exercises, in particular, can be very powerful and offer you some wonderful insights. In digesting new information within this book, you have been working at expanding your understanding of certain areas of life: energies, psychic behaviour, spiritual growth. You've been using your mind and thought processes continually to stretch yourself. You may now discover that expanding your thoughts about life was easier than expanding your thoughts about loving yourself! You may have struggled with some of the information about energies or chakras and had to re-read certain chapters to grasp new concepts, but that may seem easy in comparison to loving every part of yourself. It probably won't feel natural or right to you, at this stage. Yet go back to the hologram theory. If you believe that you are everything, how can you possibly not love yourself? Loving yourself means you love everything and everybody: the whole universe. Loving yourself makes you powerful and complete.

Many of the Exercises you've looked at so far have been expansion on a spiritual level. For a moment, let's look at self-healing in a more earthly sphere. Most of our doubts about ourselves stem from experiences we have during this life-time, and specifically from what other people say about us and how they treat us. What are your memories? Try this below:

MEMORIES

Take a large sheet of paper. Start off by writing the word 'Childhood'. Now think back to when you were a child. What did your parents and siblings say about you? How did they treat you? What is your over-riding memory of childhood? Did you feel nurtured or continually squashed? Give yourself time to remember things. The more you start to think, the more the floodgates will open. Were there things that a parent constantly said to you or did to you? What about your sisters, brothers and other relatives? How did you feel with them? Remember any particularly strong influences, people you dreaded seeing or those who made you feel good. Then think about your school friends and teachers. What did they say? Were there other figures of authority who influenced you as a child: a Sunday school teacher or a parent's close friend? Really delve back into your childhood and allow yourself to remember everything you can. If you find some of it upsetting, you can always bring your white light and waterfall down into you and cleanse. It might just seem appropriate to react however you want to react.

When you feel you have honestly studied your childhood memories, then write the heading 'Adulthood'. (You might find you need another sheet of paper if you've really been thinking thoroughly about everything!) Now look at your adult influences and what you have around you at present. If you have a partner, how does she/he make you feel and what do they say about you? If you have children, what do they say? What do your friends say to you and how does that make you feel? How do you relate to your business colleagues and what do they say? Go through your adult influences thoroughly and take your time considering exactly what they say. Try to be honest and write everything down, no matter how hurtful or untruthful the statements may be.

When you have finished, compare the two lists. Can you find similarities? If there was a strong influence in your life who criticized you in a particular way, have you found someone to recreate that scenario as an adult? If you were made to feel a failure as a child, have you got someone in your adult life who is continuing that pattern? Match up as many 'pairs' as you can with your childhood and adult scenarios. Remember to match up the positive as well. Have you discovered that most of your comments are negative ones? Is that because you only remember the negative or did you have very little encouragement as a child?

Most of us discover that we have recreated much of our childhood again in our adult life. There will be differences, of course. If you have already spent time looking at your childhood influences and have learnt from those experiences, you may find your two lists are considerably different. However, unless you have already come to terms with your childhood, you're unlikely to have sorted out your adult relationships. Our childhood is the foundation from which we build ourselves. If those foundations are unstable, it's hard to create a solid structure on top. The stronger our foundations, the stronger we are as adults.

You can't now alter those childhood situations. You can't go back and relive them again. Yet there is something you can do to help your life now. You can accept responsibility for whatever happened and know that it was right for you at the time, no matter how difficult, uncomfortable or painful it may have been. If you have taken on board the concept of karma and re-incarnation, then you can know that you chose this present life and the problems you have as your choices: to help your soul grow and develop.

This level of 'knowing' isn't about trying to convince yourself that it's a good idea to feel this way so that you can move forward in life. It's the 'knowing' that comes from that higher sense of consciousness. You don't know it because it would help you to say that; you know it because you 'know' it. You may not reach this plateau of acceptance immediately. You may have some anger or resentment or fear you need to get out of the way first and, if you feel some of those emotions are still overwhelming you and not something you can control, then you should seek further guidance from a professional body, such as a holistic centre. Any form of feeling which leaves you out of control requires a more concentrated form of help than the assistance you can get from reading a book. However, if you know you are ready to accept responsibility for everything that has happened to you so far, and you want to release some of that anger or aggression which you have concerning your childhood, then you can use the Karma Exercise and concentrate on the person involved.

This isn't a quick method to make everything suddenly feel all right. It takes time, patience and honesty to work through these emotions. You may feel you move forward one day and then slip back the next. You may feel you've sorted out a karmic situation and then it crops up again to confront you in another way. It helps if you see working on karma as an ever-increasing cycle of growth and re-birth. It's not something you just sort out so you can forget about it. It's a guidance by which you can continually grow and develop.

If you can learn to embrace each scenario and problem as a gift from which you can learn, you no longer dread the difficult patches in your life. You can welcome then as a means of learning. Sorting out childhood sadnesses is a wonderful starting point. Don't run yourself down in your efforts, either. Spend one session on the Karma Exercise and then let it go. Don't feel you have to work on it again the next day or even the next week. Your subconscious will continue working on the situation, even without you concentrating on it. You start the ball rolling with your willingness at look at a problem, and your subconscious will carry on. You have forever to sort out karmic influences. If you don't sort a problem out during this lifetime, it is carried forth into the next. Whether you want to look at it during your present lifetime, is purely your choice, not someone else's. If you listen to your inner self, you'll know whether the time is right for you to tackle a situation or not.

You have looked at how to deal with childhood influences in a spiritual, karmic sense. There is also a very basic, earthly method you can use to help your process of reprogramming negative into positive. This method uses something called 'affirmations'. Affirmations are statements which you say out loud to yourself on a regular basis, in front of a mirror if possible, which become a sort of mantra, a tool to help shift consciousness. This isn't meant to replace your meditations or spiritual development it is simply an additional tool that can be useful.

Sometimes, approaching a situation from different angles makes the results more powerful. Have a look at the statements below:

- *I can re-programme any thought that I want to*

- *I love all of my body, exactly as it is*

- *I love all of me in every way*

- *I love everyone unconditionally*

- *Everything in my life is exactly as it should be*

- *People are wonderful*

— I am the whole universe

— Every day, in every way, the world is becoming more and more wonderful

— Every single experience I have enriches me and helps me to grow

— I choose everything that happens to me in life

— I choose my reactions to everything that happens and I can change those reactions if I wish.

Some of those you may find impossible to say out loud in the beginning, but after you repeat the statement several times, you start to feel less cynical. Your mind expands to consider a new concept. Choose the one you find most difficult to accept and say it now out loud. Repeat it ten times. You don't have to say it loudly or quickly. Just keep saying it. You might try writing it down, in several ways. Write it small to begin with, then larger. Use a light-coloured pen and then change to a darker one. End up filling a large sheet of paper with the affirmation. Every time a negative thought crowds into your mind to disprove the affirmation, acknowledge the thought but tell it you have decided to try something new. You know yourself that embracing new concepts will heighten consciousness. Try repeating that affirmation every night before you go to sleep and when you wake up in the morning. When something happens to you during the day and you have a negative response, go back to your affirmation to change the situation into something constructive. Change the affirmation itself if you want to try a new response. Use another one listed above, or make up your own, if that feels more powerful.

A word about making up affirmations. Ensure that the statement is always in the positive, not the negative. For instance, instead of 'I no longer feel negative about myself', say 'I feel positive about myself in every way'. Instead of 'I won't hate my parents for what happened in my childhood', try 'I love my parents for everything they have given me'. Affirming in the positive is an important part of the reprogramming process.

If you find affirmations are making a difference in your attitude to things, you can use them in other ways. If you have difficulty with a particular affirmation, try meditating on it. Go into your opening-up process, grounding and balancing yourself, and then say the statement to yourself. Ask your inner self for guidance. Meditate on the meaning and power of the affirmation. You will probably gain some insights which will improve your relationship to the concept. Use your inner self to show you new paths into enlightenment.

You can also purchase tapes that are filled with different affirmations. You can use them at any time: when you're on a journey, when you're going off to sleep, when you're relaxing in a bath. Better still, you can record your own affirmations and play them back to yourself. Hearing your own voice and its vibrations will further enhance your connections with the affirmations.

At all times, be gentle with yourself in your self-healing process. It is sometimes slow but, provided you refuse to give up, it will be a constant progress. You can liken your self-healing path to the Flower Exercise, in which you experienced the wonderment of a seed blossoming into a beautiful flower. Your affirmations and meditations all start off as a tiny seed in your palm. At that stage, it is not recognisable as that glorious outburst of beauty and perfection. It has to be nurtured and given time to grow. Every flower has to start as a young shoot that is vulnerable and delicate. Your self-healing works the same way. While you are growing and spreading tiny shoots, you have to be kind and supportive. You didn't look at that small shoot of a flower and decide that it was pathetic and worthless, and trample upon it, did you? You regarded it with pleasure and happy anticipation. So are your early stages of self-healing and spiritual growth a deeply joyous event. Decide that you will never trample on your own development; instead, be clear that you will encourage and enjoy the path you are on, appreciating each stage and acknowledging that you, too, can culminate in that glorious explosion of a magical flower that brings joy and pleasure to others.

When you have embraced your capacity for self-love and self-expression, then you are ready for the task of healing others.

CHAPTER 16

HEALING OTHERS

Healing others takes many forms, from the simple touch of a loved one when we're feeling unhappy to the intricate, highly skilled sensitive who can take themselves into a trance and psychically enter someone's aura to cleanse and heal them. You're now going to be looking at some of those levels in between, which deal with the emotional level of healing, using the chakras up to the heart level. There is a great deal you can do in this realm to offer comfort to others.

Healing is a natural gift which we all have and which most of us have already used in some capacity; some use it more than others; some channel it more powerfully than others. Most of us use our own energies when we offer unconscious healing. To heal others on a regular basis, you should never use your own energies but draw upon those offered by the divine state of consciousness: in other words, the pure white light which you have already used in psychic development.

Let's start by looking at occasions when you have either received healing or offered it to others, probably without realizing it was happening. Have you any memory of hurting yourself as a young child and rushing to a parent so that they could kiss it better? That kiss wasn't just a token gesture. Healing vibrations were within that loving kiss; as a child you knew it without quite understanding what it all meant. Is there a person or certain people you crave to have around you when you are feeling upset or unwell, because you know they will improve your condition? It's because they offer you unconscious healing and can rebalance some of your energies. If you've had a particularly trying day, has someone given you a reassuring bear-hug, releasing your tension and filling you with a renewed sense of peace?

Their healing energies were enveloping and affecting you in a positive way. If you have sore skin and someone gently rubs a lotion on you, it isn't just the cream that is soothing; their very touch and exchange of energies is adding to your sense of well-being. A body massage can also be wonderful for that added, loving vibration. If you have a stomach ache and you ask someone close to you to gently touch the affected area, their loving connection can aid your recovery. If you stub your toe badly, isn't it your natural response to clutch it to ease the pain? This isn't simply because you want to stop the blood flow and sensation in that area, it's because your own touch can soothe and heal. Once you stop and think about healing you realize it is all around you and used every day, in different ways. You might be worried about a work situation and finally confront your boss with your problem; if they then respond in a helpful, comforting way, that very action heals and calms you. You may be dreading a presentation you are about to give at work, when a business colleague gently touches your arm and smiles understandingly at you. That simple gesture heals and rebalances you. The list is endless.

Of course, the above are all examples of unconscious healing, offered through a direct personal contact where love and affection are offered by someone you already know. Healing others also works on a much more impersonal, structured level.

What can you accomplish by healing people? You may now understand that an unwell state in someone is created by energy being blocked in different areas within the aura. Basically, healing is all about releasing blocked energy and rebalancing energy levels. In the area you'll be working with, you won't actually be balancing their energy yourself, but you will be offering them the ability to help themselves by giving them the freedom and opportunity to change their own energy and unblock some of their closed energy currents themselves.

The reason you won't actually be unblocking these channels for them is because that level of healing can only take place after years of continued study and practice. You're not yet in a position to decide whether someone's energy is ready to be fully released or not; nor are you yet capable of effecting that release. People open up in their own time, when they are ready to do so. What you can safely do, is offer them love and encouragement from a higher source, which then leaves them in a protected position of choosing for themselves how they want to progress. By leaving the decisions up to them, you are not being any less powerful. In fact, you are offering them the ultimate in power; you are respecting and nurturing their growth, and encouraging them to take responsibility for themselves. Healing is a vital part of the world's well-being. Fortunately, it is now being acknowledged and practised more and more on a world-wide scale, continually increasing our chance for awareness and holistic health.

There is one aspect of healing you must understand before you start and you must impart this information clearly and concisely to everyone on whom you practise healing. Your psychic healing is not in any way intended to replace any orthodox medical treatment that your sitter may be undergoing. Never, ever encourage anyone to think that your method of healing is in any way superior to, or can replace, a doctor's prescription. You may find that people who come to you for healing are in a low frame of mind, particularly if they've been feeling unwell for any length of time. It's extremely important you don't mislead them, or offer them any false hopes. By all means, let your healing be a complement and addition to any other form of treatment they may currently be undergoing. They may find your healing leaves them feeling better than their medication. However, at your stage of development, you are in no position to make any medical decisions. It's suggested you always, always start a healing session with something like this:

> '*I hope you receive benefit from my healing, and there is no reason why you shouldn't do so. However, I must stress that what I offer you is not intended to replace any orthodox medicine or treatment which you are currently having. If you should feel better as a result of this healing, please don't discontinue any treatment without first consulting your doctor. To do so might be detrimental to your health. My healing is intended as a complement and addition to your present situation.*'

Rephrase the words if they feel uncomfortable to you, but never forget to say them to your sitter. Your responsibilities are increased during healing work and your sensitivity to their energies needs to increase as a result.

Before your first healing session, you could help prepare yourself by practising the following meditation. This will help align your energies and focus them in a way that may increase your healing abilities.

HEALING PREPARATION NO. 1

Start by sitting in your space and closing your eyes. Concentrate on your breathing, visualize the pure white light and open up your chakras. Balance and ground yourself. By now, after considerable practice, this process should be easier and quicker for you.

Now you can use an affirmation or mantra to help focus and centre yourself. Something simple like 'Be still and know that I am God' can be powerful. Use another word other than 'god' if you prefer. Whatever you choose, repeat this mantra over and over, focusing on it and nothing else. If your mind starts to wander, bring it back again. Continue saying your mantra for as long a period of time as feels right for you; don't move on until you feel relaxed and focused.

Now concentrate on your body and imagine that your Sushumna is a long, empty golden tube. (The Sushumna is the vertical line of energy that connects all your chakras. Re-read Chapter Seven if you need a refresher). Create a ball of pure golden light above you; see it come towards you from the universe of higher consciousness. Feel the ball as it stops above your head and then slides down this golden tube to your solar plexus chakra. Feel it pulsing there, like a warm, golden sun. Now feel it filling all of you, spreading like a radiant glow throughout your entire body. It fills all of you, down to every toe and finger. Feel your whole body pulsing with energy and light.

Now feel the golden ball expanding, also filling your aura and then the entire room in which you're sitting. See it spreading beyond the room, to fill your whole home, the area around your home, the town in which you live. Slowly, see it ever expanding, growing brighter and lighter and more radiant with each expansion. See it covering the entire country in which you live and then watch it spreading to other countries, spreading around the entire globe. Feel the whole earth pulsing with this pure, divine energy. Then see it expanding out into the universe, enveloping all the planets and the entire solar sytem, and spreading into infinity, growing brighter and stronger as it spreads.

Know that you are part of that pure golden radiance and that you are all things. Know that you are connected to all higher consciousness and that you are part of the Divine spirit itself.

Now slowly contract the golden ball again. Do this gradually, step by step, reversing the process. See the golden light as vibrant and beautiful as ever. See it contracting from the universe to the earth. Then feel it contracting from the earth back to your part of the world, to your country, your town, the area around your home, your room, your aura and finally back to your body. Then feel the golden ball contract back to your solar plexus area and see the golden light slowly lift up through your Sushumna, through the top of your head and back up into the universe of higher consciousness.

Slowly cleanse and centre yourself and close down thoroughly. The warm, golden glow may still be pulsing in you, even after you have closed down. Give thanks for its divine presence and ensure you are well earthed again before you open your eyes.

Practise this meditation a few times before you hold your first healing session. The more you connect to the pure energy you are drawing upon, the more powerfully you will be able to use it.

There is also another exercise you can do which will increase your healing abilities. Your hands become a tool during healing work and the divine energy you call upon, has to be channelled down through your crown chakra, down your arms and through your hands and fingers. Use the meditation below to improve this flow:

HEALING PREPARATION NO. 2

Close your eyes and go through the opening-up and tuning-in processes. Ground yourself. Check that you are balanced.

As you breathe deeply and comfortably, think about your arms and hands and all the tasks that they perform for you each day. Think about how much easier they make your life in every way. List in your mind at least twenty vital functions that your arms and hands do for you. Feel your appreciation of their existence growing with each thought. Bless their presence and their state of health. Resolve to always acknowledge them and appreciate them in the future.

Send love from your heart chakra through to each arm and down into each hand, each finger and then let it flow out. Feel a warm green light flowing from your heart up through to both arms. Then feel the sweep as the light flows smoothly down each arm and into each hand. Let this cycle continue for a few minutes. Feel your heart, arms, hands and fingers all tingling with loving vibrations. Become aware of the power of your arms and hands for the first time. Really acknowledge their presence and beauty. Feel every cell within them pulsing with vitality. With each sweep of the green light of love, they feel more and more alive.

When you know you have fully experienced the joy of your arms and hands, slowly bring the white light in through your crown chakra and let it wash down through you, paying particular attention to your arms and hands. Let the light wash through them several times. It's possible that your hands will have become quite hot during the exercise. If they still tingle, keep using the white light to cleanse and refresh them.

When you are ready, close down and protect yourself. Make sure your cloak of protection is drawn around both your arms and hands. Make sure they feel secure and safe, before you open your eyes and reorientate yourself.

This exercise is to increase your appreciation of your arms and hands, but this isn't the actual process you use for healing itself, as you'll soon see. Healing involves the earth energies to keep you well grounded and use of your base, navel and solar plexus, as well as the heart. Again, go through this exercise several times before you first practise healing.

When your sitter arrives for the healing session, you need to ask them if they have a particular area they would like to concentrate upon and which position they would like to use for healing. If they know you well and feel comfortable, it may be best for them to lie down. It also depends on the area they would like you to heal. However, lying down can also make people feel very vulnerable and if they are nervous about healing and haven't experienced it before, it's better that they sit. You will have to accommodate their needs. It's not a good idea for them to stand during healing work. Apart from the fact that it's more difficult for them to relax, the healing session may make them feel off-balance at times. Sitting is a better grounding for them.

You also need to work out your own position during healing work. You will certainly need to stand for some of it. Remember to keep your weight evenly distributed over both feet during your session; this is important for balance as well as proper grounding with the earth energies. When you bend down, how are you doing this? If you bend your back, you'll soon end up with back-ache. You need to use your knees a lot during this work. Are you also getting your physical exercise? You will feel the benefit of it during healing. Remember you have to look after yourself as well, during healing work. You won't be an effective healer unless you are in good health yourself. It would help you to practise in front of a chair, imagining a person sitting there. How can you reach their solar plexus area and still feel comfortable yourself? If you work around their shoulders and neck, are you putting yourself into an awkward position? If they have a sore foot or ankle, how can you best spend a few minutes healing that area? Practise alone to work out what feels right for you.

Also make sure that your sitter's chair has enough space around it for you to move in all directions. It's distracting if you're half-way through a session and suddenly you realize you have to move a table and its contents before you can continue.

Another point to consider is that healing is conducted mainly in silence. With your previous psychic work, you have been speaking and offering information. Now you are working in a much quieter, more subtle way. Apart from checking how your sitter is feeling, you don't actually need to say anything. Now you really can think about sounds and whether any are appropriate. Again, this should be your sitter's choice, although you must also find the sound harmonious. Ideally, if you can create your own small collection of sound and music, all of which you like, then you can safely offer any of that to your sitter. Both of you may prefer silence. That is fine, provided you are both comfortable with that state. So often a sitter may feel they have to speak if there is silence, because they find stillness an awkward state. If they do insist on talking continually, gently suggest that some music might be soothing and put on something gentle and calming, to settle their energies.

It's also very important that you pay attention to the clothing you are wearing. Can you bend your knees and squat down without anything pulling or without revealing parts of yourself that you'd rather have covered? Make sure you don't have a waistband that cuts into you or a collar that is too tight. If you have long hair, make sure it is tied back in a comfortable way. It would be very distracting if it suddenly swung out and touched your sitter.

On the subject of touch, there is no need for you to physically touch your sitter during a healing session. You are dealing with the energies within their aura and their aura is outside their physical body. Many people don't feel secure with a physical approach and it can be misconstrued so easily. For your initial healing work, never touch their physical body, unless you ask permission first and it's for a specific reason. This is explained fully in a moment.

The sense of smell can also be heightened during healing work. If possible, choose a scent which seems appropriate for the session. If your sitter finds it unpleasant, make sure it can easily be extinguished and cleared from the room. Your own sense of smell should be sharpening and increasing in awareness through work you have done already; use your knowledge to tune in and choose the right scent for the session.

Once you have settled your sitter in a suitable position, and the sounds and smells feel right, you are ready to begin. Suggest to your sitter that they may wish to keep their eyes closed during the healing, as this can sometimes increase their awareness and relaxation. Assure them it's not essential to do so, in case they feel too vulnerable. Also re-iterate that they don't have to do anything during the session except relax and enjoy themselves. Ask them to let you know at any time if anything you do makes them feel uncomfortable in any way. Explain this is important because healing should be pleasant and uplifting and not a strain. Even though you start by telling them this, you will still need to keep checking through the session that they are all right. People can be very hesitant to give you negative feedback, unless you keep letting them know that it's fine to tell you.

HEALING

Again, go through your usual opening-up and tuning-in exercises. Make sure that your heart chakra, in particular, is fully opened, front and back. Make sure your breathing is even and deep. Spend a few moments checking that you are well-balanced. Take longer than usual pulling the white light down through your crown and into your body. Really feel the surge of the earth energy as it whooshes up through your feet and fills all of your body, right up to your crown. These energies need to be as free flowing and rich as possible. The more you concentrate on the energies, the more they can enter into you. Say a prayer to your deity and ask for help that is specific to your sitter's healing needs. Ask that you be allowed to be as powerful a tool in that process as possible. Ask for guidance to take you to whatever area of your sitter is most important. Remember your sensation of the golden ball that filled you, the world and then the whole universe. Feel yourself expanding with love as you remember the feeling. Wait until you feel as though you are an empty vessel, pulsating with energy and love. Feel the energies through your arms and hands increasing. Feel the strong surge as the white light and earth energies meet and cascade down your arms, through your hands and out through your fingers and palms. Wait until you know the energy is flowing freely before you start. Again ask for help from above as you open your eyes and approach your sitter. Keep asking for help throughout your healing session.

Lift your energies up to your heart chakra. Make sure they are resting there comfortably before you lift your arms and start your work. You may instinctively know which area of your sitter you want to approach. Remember to keep a distance away from their body itself. Remember your exercise when you felt the human aura? You don't need to be on top of them to be effective. If you are uncertain where to start, always choose the solar plexus area, being careful to keep at least a foot away from their body. The solar plexus area houses a vast amount of our energy and is often unbalanced and over-active. Feel yourself filled with love and light as you place your hands gently over the area. Empty your mind of any conscious thoughts, other than your desire to help in the best way possible. Remember to keep breathing deeply and keep balancing your own energies.

If, during the session, you start to feel light-headed, remember to cleanse and then concentrate on your feet again. Spend more time pulling up the earth energy and letting it fill all of you.

It's possible, during early stages, that your empathy may allow you to take on board the symptoms of your sitter's problems. This isn't harmful, as long as you cleanse them away immediately. If you feel uncomfortable, take a few steps away from your sitter and let the white light fill you. Cleanse under your private waterfall, directing the light and water to whichever area has picked up the unpleasant sensation. Often it will affect your solar plexus area, as this is used a great deal in healing work. Cleanse it thoroughly before you move towards your sitter again. Remember to lift your energies again to the heart level.

Never spend much time around your sitter's heart chakra or the crown chakra. The heart chakra shouldn't be dwelt upon because it holds the breath, the very life-source of your sitter. Without realising it, your energies may affect their heart area. Pass over it, but do not let your hands rest in that area. The crown chakra is also *vulnerable because it is releasing and receiving energy all the time. If you watch an experienced healer working, they may spend considerable time around both the crown and heart areas; their experience affords them safe conduct but they have spent time developing that degree of awareness.*

After a few minutes, ask your sitter how they are feeling. They may ask you to move to another area. If you do so, you may find yourself drawn back again to a different section of their body. Your sitter will not necessarily be the best judge of their needs if they have little contact with their inner self. Make sure you keep listening to your inner voice and learning from it.

If you start to feel tired after a few minutes, you are using your own energies instead of the ones being given to you by higher sources. Cleanse yourself and let yourself feel empty again. Concentrate only on the white light pouring in through your crown and the earth energies coming up through your feet. Feel both energies meeting and pouring down through your arms and out through your hands. After a few sessions, you will soon learn how not to use your own energies. You will only exhaust yourself by doing so. You should finish every healing session feeling uplifted and refreshed.

It's not uncommon for healers to cleanse literally dozens of times during each healing session. Healing is an especially powerful expression of psychic work and it's very difficult to maintain a degree of attachment. Empathy and compassion are natural human emotions and they strongly affect our solar plexus area. Remember to keep being aware of your own solar plexus and how it is feeling.

If your sitter tells you that what you are doing feels wonderful, it's naturally very gratifying and encouraging. Your instinct is to want to give even more, to increase the healing vibrations. Then you are likely to use your own energy and tire yourself.

It's possible you may find your sitter telling you that something you are doing is causing them discomfort. If this happens, move away from your sitter, consciously withdraw your aura from them, and feel the pure white light pouring down into their crown chakra. See it cleansing them and washing away any pain. Ask them if the ache is in a particular area and direct the white light through to that section and see it breaking up the pain, dissolving it and washing out through their body. You don't have to explain any of this to your sitter. Your visualization will work powerfully without you expressing what is happening. Remind them to breathe slowly and comfortably. Don't encourage them to take deep breaths at this stage, as this may make them dizzy. Speak soothingly and quietly during this process. Remember you have to be in control at all times. If your sitter senses any panic or concern from you, this fear will intensify their worry and increase any discomfort. Panic causes a great imbalance of energy flow and will affect both you and your sitter. Your higher sense of knowing will keep you calm and in control at all times. Refuse to let yourself be put off-balance. Ground yourself and increase your deep breathing. Connect with your inner self and ask for help. Explain to your sitter that nothing dreadful happened; it was purely their energy flow moving at a different rate which unnerved them. They are in no danger and have nothing to fear. Remind them to concentrate on their breathing and to keep their eyes closed.

Now slowly move back towards them. Remember to lift your energies back to your heart chakra and then visualise soft waves of comfort and peace flowing from your hands into their aura. See it as calming and gentle, gradually rebalancing their ruffled energy flow. Ask them if they still feel discomfort in any area.

If they do, ask them if you might lightly touch the area concerned. If they give you permission, very gently place your hand over the area and now ask them to direct their own breath to that area. By touching the spot, you are enabling them to focus better. Explain that as they breathe in, they need to imagine that breath is moving to the spot you are now touching. As they breathe out, imagine it dissolving the knot of discomfort and disappearing out into the distance. As you encourage them to do this, visualize their breath coming to the spot which you are lightly touching. See the breath breaking up the pain and disintegrating it into nothing. You may need to let this process continue for a few minutes. Your sitter probably won't be familiar with this technique and it may take them a few tries before they can get a sense of what you are asking them to do.

Finish your healing by returning to their solar plexus area. Ask for help from your inner self to leave your sitter in as much comfort as possible. When you feel your energies drop again to your base, you will know the healing session is complete.

Slowly move back from your sitter and retract your aura. Gently ask them to continue sitting there with their eyes closed; explain that they need a moment to balance themselves after the healing. Visualize the white light pouring into the room from above and swirling down into their body, cleansing and rejuvenating. Create this image and concentrate on it until you sense that they have fully benefitted from it. Now suggest to them that if they are feeling quite open and vulnerable after their session, they could benefit from giving themselves a little protection before they leave you. Suggest they imagine a soft cloak coming over their shoulders and down around their body, protecting and warming them. Keep your voice soft and warm as you speak; the way you speak will make them feel even more relaxed and comfortable. Ask them to use a light, happy colour for their cloak: explain that dark colours can drain energy. Suggest a comforting fabric like velvet or silk and remind them to cover their whole body with it. Now ask them to remain seated for a few minutes while you close yourself down.

Take time to cleanse yourself. Never rush this part during healing work. Strengthen the power of the white light by continually recreating it, feeling it becoming brighter and richer all the time. Step under your private waterfall and really enjoy the cleansing process. Check if any part of you is feeling the effect of your sitter's energies and wash it away. Listen to all of your body. Let energy sweep through your arms and hands, making sure you release any tension that may have built up during your session. You may find your hands and fingers feeling hot and slightly sweaty. They may *tingle or even ache slightly. They may feel cooler than usual. Just wash away anything you don't want and feel your sense of equilibrium returning as you do so.*

Ensure you ground yourself thoroughly; the pleasures of healing sessions can make you very 'heady'. Pay extra attention to closing down all your chakras, especially your solar plexus and heart centres. Put an extra cloak of protection around yourself and sit quietly for a few minutes before you open your eyes again. You will probably find your sitter is more than happy just to sit and relax. If you were able to focus and use your healing energy well, it's quite likely that they will have found the whole experience highly enjoyable. In fact, they may not want to leave!

Make sure you have a good chat with your sitter afterwards. Encourage them to tell you everything they felt. You may find they only told you half the story during the session itself. If they had a particularly strong sensation during one moment, ask yourself if you felt anything different at that point. Were you doing something slightly new in your approach? When, if at all, were they uncomfortable? What were you doing then?

You may find your sitter can't say anything specific about what felt right or wrong for them. They may just have a vague sense of feeling better, calmer now. That is fine. Something has shifted within their energies on a subtle level. Even if they say they felt practically nothing, don't take that personally or feel you must be ineffective. It depends how well someone is in touch with their own energies as to how much they sense what has happened. It doesn't mean things haven't shifted. They may notice a difference when they get home or when they next speak to someone else. Other people may notice the change in them. Or perhaps they will choose to shift and unblock some energy at a later stage: when they're relaxing in the bath or before they drift off to sleep. Perhaps it didn't feel right to make that shift whilst they were with you. Healing continues after the session has finished. Whatever response you receive, know that it is right.

It's possible that your sitter may say they felt absolutely nothing and nothing feels different now. That can happen. This is not necessarily because you weren't working properly. This may be a reflection of their thoughts on healing. There is a subtle understanding you need to grasp with healing work. Your sitter doesn't need to believe in the power of healing to get a positive effect from it. This is proven by absent healing, which we'll be looking at in a minute. So it's fine for you to reassure your sitter that belief in you or your powers isn't necessary. They don't need to have faith in God or any religious or spiritual doctrine. Most people are surprised when you say this to them because most assume that implicit faith is part of healing. It isn't. However, there is one extremely important area in which they do have to believe. They have to believe in the power of change. In other words, they have to believe that nothing is set in stone or has to stay the same; that everything can be shifted in some way. This is the pivotal distinction that creates the possibility for healing.

Let's use an example to clarify this point. Your sitter has come to you because they are in emotional turmoil after the break-up of a relationship. They can know little or nothing about healing and how it works. They may not know much about you or have much confidence in your abilities as a healer. They may feel that healing sounds like something that can't really work. They may only be there because they're feeling lonely and despondent and thought some company would be better than nothing. Basically, they're not in a very positive frame of mind! None of this matters. However, how they reply to the following question does matter. Do they believe that something is capable of shifting the emotional pain they are feeling, even though they don't know how it might work? Or to put it another way, can they believe that it is possible to let go of the pain, although at this stage they haven't the slightest idea of how to do that? If they answer 'yes' to that question, there is every indication they will benefit from healing. If they answer 'no', then it's unlikely that anyone could help them at that stage. Healing is about embracing the capacity for something to change, without necessarily understanding how that process works. Someone who is rigidly convinced that no one and nothing can help them, who is firm in their belief that, no matter what happens, they are destined to live with a certain pain, will never allow the possibility of letting go. They will have built up so many layers of steel walls around them that no one can help them. This is the subtle difference between

DISCOVER YOUR PSYCHIC POWERS

effective and non-effective healing. Talk to people about this area of belief before you suggest some healing work. Make sure you are clear about the distinction yourself: they can be as cynical as they like about healing, your abilities and life itself, but if they believe in the possibility of change, they could benefit from healing.

You may still find it difficult to believe that someone who is cynical about healing could still be helped. Let's now look at absent healing to see how this works. Using this form of healing will afford you proof of this phenomenon.

Absent healing is literally what is says: healing someone who is absent from your presence. It's extremely powerful. Absent healing has been practised successfully around the world for many years. Its positive results have ensured it remains a powerful form of healing today. When you first work with absent healing, your natural reaction is to doubt how it could possibly work. How can healing someone in a visualization technique have any power, when you aren't actually with that person to interrelate with their energies? It's because all our energies are being given out at all times into the universe and we are all receiving different energies all the time. In absent healing, you are simply focusing your energy channels in a particularly concentrated and loving manner. It's like tuning in to the right radio or television station. When you are tuned in, the reception is clear. You can learn to tune your own channels so that you can receive and give healing energy. What is wonderful is that although your absent sitter won't be tuned in to your wavelength, all it needs is for you to tune in to theirs, to enable you to give them help.

Absent healing requires a powerful focus. You may find that going through The Candle and Numbers Exercises helps you to prepare for absent healing. The Healing Preparation No. 1 Exercise is also particularly good. When you feel you have strengthened your focusing techniques and when you feel you want to practise absent healing, you can do this at any time in your space. You don't need anyone with you, nor do you need to let anyone know what you're doing. Of course, if you prefer to contact your absent sitter and let them know you are doing some absent healing on them, there is nothing wrong with that, unless you feel that by telling them what you are doing you will make them nervous and have them retreat from the experience. Absent healing works on a very different level from the earlier Connecting With a Person Exercise in Chapter 9, when you practised concentrating on somebody's whereabouts and actions. Then you were advised never to do this without asking the person's permission first. Absent healing doesn't work on this level. With absent healing you are using energies from the state of higher consciousness and rather than intruding on someone's personal space, you are positively assisting them through higher awareness. The energy levels we're dealing with now are much finer and subtler. Any effects they feel from absent healing could be likened to a spiritual experience or an inexplicable sense of peace and well-being. They will not feel violated in any way, because of the higher source of power connected with absent healing.

So, choose one person whom you feel would benefit from absent healing. If you aren't certain who it should be, then close your eyes and ask your inner self for help. Wait until you hear that person's name, or see them in front of you, to know who it is. Now you are ready to try your first absent healing session.

ABSENT HEALING

Go into your space, giving consideration to the sounds and smells around you. What do you think your absent sitter would like? What would they find uplifting? If you close your eyes and concentrate, you will probably find the right scent and sound coming to you quite easily. Use any other techniques that seem appropriate to you. If you have something they gave you or you have a favourite item you want to hold, such as a soft piece of fabric, then do so. This is you relaxing within your own space and you can use whatever tools you wish to make you feel good. Just ensure they are not distracting for you; you want to create a space where you enhance your sense of focus. When you are ready, sit down, close your eyes and go through your opening-up and tuning-in processes.

Once you are open, balanced and relaxed, spend an extra few minutes pulling the beautiful white light down into the room. Keep your eyes closed throughout; this will intensify your concentration.

Now see your chosen person in front of you. See them glowing vibrantly with health and happiness. This is most important. If your last image of them was one of sadness or pain, then wash that image from your mind. The healthier and brighter you visualize them, the more powerful your absent healing will be. If they are someone who laughs often and easily, see them smiling contentedly or see them laughing. See their eyes sparkling with joy. See them dressed in their favourite mode of dress. Choose colours that you know are right for their sense of well-being. See their hair and skin radiating a happy glow. Spend as much time as you like, creating this joyous picture of them. You will find yourself feeling wonderful as you create them in front of you, happy and at peace. Their sense of well-being also makes you feel terrific. Make sure every part of them is positive and uplifting. This means seeing them in a holistic sense. Sense or see their energy as free-flowing and brilliant in its spiritual luminescence. Every part of them is well: mind, body and spirit. Create the image as strongly and beautifully as you can. Nothing else should be in your thoughts, other than their inspirational beauty and health.

When you have created their glowing image, then see the white light in the room pouring down onto them and sweeping through them, adding extra light and health. See it surrounding them, protecting them and flowing through them, completely bathing them in pure divine light and energy.

Now you may choose to add your own special love to them. See streams of rich green energy pouring from your heart chakra into their image. See your love being accepted by and mingling with their energy. (If, for any reason, you are feeling depleted in energy yourself, choose not to offer this personal expression of love. It's not essential you do so, especially if you know you need to nurture your own sense of well-being.)

When you know they have received the full benefit of the cosmic energy and your own love, then release their healthy and happy image up into the white light above. See this happen as a gentle ascension up into the universe above. Feel them become lighter *and brighter as they slowly disappear into the realms of higher consciousness.*

Say a prayer that feels right for you, blessing their healing process and asking that they may be guided as necessary to help them in their own learning processes. Thank your inner self for its help in this absent healing.

Now thoroughly cleanse yourself. As with any form of healing, you may have unconsciously taken on board some of your person's pains. This is most likely to have happened if you initially saw them as unwell and had to concentrate to let go of that image and create a healthier picture. Some of those problems may have gone into your aura. Is any part of you feeling unwell in any way? How are your solar plexus and heart chakras feeling? Stand under your psychic waterfall for as long as you like. Enjoy the refreshing sensation. Don't close down until you feel ready to do so. Protect yourself well and ensure you are well grounded before you open your eyes again.

If you were able to create a strong image of your absent sitter as healthy and happy, then those focused energies are likely to have affected them on some positive level. You may know, just from one absent healing session, that it was powerful. Again, this is the higher sense of knowing that renders physical discussion unnecessary. If you feel what you visualized was not strong and you doubt your ability to have made any difference, you could start keeping a note of when you offer absent heaing and to whom and then document the results.

Some people want to add colours into their healing techniques, as they feel that will make them more powerful. Colours are a wonderful form of focus and can aid healing in many ways. However, it's a subject that requires a lot of study and using the wrong colour can be much more damaging than using no colours at all. For early stages, until you develop your own very personal relationship with colours and until your awareness of them reaches a higher level, you are safer to use the image of pure white light. Did you know that white is the sum of all the other chakra colours put together? Therefore, in a sense, you are already using all colours, when you use white. If you really feel the need to add another colour, the safest is green, the colour of the heart chakra. Symbolizing love and peace, it is most likely to harmonize with others' energies.

You can put more than one person into your absent healing, once you have practised for a while and know you can create healthy images without difficulty. If you know that a couple are struggling with their relationship, or that your friend is having problems with a child, or a relative is not getting on well with their boss, then you can create a harmonious and healthy image of the two of them together (of course, you need to know what both parties look like). You need to understand that what you are doing in the case of two parties is not making any decision about their way forward together. For instance, you may know that a close friend and their partner are arguing a great deal. The purpose of absent healing is not for you to decide that they should get married or split up. You are not in position to decide what is right for them. By picturing them as healthy and contented together, you are asking higher sources to help them find the path that is right for them. This is the healing process that you are facilitating: a tool for them to learn how to make their own changes. Being a healer is about helping people to discover themselves in the physical, mental and spiritual realms. It shouldn't be confused with thinking that a healer has special divine or god-like qualities. Any healer is a human being who is learning how to focus and channel energies. Notice the choice of words 'is learning'; healing is a subject which is ever-expanding in possibilities. What you are learning at present is only the tiniest tip of an enormously complex and powerful expression of human development. You are not likely to learn and understand all there is to know about healing in one life-time.

Now let's look at crystals and how they can benefit you, not just during healing work, but in all aspects of psychic and spiritual development.

CHAPTER 17

USING CRYSTALS

Crystals have been around on Earth since long before man even came into primitive existence; many of the crystals you see around you today were formed thousands of years ago. Crystals are unique in that they have a geometrically perfect atomic structure. Quartz crystals are a natural substance; they're made from movement in the earth's crust. This ancient, perfect substance has extremely special properties. It receives, focuses and converts energy. You may already know that quartz crystals are used in many of our modern appliances. Their electrical properties mean that they amplify sound waves in a radio and amplify light waves within a television. At their most esoteric level, crystals are said to be mineral transmitters and storers of the cosmic energy contained deep within the Earth's core.

If that sounds somewhat fanciful to you, consider how much you know at present about the composition of our planet Earth. For instance, did you know that although the diameter of our Earth is nearly 8,000 miles, our land mass is only 22 miles thick? Under the ocean, it's only 4 miles thick. Beneath that crust is molten lava; scientists estimate that the innermost core of our Earth could be as hot as 6,000 degrees Celsius, which is as hot as the surface of the sun. Can you imagine the powerhouse of heat and energy which lies within the centre of our planet? It's because crystals have a perfect molecular structure, that they're believed to be in complete alignment with the earth's energy.

However powerful you believe they may or may not be, crystals are certainly worthy of some study and experimentation. Many healers use crystals on a regular basis: they either hold them in their hand during a healing session, have their sitter hold them, or they are placed in specific areas around the room. At the very least, because of their atomic make-up, crystals can become excellent tools for you to use; they are easily imbued with your own energy and can be used to focus and re-direct energy in many positive ways.

Everyone's relationship to crystals becomes very personal. There are no clear rules for what does or doesn't make a suitable crystal. You have to discover for yourself which crystals resonate for you in a powerful way.

You can only find out by studying them. The next time you take a walk along a beach, stop and study the stones and crystals around you. Pick one up and hold it in your hand. Do you feel anything? Transfer it to your other hand. Close your fingers around it. Place it against your solar plexus or your third eye chakras. Do you feel anything? Try another stone and experiment. You may feel a surge of energy flow up through your hand and into your arm. You may feel nothing.

Do you know anyone who owns a crystal? Ask if you may pick it up. See what happens when you do. Stare into it and enjoy the amazing swirls of frost-like fog. It's easy to lose yourself into a crystal. Once you have handled it, a crystal belonging to someone else needs to be cleansed. Details of how to do this are explained in a moment.

Almost all New Age shops now sell a variety of crystals. Some can be incredibly expensive. Expensive doesn't necessarily mean the most powerful. Bigger isn't always best. You may find a smaller crystal reverberates better with your energies. Each crystal is unique in its make-up and gives out energy at a different speed. If you choose a crystal that vibrates too quickly or powerfully for you, you will end up tired, as you try to force your metabolism to keep up with the crystal's energies. If you own a crystal that is too slow in its vibrations, you will find yourself slowing down to its level and not using your own energy effectively. You want to choose a crystal with energy that is just slighter stronger than yours. Then it becomes an enhancement to your own state. Finding the crystal that is right for you, is a process of trial and error.

You can also use it in a passive or active way. For instance, you may choose to have the crystal in your space with you and leave it untouched, having it absorb negative energy for you. Or you may imbue it with your energy by keeping it in the room and using it as a powerhouse of energy that complements your space. If you want to use it in a more active way, you may decide to choose a small crystal which you wear around your neck or hold in your hand during meditation.

When trying to choose the right crystal, simply hold it in your hand for a few minutes. Close your eyes, breathe deeply and regularly, and feel what the crystal is saying to you. If you have been practicing psychometry, your senses will be getting higher and brighter. You should know quite quickly if a crystal feels right to you or not. If you feel nothing much is happening, then quickly do your Hand Brushing Exercise to activate your chakras. If you know your solar plexus or third eye chakras are good sensors for you, hold it against either area. Ask your inner self to guide you. You will know when the crystal is right for you. Never be influenced by a person trying to push a sale. Only you know what is a good purchase.

Different coloured crystals also offer different strengths and areas upon which you can focus. Again, this is also a personal choice, although if you go into a shop which sells different crystals, you will quite likely see a description of each article and its intended purpose with it. If you aren't certain what is right for you, you can always try relating the crystals to colours within your chakras. By now, you will hopefully be strengthening your relationship to all seven of your energy centres and you should be developing an understanding of the areas in which you need to do more work. Below is a guide:

Base — ruby, garnet

Navel — topaz, carnelian

Solar Plexus — yellow sapphire, citrine

Heart — emerald, jade

Throat — blue sapphire

Third Eye – lapis lazuli

Crown – amethyst

Crystals are also used as a means of protection. If you feel you are vulnerable and easily influenced, you may choose a stone that is good for self-preservation. Tiger's eye is considered particularly effective in this field, whilst also helping you to tap into your inner power. Black jade and black jet are also used to provide a barrier against negative energy. Tourmaline can again provide a good shield. Turquoise is also considered a protector, whilst at the same time encouraging positive thinking and a state of 'Oneness'. These crystals are best worn around or against your body in the most comfortable fashion for you.

Do you or does someone you know have a jewellery box with items in it that you haven't looked at for years? Often old jewellery may contain crystals which you hadn't considered before. Use a good reference book to help you identify the stones, or ask a reputable jeweller for assistance.

However you acquire your stones, you need to cleanse the crystals of previous energy. You know from psychometry how important this is. It's even more essential with crystals given their powerful receptive qualities. Just as they can be imbued with your own positive energy, so they will soak up all negative influences as well. This makes it a wonderful tool to cleanse atmospheres and influences, but you must remember to cleanse it. Otherwise, it then starts to reflect that negative energy.

There are several established methods for cleansing crystals:

1 – *Soak the crystal in a mixture of sea salt and spring water. Use approximately a teaspoonful of salt to every three pints of water. Use sea salt as opposed to table salt; its properties are purer. Leave it for several hours, preferably overnight.*

2 – *Leave the crystal in direct sunlight for a day.*

3 – *Burn some sage and surround it with its smoke; this is an ancient Native American tradition.*

4 – *Cleanse the crystal using your pure white light from above. Imagine the white light flowing through your crystal and removing all blockages and impurities.*

5 – *Put the crystal into your special waterfall and let it be cleansed. This will also strengthen your own personal bond with the crystal, as no one and nothing else is allowed to enter your private cleansing space.*

Various other techniques are also considered effective, such as leaving the crystal in a clear, running stream for several hours or burying it in the sand and allowing the ocean to wash over it. Be careful not to lose the crystal while following these methods. Think about the cleansing process that feels most suitable for the crystal. Hold it in your hand and ask yourself what feels right. Different crystals may seem to need different cleansing processes.

When you have cleansed the crystal, you can try your first meditation upon it, to increase your relationship with its energies and to imbue it with yours.

THE CRYSTAL
Go into your space and sit down with the crystal resting in your hands. Close your eyes and open up as usual. Balance and ground yourself.

Firstly, open your eyes and look at the crystal in your hands. Really study its shape. What is it about the shape that you like? Look at it from different angles. Does it make you think of different things? Look at its colour. How many different shades are there within it? If it's clear or semi-opaque, look into the crystal. What can you see? Notice all the extraordinary shapes and designs within your crystal. Turn it over and study it from a different angle. Does one side feel more expressive than the other? Let the light play across the crystal and see how it shimmers, reflecting and deflecting the light.

Hold it up to your nose and smell it. What does it smell like? What does it make you think of? You may find the scent is very subtle, very delicate. You may have to be well focused to smell anything at all.

Place it against your ear. Does it say anything to you? If you picked it up from a seashore, you may hear a faint roar of the sea. Or is it saying something else to you? Let it rest against your ear for a moment, then transfer it to your other ear. If you hear nothing, that's fine.

Now close your eyes and have the crystal rest comfortably again in your hands. Let your hands rest on your thighs so there is no strain. Keeping your eyes closed, focus on the crystal resting in your hands. Feel its texture under your fingertips. Run your hands lightly over the whole surface, using your touch to explore every crack and crevice. Notice where it feels smooth and where it roughens to the touch. Throughout all this exploration, be aware if your inner self wants to speak. It doesn't matter if it remains silent, but be open to its presence and power. Does the crystal feel hot or cold? Is it pulsating? Is it making your heart rate speed up or slow down, or does it feel in harmony with you? Concentrate fully to make sure you know what is happening. Ask your crystal why it has come into your life. What do you have to learn from it? If you receive no answer at this stage, don't worry. It isn't important. Know that you will when you have bonded more fully with it. When you know you have held the crystal for long enough, gently place it on a nearby surface. Now close your eyes again.

See the crystal in your mind's eye. You should know its appearance quite well by now after your study. Keep looking at the crystal, moving around it. Then you notice there is a door in one section of it, which you hadn't noticed before. As you stare at the door in pleasant surprise, the crystal grows in front of you. It becomes large enough for you to be able to open the door and walk through.

When you walk into your crystal, you are in a large, beautiful room.

Rainbow-coloured light is being reflected through the glass walls; everything shimmers with the seven chakra colours. It is an empty space, perfect in its shape, colour and feel. You move into the centre of the room, sit down and close your eyes.

Now you feel completely in touch with your crystal. As you sit there and relax, you have different sensations wash over you. You may suddenly 'see' areas of your life that you know you are ready to work on. The crystal will help you in these areas. You may understand the particular purpose of this crystal and know where it is meant to rest. It may show itself positioned in a corner of your room, or you may see it on a chain around your neck or wrist. It's possible you might be surprised; you might see it resting on your bath or on your desk, or even in your refrigerator. You might see yourself holding it in your hand as you heal someone. Let all the sensations wash over you and know you are attuned to your higher needs and abilities. You may realize there are worries in your life that you can shed because you no longer need them. You may see the Earth more clearly and its position within the universe on a spiritual level. You may receive powerful insights about people and their relationship to Earth. Be open to whatever experience the crystal is showing you, and you will keep the energies flowing.

Bless the crystal for its presence in your life and the gifts it is offering you. Resolve that you will embrace the opportunity and grow from its teaching. Ask the crystal to continue nurturing you through your time together. Now it is time for you to leave its protective womb and return to the outside world. As you get up and walk towards the door, know you can return on another occasion. Know that the energies of the crystal are always there for you to draw upon.

As you go through the door, you find yourself back in your seat again. The crystal has shrunk back to its usual size and you know it's sitting in front of you again.

Feel your weight back on your seat again. Become aware of how heavy you feel in your physical body. Cleanse any unwanted sensations away with your waterfall and then slowly close down and protect yourself. When you feel centred and ready, open your eyes and pick up your crystal once more. Does it now feel right in your hand? Does it vibrate in harmony with your own energies? You may want to repeat this exercise several times with a new crystal.

If the sensations you receive when tuning in to your crystal are not pleasant, you may realize the crystal is not compatible with you. Ask your inner self who may benefit from it, if it's not right for you. Perhaps you were meant to find it, so that you could pass it on to someone else. It's also possible that you hadn't cleansed the crystal properly so that you were picking up outside influences. By focusing on the crystal's energy yourself, you will know what is happening.

Crystals are often used to enhance chakra meditation. You read earlier about sympathetic chakra stones; if you have access to any that are suitable, you can try meditating on a chakra with the relevant stone placed upon that area. You need to lie down for this, unless you tape a small stone onto the area. If you haven't tried meditation in a horizontal position yet, you could do so with a crystal. You can either place the stone on your front chakra or the back opening; it depends whether you prefer lying on your back or your stomach. Experiment with both. Simply place the stone upon your chakra and then close your eyes and use your usual process to open up and tune in to the chakra. Using crystals this way has been known to help many people.

There are other simple experiments you can conduct. Do you have an ailing plant? Place the crystal in the earth, or by the pot itself. Notice if there is any difference after a few days. Put a small crystal into a vase and then fill it with flowers and water. Do the flowers last longer than usual? Try putting a stone on top of your television or computer; it's supposed to absorb the negative radiation from the screen. Do you notice any difference in the atmosphere by doing this? Do you know someone who is unwell at present? If you have a photo of them, place a crystal in front of it to direct healing rays towards them. Try doing this at different times and see if the person feels any effect. A crystal placed in the refrigerator is said to absorb odours and keep the food fresher. Keep a stone in your working environment and notice if it helps your creativity. Put one under your pillow and see if it helps you to sleep. The list of possibilities is endless; after you have experimented for a while, you will create your own uses for crystals.

Wherever you place your crystal, let it stay there for a few days, before you decide if its location is right or not. Often, when energies first change within a space, the change in atmosphere can feel unnerving. It's not because it's wrong, it's because it feels different. Anything different often feels threatening, especially initially. So let the stone rest in a spot before you decide if it should stay there. If after a couple of days you know it isn't right, then move the crystal. Keep moving it around until you find the right place for it.

At some time during your healing work, try working with a crystal and see if it's a helpful tool for you. Make sure you have already cleansed the crystal thoroughly and that its energies are compatible with yours. Don't suddenly decide you'll use a stone that's new to you because the energies can become unbalanced within your space and affect your work. When you've chosen the right piece, then either hold it in your hand, wear it on your body, place it nearby in the room, or ask your sitter to hold it. You'll have to use the same crystal in several different healing sessions, and with different people, before you'll properly know whether it has had an effect. Then try introducing other crystals and see how they compare. When using crystals for healing, remember the rule of not directing them for any length of time around the heart or crown chakras. Always listen to your inner self and be guided by its wisdom. Listen to what each crystal has to say to you and use it appropriately. If you feel that crystals are a valuable enhancement to your work, then read as much as you can on the subject, experiment with as many different crystals as possible and attend any workshops or lectures that you can find. Learn from more than one source and develop your knowledge as much as possible so that you make full use of your special relationship with these gifts from nature.

Now you're ready to look at another area of psychic development where you can use a 'tool' to assist your work. By using no more than a pen or pencil and a piece of paper, you can develop yourself in another way, by creating auragraphs.

CHAPTER 18

DISCOVERING AURAGRAPHS

There is another area of psychic development that you have yet to explore: auragraphs. An auragraph is basically a drawing that you do whilst you are open and tuned in to your sitter. This drawing is nothing to do with artistic ability or technical skill, because you are not using your own talents for this. As healing involves a free flow of energy through your arms and hands, so psychic drawing requires a similar level of unhindered flow, which does not involve using your own energies. Many people assume that if they're no good at drawing, then any form of auragraph would be uninspired. It needn't be that way at all. You can now start to explore another part of yourself that may prove to be much more powerful than you expected.

As in all psychic work, you need to leave your own self out of psychic drawing as much as possible. Not only do you want your hand to move without conscious effort, you also want to leave your own thoughts and ideas behind, so that what appears on the paper is from a higher level of awareness in which your own conscious mind doesn't interfere. Although this may sound difficult, it can actually be a very uninhibiting and expressive form of psychic development. Trust in your inner self and you can enjoy a flow of artistic energy that you may never have tapped into before.

You may already be familiar with psychic drawings. There are psychic artists across the world who, with spiritual guidance, can draw likenesses of your spirit guides or images of departed friends and family. This is a fascinating area of work. However, it requires communication with spirit and a degree of focus and discipline which is only afforded to the highly-trained. It is a level to which many can aspire, although relatively few can achieve consistently accurate results. To start on this path, you need to explore your own relationship with drawing. No one can say what makes a budding psychic artist, although most describe having an interest in drawing at some level prior to psychic work. Many also describe sensations in their fingers and hands. They say they feel particularly hot or cold before they start to work psychically, or their palms start to itch or feel restless and twitchy. If you have had any of these sorts of feelings, it may be because you have untapped ability in your hands.

It's time to ask yourself some questions. Do you like art? Do you enjoy walking around art galleries? Do you spend ages choosing a birthday or Christmas card for someone because you are studying the pictures? Is it important for you to have photographs of people around you? Are there a lot dotted around in your home or your office? Do you like taking photos of people? Can you look into someone's eyes in a photo and get information from them? Can you pick up a photo and feel in touch with that person? Do you have drawings in your home that friends or relatives have done? Can you feel their presence simply by looking at the picture?

If you answered 'yes' to more than one of the above questions, then you may well find auragraphs to be a useful form of psychic expression. You won't know unless you try, preferably on several occasions.

Start by explaining to your sitter that you would like to try drawing an auragraph. Explain that you're not a trained artist and the result may not be highly artistic. It's important they don't have false hopes, imagining that you are going to produce a beautiful, spiritual likeness of them. Assure them that all they have to do is relax and let them know they can shift in their chair if they want. (Otherwise, they may be under the impression that they have to keep still, like an artist's model.) Honestly explain this is an experiment because you aren't experienced in this field. Thank them for bearing with you. You need a large pad, preferably with a hard back to make drawing easier. For your first attempts, use a good, solid pencil, not a pen.

PENCIL DRAWING

Go through your usual opening-up process. Balance and ground yourself. Ask your inner self for guidance in this new field. Concentrate on emptying yourself of everything. Practise with the white light and earth energies, feeling them sweeping through you, down your arms and hands and into each finger. Go through this process several times, feeling the energy increase all the time.

When you feel ready, pick up your pad and pencil. Place the pad on your lap or on a table in front of you. Make sure you are sitting comfortably. Hold the pencil loosely in your fingers. Did your fingers and arm become tense as soon as you held the pencil? This usually happens the first time. Feel the white light washing away the tension. Feel your muscles relaxing through your arm, and become aware that your grip on the pencil is effortless. It feels natural and unpressured. Keep feeling the energy flowing through you.

Now lift your energies to the solar plexus. If you've been practicing healing or flower reading recently, your energies may shoot up to the heart. Make sure you pull them down again. Ensure they are resting at your solar plexus chakra.

Place the pencil tip loosely on the paper in front of you. Now you may choose to close your eyes, to help you relax and concentrate. Keep them open if that feels right. Whatever you do, don't try to draw or write anything. If nothing happens on your first attempt, that is fine. Remember to keep breathing deeply and regularly. Psychic drawing is all about flow. It should feel unrushed and easy. You may not achieve this until you have held a few sessions, but do persevere. It's a wonderful feeling when it does start to flow.

If your pencil does start to work, don't then decide which part of the paper it will cover or what you want to draw. It's not to do with you! Let your pencil go where it wants to and let yourself be the facilitator, not the guide. You can keep your eyes closed and still not have the pencil slide off the paper; your inner self will control it for you. Keep breathing comfortably and enjoy the freeing sensation of the pencil as it moves. Keep checking that your arm feels nicely heavy and relaxed. Release any tension, especially in the shoulders, and keep washing through with the white light. Remember that once you start drawing, your energies will slide again down to your base chakra. Remember to keep lifting them again to your solar plexus.

When you feel your pencil stop, keep the energy flowing through your arms and hands. You may not be finished yet. Your inner self may be having a breather but they may wish to continue. Tune in to yourself and see if you have more to draw. Lift your energies again to the solar plexus. Let your pencil continue in any way it wants.

When you have finished, your energies will probably drop quite quickly. Put your pencil down, have a cleanse under your waterfall and make sure you are grounded. However, you still want to remain open for your interpretation.

Open your eyes and study what you have drawn. Always, always go with your first instinctive reaction. Do you see an animal? Is it an emotion which hits you? Is it a symbol or inanimate object? Do you see an initial? What does that first impression tell you? Don't stop to rationalize about what the picture should be or what it is meant to be. You drew exactly what you did for a reason. Keep focusing on the picture. Try to leave your critical thoughts out of it, such as 'This isn't very good' or 'This just looks a mess'. You never draw what you think you're going to draw, if you are leaving conscious thought out of it. You must also use your inner self whilst you interpret it. Ask for help if you're confused. There may be a section of the drawing you just can't understand. Always ask for guidance. Only when you feel you have offered everything to the drawing, should you ask your sitter for their comments on it. Don't let yourself be influenced by them initially because you drew it and only you can properly interpret your own work. However, they may offer valuable insights as well.

Listen closely to what they say. They may see the picture and be able to identify with it for other reasons. If there's a particular part of the picture which means a great deal to them, try to remember how you felt as you drew that section. Was it a different sensation? Encourage them to say whatever they like about it and let them know you won't be offended.

When you've both explored the drawing as much as possible, then ask your sitter to quietly hold the drawing and look at it, whilst you close down and protect yourself.

You may find you have very few results for the first session or two. The more sceptical you are about your artistic abilities, the more you will block yourself in your attempts. Again, this is an excellent example of needing to let go of your own ego. You may draw nothing except a single line across the page; however, if you know that you didn't consciously draw the line yourself, then you should acknowledge that you've had a result. It doesn't matter what other people may think of it, because you've experienced another level of psychic expression. Risk looking silly and accomplishing very little, and you'll be able to move forward.

When you've had a few sittings with your pencil and pad, you'll then be in a position to try going on to another stage. Now you can try using colours with your auragraphs. Colours add a further dimension in that, with a knowledgeable interpretation, they can become a very expressive addition. Of course, you will need to develop your relationship with colours to a deeper level before you can work powerfully with them, but you can try using colours and see what effect they have on your work.

When you start, it's easiest if you limit yourself to the seven chakra colours. This makes interpretation less confusing. After a while, you can then add others such as gold, silver, pink, brown and black, but try to make it as uncomplicated as possible when you first introduce colours. You can use coloured pencils or pens, paints or chalks; try anything available and see which feels right for you. You may find the feel of a pen isn't comfortable and the flow of a piece of chalk is preferable. Others find a pen solid and comforting and the chalk messy and distracting. Experiment as much as possible. Colour auragraphs work in a slightly different way.

COLOUR AURAGRAPHS

Open up as usual. Ground yourself well. Check you are nicely balanced. Practise sweeping the white light and earth energies through your arms and hands. Ask for help in your work with colours; ask your inner self to help you choose colours and to guide you in your drawing.

Put the pad in front of yourself and have your seven colours laid out in front of you. You don't need to have bright lighting for this work; seeing the colours clearly isn't important because you want your hand to be guided to what is right without you choosing anything yourself. If you work with a candle normally and the lights are dim, that is fine. Continue to do this.

Now you want to increase your energies and consciously connect to your sitter's aura. Breathe comfortably and lift your energies to the solar plexus. Now practise the auric egg of energy that you use with auric readings. Breathe out to your sitter's aura and then pull some of their aura back to you. Keep your energies at your solar plexus. Now ask your inner self to pick up the colour which is appropriate. Don't worry if you pick up the colour you least expected. Hold it over the paper but don't force any movement with it. Let it move across the paper when it wants to do so. It may start to draw and then decide it isn't the right colour. Let that energy sweep down through your arm and hand and focus on keeping the two separate movements in harmony: the auric egg of energy spiralling back and forth between you and your sitter, as well as the energy sweeping through your arm and hand, down into your fingers.

You won't be able to accomplish this all at once. Be patient with yourself and let your development happen gradually. Keep asking for help from above. Don't worry about how much or how little you are using of each colour, or how you are filling the paper. None of this is up to you and you aren't trying to create an artistic masterpiece! Keep trusting in your higher abilities and keep breathing deeply. Keep lifting the energies up to your solar plexus; as soon as you start to draw, they will drop.

Wait until your energies drop completely. You will find your hands put the colours down and return to your lap when you have finished. Remember to have a quick cleanse and to balance yourself, before you study your drawing.

The first time you work with colours, you may have an added surge of understanding as you look at your drawing. The colours can fill in the missing sections that you didn't fully understand before. Colours can be wonderfully expressive in that they seem to actually 'speak' to people, rather like crystals can do for those who resonate well with them. Enjoy your colours. Enjoy the freedom of expression which they offer you. You may find interpretation much easier now. That sweep of yellow will seem to tell you what it means. That patch of blue is so obvious. The red circle is clear. Always remember your responsibility to your sitter as you speak. You may get carried away by the depth of your knowledge and forget your position. Use tact, empathy and appropriate words as you discuss the auragraph with your sitter.

Then show them and encourage their feed-back. Again, you may find that they understand your drawing better than you expect. You may find they love what you have drawn, although to you it may not seem that special. It's also possible you may really like it, only to have their face drop as they look at it! Both reactions are fine and relevant for them. Again, try to leave your ego out of the sitting.

When you feel ready or when your time is up, hand them the picture and ask them to continue looking at it quietly while you close down.

If you now feel you are learning and growing from auragraph work, you need to develop your feelings about colour. Work with your chakras will have helped you a great deal, but if you still feel very uncertain, here is a run-down of some basic colour interpretations:

Red –   the 'root' of you, often referring to your childhood; feelings such as passion or anger; physical strength and vitality for life.

Orange – ambition; sexual energy and emotions; relationships.

Yellow – intellect; clarity of thought; feeling of belonging; willpower and self-purpose.

Green –   loving in a holistic sense; healing and nurturing qualities; feeling of everything being all right.

Blue –   peace; a sense of tranquility; seeker of truth; sensitivity; speech and creativity; communication and meditation.

Purple –   connection to spiritual states; transcending the earthly; respect and sense of leadership; ideals and dream-like conditions of far-seeing knowledge.

White –   purity; a state of divine being; truth; fulfilment; (or Violet) completion; enlightenment.

This is a very basic guide and can only be used as a starting point. Your own feelings about colours should grow and become intensely personal to you. You will gradually want to add all sorts of further colours and express your work even more vividly.

You also need to look at the shapes you draw and develop a relationship with them as well. This will again be a personal experience for you. A circle in your auragraph may have a different meaning for you than for someone else. You may see a circle as completion in an area of your sitter's life; someone else may draw a circle and it will indicate a sensation of going round in circles and getting nowhere in a situation. It's also possible that a circle can mean more than one thing to you and you will interpret it differently for different sitters. This knowledge will come with practice, but you can choose to work on your understanding of shapes by yourself. There's a simple method you can use to do this.

UNDERSTANDING SHAPES

Take a small pad of plain white paper. On each page, draw a different shape in thick, black pen. Apart from the obvious shapes such as a square, triangle, and circle, let your hand do what it likes and draw any shape it wants to. This needs to be simple. Only draw one shape per page and don't let your hand come off the page during each drawing. Simplicity is paramount to help your process. Draw at least ten different shapes.

Now settle yourself comfortably into a relaxed state. You don't have to fully open up unless you particularly want to do so. Choose just one shape and look at it. What is the first thing that comes into your mind? Ask your inner self for confirmation. Keep looking at it, but remember your first impression. After looking at it for a while, close your eyes. You will probably still see the shape in front of you. Go deeper into a meditation and decide what that shape means to you. Repeat this process for all the other shapes but don't try to do them all in one sitting. If there is a shape which you find difficult to work with, then prop it up in an area where your eyes will often fall upon it. Let your thoughts spiral when you have the time. Often insights will come when we are very relaxed and not straining for understanding.

Of course, you could do this with colours as well: using different sheets of coloured paper. However, it's not always easy to create the pure colours on paper. We may see ten different shades of blue, but none of them are quite the sky blue of the throat chakra. Purple and violet can likewise be particularly difficult. Often the colours we create through visualization have a beauty and intensity which we can't describe. Their very richness makes them inspirational. If you can create the colours in your mind already, continue to use that method and let your higher consciousness show you the incandescent beauty of colours.

Auragraphs are a particularly helpful way of learning how to leave yourself behind during psychic work. Once you have experienced drawing something where you know you haven't consciously been interfering, you will truly know what it's like to use your higher senses and trust your inner self. Persevere with this form of psychic development, even if you feel uncomfortable or untalented. It's a very valuable part of the learning process. Once you have let go of your own ego and drawn something, anything, you can acknowledge that your development has reached another level. As so many of our blocks in psychic work are about us stopping our own free flow of energy, this is a good chance for you to let go. So enjoy yourself. Enjoy your new-found sense of freedom and relish your results, no matter how small or large they may be. This is the chance for you to stop judging yourself.

Now we're going to look at yet another area of psychic expression where you can use the movement of rods and/or pendulums to access information from a higher source.

CHAPTER 19

PENDULUMS & DOWSING

If you haven't heard of dowsing before, this is a technique whereby you use rods or pendulums to gain a variety of types of information. By observing the way in which a rod or pendulum moves in your hand, you may be able to pick up a great deal of information. You may be searching for water, oil, gold or energy lines within the Earth; you may want guidance on personal or spiritual matters; you may be trying to find a lost article or person. Dowsing has a wealth of uses, although it's also true to say that some people find it a much more powerful tool than others. Now is your chance to experiment for yourself. Doing this is simple and enjoyable, although you can only learn to be consistently successful with practice.

Let's start by looking at a brief history of dowsing. Its origins are uncertain, although there are carvings on a cave wall in south eastern Algeria that depict what appears to be a person holding a dowsing rod. As these drawings date back approximately 8,000 years, this indicates that dowsing could be an ancient application. In Egyptian mythology, the god Thoth is said to have developed the pendulum, but the Greeks believe their own inventor, Daedalus, to be responsible for its discovery. The earliest known dowser dates back to 3,000 BC: a Chinese adventurer named Yu who is believed to have explored the Grand Canyon area of the U.S.A. and later became Emperor during the Hsia Dynasty. References to dowsing can even be found in the Bible when Moses is commanded to take a rod from the Lord and find water within a rock (Numbers 20:1-12). Although some organized religions found dowsing threatening, in that they perceived it as direct communication with spiritual powers, some skills such as water-divining were so successful, and so necessary for survival, that dowsing survived.

It had an enormous revival in the 1500's and 1600's in Germany, when miners discovered that they could locate veins of metal ore beneath the earth's surface by using forked twigs as divining tools. At Queen Elizabeth I's request, German miners then brought this skill to Britain and assisted British miners in finding lead and zinc ore in Somerset and tin throughout Devon and Cornwall. This form of divining then continued for at least 200 years, although its popularity slowly waned.

Water-divining, however, was still used with a consistently high success rate. Many books from the 1600's onwards document the amazing abilities of famous water-diviners such as the French Baroness Martine de Beausoleil (early 1600's), French herdsman Bathelemy Breton (mid 1700's), and Britain's Benjamin Tompkins, William Stone and John Mullins (late 1800's). Reading about their abilities gives a fascinating insight into this little-understood realm of psychic expression.

Today, there are a number of dowsers (water-diviners and others) who continue to work with a great degree of success, and who have published their experiences and results. Their names and books are too numerous to mention but are easily available from most New Age shops and many libraries. If you want to explore pendulum and dowsing further, reading about people's personal experiences helps cement your understanding of this unusual phenomenon.

So what exactly do you do as a 'dowser'? Although there are several methods people use, we're going to look at just two: pendulums and rods.

Whichever you choose, dowsers seem clear about one aspect of their work. The pendulum or rods are purely tools that they use to accentuate or magnify their responses to certain situations. In other words, the rods and pendulums do not possess any magical power on their own; rather they are a means through which the dowser amplifies and clarifies his personal response.

Dowsing never works exactly the same way for any two people. Just as two psychometrists will have different responses to the same object, and no psychic will draw the same auragraph as another, so each dowser develops his own method of working. Dowsing is a way of learning more about yourself and learning to recognize what you respond best to. For instance, dowsers who have success finding energy lines (also known as ley lines) across the Earth's surface may not have the same degree of success if they were to dowse for water or oil. They only learn where their abilities lie through practice and patience.

You also have to experiment to see what sort of pendulum or rod works best for you, just as you need to choose your own crystal with care, or work out if you prefer chalks or pens for drawing. Choosing your dowsing tool needn't involve great expense or be very time-consuming.

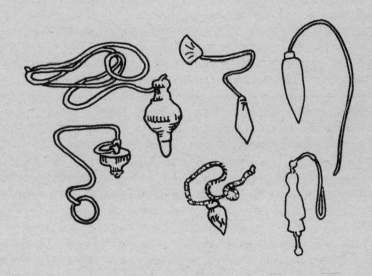

Different types of Pendulums

Let's start by looking at how you can construct a simple pendulum. Almost anything can be used, within reason. If you look at the diagram above, you will see examples of different pendulums. They can be a variety of shapes, colours, textures and sizes. To begin with, you can make yours as basic as you like. Cut a length of strong thread or fine string that is at least ten inches in length. Now you need to find a suitable object to act as your pendulum. Try choosing from any of the following: a curtain ring, a cork, a spool of thread, a lump of plasticine moulded into a point, a small piece of stone, wood, metal or glass. Do you prefer the feel of wood or glass? Where possible, use something that you actually like. This makes your connection with the pendulum even stronger. Ideally, you want an object that comes to some sort of a point as this makes interpretation easier when you start to work with it. Don't choose a long or thin item such as a pencil as this will make things more difficult for you; you need an object that can be held in neutral balance when suspended from a piece of string. Don't choose anything that is too large or too heavy, but it can be any colour, texture or substance. Now you need to attach it to your piece of thread or string. If there is nothing through which you can thread it, try using a piece of Blue Tack to do this, or a drop of glue. You will have to experiment to see how long you want the string to be, but somewhere between seven and ten inches is a good guide. Once your make-shift pendulum is constructed, you can start experimenting.

THE PENDULUM

Firstly, sit in your comfortable space and hold your pendulum up by taking the end of the string between your thumb and first finger. Use whichever hand feels most comfortable for you; it doesn't matter which one. Hold the pendulum away from your body, keeping a distance of at least twelve inches. With your other hand gently steady the pendulum until it isn't swinging but just hangs, straight and still. Move your free hand away once you have done that.

Now focus upon that immobile pendulum and ask it quietly to start moving for you. You don't have to say it out loud: using your thought process alone is just as powerful. At this stage, don't expect a particular type of movement. It doesn't matter if it swings back and forth or side to side, or goes around in circles, clockwise or anti-clockwise. Just wait until it starts moving. If you are relaxed and open, it will start to happen quite quickly. If you're worried or uncertain, it might take you a few sessions before it happens. Wait until it is moving in a discernible pattern (it will be one of the four mentioned above) and acknowledge that the pendulum is moving without your apparent intervention. This means that your hand and fingers appear perfectly still. In fact, your whole body should feel relaxed but unmoving.

Thank the pendulum for the movement and then ask it to please change its movement and show you something else. You may find it gradually goes into some indecipherable pattern before settling into another recognizable rhythm. Thank the pendulum and then request another movement. Keep doing this until the pendulum has demonstrated all four patterns. This may take a few minutes. At this stage, neither you nor your pendulum will be feeling very sure of themselves. You have to slowly build up a relationship to this new object before it will respond quickly and easily. Once all the movements have been shown, gently ask the pendulum to stop swinging altogether. If it doesn't do so after a minute or so, stop it with your other hand.

When it is still, decide that you would like the pendulum to swing in a certain manner, i.e. a clockwise circle. Politely ask it to do this. If it swings into another pattern, gently stop it again and repeat the process. You need to show that you are in control. Once it has moved into the rhythm you asked, then still the pendulum once more and request a further pattern. Do this until you have persuaded the pendulum to move in all directions, at your request. This may take several attempts but that is normal.

Now, as the pendulum has limited movement and can't 'speak' as such, you need to determine what its movements mean. You will be asking it questions that require a 'yes' or 'no' answer, so you need to know which movement means which. To work this out, take a large sheet of paper and write 'yes' very clearly in one corner and 'no' in the other. Now pick up your pendulum again and hold it over the word 'yes'. Use your other hand to still it in the beginning, then take your free hand away and let the pendulum *quietly rest over the word. You may want to ask the pendulum to let you know what is a 'yes' response or you may want to say nothing. After a while, the pendulum should start to move. It may be hesitant and it may take a good minute or so before it settles into an obvious pattern. Don't rush the process. Once you know the pattern which means 'yes', then move over to the word 'no' and repeat the procedure.*

Once you have done that, you need to test the yes and no responses. Choose a very simple question that can only have a positive response, such as 'Am I wearing a blue shirt now?' or 'Am I sitting down now?' Check whether your pendulum moves into the correct response pattern. Then choose an equally simple negative response and check what happens. If the movements aren't as you expected, go back to the piece of paper and start again.

When you are clear about 'yes' and 'no', there is another response that is used, although not all dowsers need it. This is called the 'neutral' position. It is often easier to get quick responses when the pendulum is already swinging, rather than to get it to stop in between each question and answer. If you want the pendulum to swing in limbo, as it were, then you need to determine which is the neutral position. So you need to write 'neutral' on a piece of paper and ask the pendulum to show you this movement. If nothing happens and the pendulum remains completely still, then you know that your neutral position is when it stops. On the other hand, your pendulum may offer you a neutral, moving position to which it will swing back between questions. You won't know this unless you check it via the 'neutral' test.

When you know your yes, no and neutral movements, then you can try asking your first question. This can now be a question to which you don't know the answer, although it must only require a negative or positive response. Phrase your question carefully. It's important that, as you ask the question, you aren't already determining in your own mind what the answer should be, or what you would like it to be. This is again where you have to leave your own self behind. You have to accept that your infinitesimal reflexes are affecting the pendulum swing, so you are responsible for the movement. It's only through accessing your higher mind, that you will get a true response. Anyone can learn how to make the pendulum move any way they want it to. This won't make dowsing a powerful tool. Practise letting your own thoughts go as you ask the question. If you prefer to be fully opened up before you try it, that is fine. You may just wish to stand under your white light and feel yourself as empty and free-flowing as possible. You may want to consciously ask your higher self for guidance.

Ask the pendulum no more than two or three questions on your first attempt. Then cleanse yourself and the pendulum under your waterfall. Make sure you feel free of any unpleasant sensations and make sure you are well grounded again afterwards.

Did you find it easy or difficult to make the pendulum move? Some people find that their pendulum actually swings wildly almost as soon as they touch it. It feels as though it is actually speaking to them. It's an odd sensation, to see a pendulum twirling quickly in somebody's seemingly still hand. However, it's important that you realize that no trickery is involved. It's not magical in any sense, although it can seem that way. Your impulses are creating the movement. To be certain of this, you can place your pendulum on a door handle or suspend it from a bookshelf. Then ask it to move. No matter how patient you are, it's almost certain that nothing will happen. It's good for you to do this, to fully know you are the perpetrator of the movement, because sometimes it's so hard to remember it.

A few people find it impossible to make the pendulum move at all. They can hold it for ten minutes at a stretch and the pendulum remains still and lifeless; no matter how much they concentrate, it won't respond it any way. If you are one of these people, it doesn't mean anything is wrong with you. It simply means dowsing isn't a powerful form of psychic expression for you. That's why you needn't buy a pendulum to begin with. If dowsing is good for your energies, you will be able to make any home-made pendulum work for you. If you really feel an affinity with dowsing, then you can gradually acquire more sophisticated pendulums. Again, it is only a tool with which you work.

The most expensive and beautiful pendulum in the world means nothing unless your own energies are compatible with it.

Provided you had some sort of response with the pendulum, you can now try a further form of dowsing, using rods. Even if you had little reaction with pendulum work, you could try the rods. It may be that they are a more powerful tool for you. The feeling of using rods is very different from holding a pendulum.

RODS

Firstly, you need to make your own pair of rods. Again, this can be simple and inexpensive. Two wire coat hangers would be ideal. If you look at the diagrams opposite, you can see that all you need to do is cut a length from each coat hanger and then gently bend the shorter length out, so that it rests at right angles. Wrap some tape or tissues and tape around the sharp edges on the shorter length, as this is where you'll be holding the rods.

Now look at how you need to hold them by studying the diagram opposite. You don't need to grasp the rods firmly; the more relaxed and comfortable you feel, the better your results. Hold them gently in each hand and keep your arms body-width apart. Make sure your shoulders feel heavy and relaxed. You need to keep each long arm of each rod in a horizontal position, as this is the equivalent of the 'neutral' position you were reading about with pendulums. That neutral position is important because the rods will be most susceptible to your responses whilst they are in that position. Just as in pendulum dowsing, so your rods will be moving through tiny, imperceptible movements in your hands and wrists. You won't necessarily feel or see these movements, but they will activate the rods.

To get used to your rods, start by gently rotating your wrists in clockwise and anticlockwise movements. Note how the rods respond. If you twist both your wrists inwards, then the rods cross each other. If you move your wrists outwards, the rods move apart. Now tilt your rods up slightly and notice what little control you have over them. Tilt them down and notice what happens.

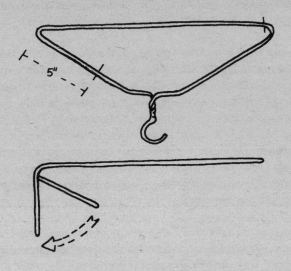

5"

Making Rods

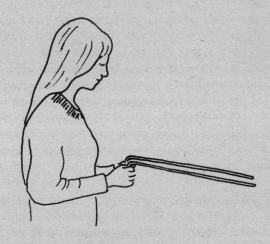

Holding Rods

You can see why that horizontal position is important to maintain control.

Now you have seen how you can move the rods, take them back to their neutral position. Without seeming to try, ask them to move in a certain direction, say to the right. Focus on the tips of the long rods and watch as they gently move. Now ask that they move back to the centre. Then ask them to move to the right. Then back to the centre. Now ask them to cross over. Then get them to uncross themselves. Do you feel that you are actually moving them? If you do, don't worry. If you keep practising, at some point you will feel that they are moving of their own accord. When this happens, the movement becomes more fluid.

After you have practised the movement of your rods and feel comfortable with them, you can then try walking around your home or garden with them. You might prefer to do this when you're on your own if you feel self-conscious. Remember to start with your rods in their neutral position and walk slowly and smoothly. Your rods will jump if you slip on the edge of a carpet or round a corner too quickly, so try to keep your own movement as fluid as possible. At some point, your rods will probably move into a crossed position. This may happen very quickly and unnerve you with its speed. This crossed position means you have encountered something. It may be a water pipe, electricity wire, gas pipe, or even a flow of energy. Initially, you won't know which but it doesn't matter. This is all experimentation and you are just trying to get a response without limiting yourself. You could try going to an area that you know will have a water pipe, like the kitchen or bathroom. Do the rods respond then? Try the approach to a gas stove or a radiator. Is there any movement then? Don't worry that the rods respond to some and not others. Just acknowledge that you are getting a response.

After a few turns around the garden and house, you can decide if you would like to be more specific. If you want to practise further, you can now focus on one thing only. Decide if you want to find water, gas, electricity, energy or whatever. Then spend a few minutes concentrating on your chosen material. You may wish to open up properly and meditate for a few moments on the substance you want to find. What is its smell? How do you visualize its shape? How does the thought of it make you feel?

Now return to your rods and hold them in their neutral position. Again reiterate what you want them to hunt for. Say it to yourself, or say it out loud if you prefer. Keep your mind focused on the material. Try not to let other thoughts and images come into your mind. Now slowly make your way through the house or garden. What sort of response do you get now? Is the movement more definite, more sudden? Depending upon what substance you chose to look for, you may not be able to validate your findings. However, if you communicate with your inner self, you will know whether the reactions you are getting are true or false. Notice how strong a response you got in a certain area and then move towards an area where you know that material can be found. For instance, if you were looking for water pipes, move towards the kitchen or bathroom taps. Do you get exactly the same reaction? Remember you need to keep your own thoughts out of the experience as much as possible.If you start to think 'I'm sure there should be a pipe near here', then you are letting yourself interfere and stopping the energy flow.

Don't spend too long a time on your first experiment. Your arms will probably get tired and the longer you work, the more they will probably twitch or ache. Then it's harder to stay relaxed and focused.

When you've finished, make sure you cleanse yourself and the rods under your waterfall of white light and energy. Let go of any uncomfortable feelings or emotions. Close down well and ground yourself again.

Once you have made your pendulum and dowsing rods, and if you plan to use them again, make sure you keep them in a safe and suitable place. Keep them dry, preferably in a dark place, out of direct sunlight. Just as a workman keeps his tools in good order, so you want to treat your own psychic tools with respect and affection. After several sessions, you can decide whether you want to continue using the tools you have made, or move on to others.

Dowsing or divining is often done with forked twigs, traditionally of hazel. Apple, willow, hawthorn, cherry, and dogwood are also popular. However, there is no hard rule about what you use. Some dowsers swear by copper rods, others by a piece of bone. The shape is important because you want something that will respond to your lightest and slightest movement. Once you have developed a relationship with whatever you use, there are many ways in which you can dowse. The pendulum can be used in a variety of ways for advice and guidance.

Many healers and holistic doctors use pendulums as a means of determining which area needs healing or which remedy is best for a patient. For instance, if you want to offer a person some healing and want a method to show you which area could best benefit from your attention, you could ask your patient to lie flat and then hold the pendulum over each chakra. Ask whether that chakra needs healing. Watch your pendulum's response over each area. Again, you have to ensure you leave your own conscious thought out because it's your inner self who needs to guide you. Of course, some of you may feel you do that already in healing without using a penduluum. That is fine; it doesn't matter which method you use, provided you feel comfortable with your choice. Often holistic doctors take a patient's details and then dowse over a selection of remedies to see which would work best for them.

Dowsing is also used in an environmental way to assist general health. Over the years, in areas where persistent health problems have occurred, dowsers have worked to understand the cause and exact location of environmental hazards which have been affecting health. One of the greatest dangers is known to come from radon, a radioactive gaseous chemical element that is formed from radium. Experienced dowsers can use their skills to determine the presence of harmful substances such as radon. They are often able to pinpoint the exact location where penetration is taking place into the home. The leakages can then be stopped quickly and safely.

Many of you may already have heard of ley lines, or lines of energy that have been charted around and above the earth in a variety of patterns. Initially, there was scepticism about their existence but continued research and its findings has led to a tremendous interest and belief in their power. Dowsers are also known to be able to trace these energy lines and advise home owners accordingly as to their influence.

Many sacred sites and monuments have been known to respond in specific ways to dowsing techniques. A clue to their unique formations and powers may lie in their direct relation to ley lines and water lines within a given area.

This study can then become part of Geomancy, which is a system of divination used to delve into the ancient secrets of our planet Earth. Geomancy works on two levels, although they are complementary: oracular, which is about predictions, and locational, which refers to positive and negative places within our landscape. Geomancy messages are received through forming distinct patterns. There is a group of sixteen different figures, each composed of dots. Each figure has a name and universal meaning, although each figure can react to another and can therefore affect interpretation. By studying patterns of earth and astrological formations, mysteries and secrets of the earth are said to unfold. People are also said to gain higher understanding by asking soul-searching questions whilst they draw a series of dots. These dots are then reformed into a specific series of patterns, from which a reading can be taken. Again, there are a number of books now available on the subject of geomancy and, again, they make fascinating reading.

However, to return to the specifics of dowsing. If you have developed an interest in this form of divination but want to be able to test your own accuracy with your pendulum or rods, then you could try a simple experiment. Ask someone you know to hide something anywhere in your house. Choose a small object such as a pen or stone. When they have done so, start working with your rods or pendulum to see if you can locate it. If you're using the rods, then walk very slowly around the house, remembering to focus on the object. Your concentration is an important factor in your success. Although dowsing doesn't have to be done under the strict tuition of psychic development, it becomes more powerful if you are disciplined. If you want to use your pendulum for this experiment, then you need to start asking simple questions, such as 'Is the object upstairs?' Narrow the questions gradually and give your pendulum plenty of time to answer. Again, stay focused on the image of what you what and let your other thoughts go as much as possible. Try this experiment at different times with a variety of objects and other people to get a clear idea of your success rate.

Some dowsers use their pendulum in a whole host of ways through their day. They dowse to decide which item of clothing to put on, which perfume and jewellery to wear, what breakfast to eat, how many vitamins to swallow that morning, what form of transport is best to use, which food to buy at the supermarket, who they should see that day, whether to have a cup of tea or coffee, if it's going to rain or not... In other words, it can become an obsession, particularly if you feel you work well with a pendulum. By all means use it for guidance but, as in all forms of psychic expression, none of it should be taken to excess.

You can't maintain a healthy, holistic balance if you rely solely on one item to guide you through life. The pendulum is an expression of the inner 'you' but you can, and should, use other means of discovering yourself, too. Remember, we can't be healthy unless everything within us is balanced. Just as eating nothing but carrots all day isn't healthy (no matter how nutritionally sound carrots are), so using nothing but a pendulum or rods in psychic development isn't healthy either (no matter how useful they are for you). Make sure you embrace other experiments as well, such as the 'tools' suggested in the forthcoming chapters.

The next area we're going to study is crystal balls and their ability to act as a channel through which you can receive a variety of types of information.

CHAPTER 20

CRYSTAL BALLS

What is your first thought when you think of a crystal ball reading? Does it conjure up images of a foreign accent, a mop of dark hair swathed in a scarf and heavy incense – all in a tiny booth at the end of a pier? So many people can't help but view crystal ball work in this light. Unfortunately, there are plenty of examples of the above scenario, so one can understand how the reputation of crystal balls has fallen into such decline. The truth is that using a crystal ball is intended to be yet another means of mind expansion and spiritual growth. Again, the ball has no direct powers of its own; it is dependent upon the person who uses it. It's a means of focusing your mind through intense and prolonged concentration.

Crystal ball reading, also known as 'scrying', has been around in a variety of forms for centuries. People haven't always used a crystal ball; they have used other methods as well. Babylonians put liquid into sacred bowls, the Hindus used a bowl of molasses, the Egyptians favoured a pool of ink in their hands and the Greeks lowered mirrors into holy waters. Others have used a still, dark pool of water or black stones such as coal or jet. Wet slabs of slate have also been used as a sort of mirror. In fact, the possibilities are endless: the flame of a candle or burning embers, a glass of dark red wine – even a wetted fingernail! This demonstrates that the object itself is not the bearer of the power; the power lies in whichever object a person finds to be a valuable source of focus and concentration for them.

There have been famous 'scryers' throughout history. John Dee, scientist and astrologer to Queen Elizabeth I, is known to have used crystal balls and mirrors during his work. However, the most famous, without doubt, is Nostradamus (1503-66). Many people know of his famous and uncannily accurate predictions of future world events; however, not that many know that the method he used to 'see' into the future was a form of scrying.

Nostradamus filled a brass bowl with water, placed it upon a brass tripod and then gazed into it. By meditating for lengthy periods at a time, he received his extraordinary insights which have since become world-famous and have been analysed and verified by historians throughout the years. The transcripts of Nostradamus's predictions are fascinating and thought-provoking. They are also complicated and controversial in content, making it difficult to make literal comparisons to present world conditions. Some scholars have claimed that not all of Nostradamus's predictions came true; this leads some to say he was inaccurate, whilst others would argue that this simply indicates that no future event is set in stone and that fate can be shifted and altered by people's consciousness. Whatever people may say, there is no doubt that Nostradamus was able to tap into a great world of higher consciousness through gazing into his brass bowl filled with water.

Of course, it wasn't as simple as sitting over a bowl of water and suddenly being able to see a host of events swimming beneath you in the water. Whatever object you use, whether it be a mirror, water or crystal, does not actually hold these images within it. You project the images yourself, using the object as a means of focus. In other words, your scrying tool is used like a key that helps unlock your subconscious and lead you to higher awareness. To work as Nostradamus did, the degree of concentration has to be enormous and can't be obtained quickly. It's important that you don't see a crystal ball as a bearer of information. It is your friend and your support; your relationship with it will grow according to how you treat it and learn to work with it.

It's interesting to learn that all forms of early scrying took place amidst a series of complex rituals. The scrying itself was only obtained after a lengthy period of initiation. This makes sense when you consider that unless you have great powers of concentration, you'll be unlikely to receive much information. These complicated preparatory rituals took the form of prayers and fasting. It's no coincidence that today psychics use meditation as their form of prayers and, although they may not fast, most are fastidious about not eating a large meal before working. These beliefs are not recent; they are steeped in tradition which is born from understanding on a higher level.

Apart from fasting and praying, a 'lamen' was also an important element of scrying. This is a circular table which is usually engraved with ornate symbols and pictures. The lamen then stands within a 'magic circle'. This circle is engraved with mystical names and spiritual images, all designed for protection and spiritual enhancement. The scryer wore protective talismans and stones, showing great respect for the powers of spiritual work and acknowledging both the good and bad influences within it. Although some psychics still use a lamen and magic circle today, much of the respect and appreciation with crystal ball work has dwindled over the years. It can be likened to some people referring to the chakras as though they were no more than a pimple on the skin's surface. As in all levels of psychic work, the depths at which it is possible to work are literally limitless. Only we as humans limit those possibilities. The greater our knowledge and consequent sensitivity, the more we can accomplish.

It may help you, as you practise early forms of scrying, to know that you are looking at an ancient art of focusing your mind and attaining higher consciousness. You have, hopefully, been continuing with your meditations each day and remembering not to eat heavy meals before working. So, you, too, are adhering to your own rituals in your process of psychic and spiritual growth. There is no reason why you shouldn't also find crystal balls helpful: interesting at the very least, deeply inspirational at the most.

To start with, try the exercise below which costs nothing and can give you a good indication of whether scrying may work for you.

WATER SCRYING
Find a bowl that is no more than five inches in diameter. Preferably it should be made of clear glass, although that's not essential. Fill it three-quarters full of tepid or room-temperature water. Choose a table that is at a comfortable height whereby you can sit and gaze

into the bowl of water. Now place a dark cloth over that table. If you have black velvet that would be ideal but any very dark colour will suffice. Place the bowl of water on top of your dark cloth.

Lighting is very important during scrying work. You don't want bright sunlight. The softer the lighting, the more it will help you. Candlelight is often a popular choice. Whatever you choose, you want to create as few reflections as possible within the bowl itself, as that will distract your sense of focus. You'll have to experiment with this to get it right. Move the lighting around and keep checking your bowl of water. When it is as free from other lights and reflections as possible, then you are ready.

Sit down in front of your bowl of water and go through your usual opening-up process. Ground yourself and make sure you are well-balanced. Take a few deep breaths and ask your inner self for guidance in this new field. Ask for protection from unwanted influences during your session. Let the white light flush through you several times. Wait until you're ready before you open your eyes. Now lean forward and gaze down into your bowl of water. You don't need consciously to raise your own energies to a specific level with crystal ball work, but you do need to maintain the free flow of white light and earth energies through you.

When you feel tired or uninspired during your gazing, don't look away. Just keep breathing and letting the energies flow comfortably. You don't need to stare hard into the bowl. Just keep a soft gaze focused on the water and let any thoughts and worries float off into the distance. See nothing but the bowl of water in front of you and feel nothing but the softness of your breath as it nourishes and relaxes your body. It doesn't matter how long you sit there. There is no time limit for this exercise. Some people see nothing for a long time.

If you do start to experience anything, the first stage is usually to see a sort of swirling mist. It's a milky shade and can often look like wisps of cloud. Even this form of visualization can take a high level of concentration, so don't feel discouraged if you see nothing. It *may take several sessions before anything happens for you. Remember to ask your inner self for some help. If you do see this twirling fog, that may be as far as you can progress for a while.*

When you do move forward after that, the water will then appear to become completely black. It's only after that stage, that visions and images will present themselves within the water. It's unlikely you'll progress to that level on your first attempt. If you should and you receive unpleasant or disturbing images, cleanse through with the white light. Also feel the white light cleansing the bowl of water. Ask your inner self for protection.

As concentration on any new form of work is difficult, you may also find that your back or neck starts to ache quite quickly; next time try a different table or chair. It takes a few sessions before you learn what is comfortable for your body. You'll also find that reflections somehow seem to creep into the water and distract your focus. It's possible that you may just find yourself thinking that you're staring into a bowl of water and that you're feeling very bored and tired. Any scryer could feel that way on their first attempt. It's the perseverance that creates the difference.

When you feel you have progressed as much as you can for that session, sit back from your bowl and have a good cleanse. Especially notice if your body is aching from having held it in an unfamiliar position and remember to direct the white light to that spot. You may want to use the Energy and Breath Exercise on page 147, where you transfer your energy from your solar plexus to the aching spot using your fingers. Make sure you stand under the waterfall for as long as you need. Then close down and protect yourself. Put an extra mantle of protection around yourself, in case you have unwittingly attracted any unwanted influences.

When you are grounded again, make sure you rinse the bowl out and wash it thoroughly in hot, soapy water.

Some of you may have been pleasantly surprised by what happened to you. Although many won't have experienced the milky fog or seen the water go black, it's possible to find scrying useful in a meditative way. You may have found yourself suddenly receiving a new insight. You might have had a flash of some memory that unlocked another door into the subconscious. You may just have been still for a long time, contemplating an issue in life which you hadn't looked at before. You may be surprised how quickly earth time passes when you're scrying. A few of you will have experienced nothing. Then no doubt time will have seemed to drag by and you will have noticed every twinge in every muscle as you were sitting there. You'll have felt rather odd or silly throughout the experiment and you'll have ended up telling yourself that scrying with water or crystal balls definitely does nothing for you. You'll have been glad to tip the water down the sink at the end!

Before you completely dismiss this form of psychic expression, and for those of you who feel scrying could be powerful, given time and practice, there is a method you can use to help you start visualizing objects within the water or ball. If you really want to work further but can't seem to see anything yet, you could try the following exercise. It's important that you realize this is only an exercise to help your progress, as opposed to being a psychic experience.

TRANSFERRING OBJECTS IN SCRYING

You again need your small bowl of tepid water. Place it on your dark cloth and sit comfortably. Try a different chair or table this time to help yourself relax more. Try another form of lighting. Perhaps a low wattage pearl bulb suits you better than candlelight. Check you have eradicated any reflections before you start.

You don't have to open up for this exercise, but you need to be relaxed and grounded. Check that you are both. Pay attention to your breathing for a minute or two and feel it caressing the inside of you, relaxing you more and more with each breath you take. When you feel ready, open your eyes.

Now focus your gaze on an object within your space. Make it something with which you feel compatible. As this should be happening within your own personal space, hopefully every object will come into that category. Choose something reasonably small in size, such as a picture frame or stone, but make sure the light is bright enough for you to see the object and its shape and colour quite clearly. Stare at it for at least one minute. Don't let your look waver; focus on that object so that you are aware of nothing else. After at least a minute of staring, close your eyes and turn back to your bowl of water. Know that as you open your eyes, you will see that object within the water.

Open your eyes and look into the bowl. Can you see the object? If you can't, repeat the process, but choose another item and this time take longer staring at it. Do you see the object within the water now? It may take a few attempts before it happens but it can often be a useful reinforcement in the early stages of scrying.

Do remember that this is you using your ability to create imagery, as opposed to psychic development. Both are equally valid, but you should acknowledge the very different sensation between psychic work and doing a physical exercise. The item you choose to transfer to the water is also important. You'll only know through experimenting which items work best. Often they are the brightest in colour and most definite in shape. Just ensure it's an object which creates a loving reaction in you. The happier you feel about the object you use, the easier it will be to make the exercise work.

If you have enjoyed the two scrying experiences, then you may wish to move on to using a crystal ball. You may find the ball is a more powerful tool for you than the water. Of course, some prefer water, but you need to try both before you will know.

Crystal balls come in a wealth of sizes and substances. The most expensive are the beryl or quartz; it's said they have the most powerful influence because of their molecular structure. However, their cost makes them prohibitive to many people, to say nothing of the fact that it isn't necessary as a beginner to have that sort of crystal ball. Start off gently and slowly with any new field of psychic work because you will probably be surprised where it will eventually lead you. You could end up with a little used but very costly crystal ball that lies at the back of your closet.

You could start with a small glass ball, or even an acrylic (plastic) one. Scrying balls are becoming more and more easily available on the market today. Whilst their accessibility is a bonus, it makes your work more difficult because you somehow have to choose which ball is right for you. Don't look at cost and decide the most expensive glass or acrylic ball has to be the best one. Don't look at the largest in the cabinet and believe that is the most suitable. Let your intuition and inner self guide you. Don't rush your decision either. If the shop is a reputable one, they will leave you alone while you choose and not try to influence you. Ask if you may hold one in your hand. Feel its energy. Then try another. Which feels right to you? If nothing feels right, don't be pressured into buying one. You may need to find another shop or maybe you just need to wait a while before purchasing a ball. Perhaps you aren't yet ready for its energies.

When you find the right one, you will know it. The ball will seem to leap out at you from the others and you won't even doubt that it is meant to be with you. When you take it home, you should respect its presence in your life by some small ceremony. You don't have to tell anyone you're doing this, if it feels odd, but all you are doing is honouring an ancient tradition. This isn't to say that you need to purchase a lamen and then draw a magic circle. However, you need to create a bond with your new tool. After all, it is hopefully going to become your gateway into your higher consciousness. The more compatible your energies are together, the better the work you will do.

So find a little quiet time when you can be alone. Unwrap your crystal ball (the shop owner should already have told you to keep it wrapped and out of bright sunlight at all times). It would be best if you have a small length of black velvet in which to wrap the ball. At least ensure the wrapping is dark in colour and soft in texture.

Firstly, you need to cleanse your ball. You know from psychometry and studying crystals how susceptible objects are to energies around them. If your ball has been sitting in a shop for a lengthy period of time, it may have picked up all sorts of influences from a variety of people. As has already been mentioned, psychic work can also attract a large number of unbalanced souls. You can cleanse your ball by creating your white light and placing your ball in the midst of it; you may wish to use your waterfall and place it under that. Some people believe moonlight to be a great cleanser, but if you choose that method, make sure it isn't left out to become affected by the sunlight. Sunlight and crystal balls are not compatible.

Once you have cleansed the ball, place your hands gently around its aura. Does it feel fresh? Does it feel clean in the psychic sense? If you are in doubt, repeat the cleansing process. Make sure you feel happy with it before you continue.

Now you could have a small ceremony with your ball. How you do this is a personal matter, but you might want to light a purifying incense, or use a cleansing aromatherapy oil in your space such as peppermint, pine, eucalyptus or sage. You might want to put on a favourite piece of music. Dim the lights; use candles if you want. Sit comfortably with your ball in front of you or resting lightly in your hands. Ask your inner self to bless your new acquisition. Ask that you be helped to treat it with respect and love. Say any sort of prayer that feels right for you. Use any meditation that seems appropriate to imbue your ball with your love and light. You might wish to actually perform some healing on it or to place it within a green or golden circle of light. There isn't a right or wrong way to do any of this, provided each thought and action is coming from a state of love and respect.

When you have finished your ceremony, make sure you wrap your ball well in its soft, dark cloth and place it safely out of sight, in a dark location with a moderate temperature. Extreme cold or heat is unhealthy. Let no one else touch your ball or look into it. This is your tool.

Only after you have performed your little ceremony, are you ready to try working with your ball. It will probably take a lot of practice before you are able to see a great deal within your ball, but the more often you can sit down with it, the more you will increase the energies between you. Working with your crystal ball is similar to water scrying, although you can gradually learn to be more specific as the number of images increase within your ball.

BALL READING

As with water scrying, you need to have a dark background for your crystal ball. You may choose to spread a black cloth on your lap and then hold your ball in both hands. You might prefer to put the cloth on the table and let the ball rest on that, without touching it. Try both to see which feels best for you. When you have a comfortable position, then you need to open up in your own time. Ground and balance yourself. Concentrate on your breathing and feel the white light pouring through you. Pull the earth energies up through your feet and feel those energies meeting the white light at the top of your head. Bless the ball in front of you and ask your inner self for help in your new field of work. Make sure that you feel the energies flowing freely through your body before you open your eyes.

Now gaze deep into your ball. Focus so that the ball is everything you see; it becomes your entire universe and you know that everything you need to know is contained within its core. Remember to keep breathing deeply; often as you concentrate, your breathing returns to shallow levels. Don't take your eyes from the ball. Stay there looking into it for as long as you can. You may find the amazing depths of a ball make visualization easier than with the bowl of water.

If you are still finding it difficult, you could try focusing on one particular question or scenario about which you'd like to know more. Being specific about something can often help create that extra level of concentration that can lead to a breakthrough.

You may see the swirling fog more quickly now and then see the ball go completely black. Then the images will start, slowly, to come through. Occasionally, you may find them moving at speed, rather as though they were sequences in a film. In the beginning, your images within the ball need interpretation, just as the images in your head during other psychic work also have to be explained. By now, you will have developed a degree of understanding about your own personal method of working. There are a few general rules with ball work that may initially help you.

The left-hand side of your ball, as you look at it, will usually indicate day-to-day life and what is happening now. Often you may get actual scenes or objects within this area that directly relate to the present situation.

What you see on the right-hand side of the ball is more likely to be symbolic. This area may require more experience and intuition before you fully understand what you are seeing. The images may also be less clear.

The front of the ball tends to show the immediate future, and the back refers to either the remote past or the distant future. Again, knowing which is which comes with a deeper contact with your inner self and developing your 'knowing' skills.

You will probably see colours within your ball and they can also be interpreted. Below is a very rough guide as to what they may mean, although you are encouraged to develop your own relationship with colours and make them work for you on a personal level.

Red: caution, possible danger or illness
Orange: a material or spiritual loss
Yellow: betrayal and deceit
Green: joy, love
Blue: happiness, laughter and respect
Violet: hidden abilities and awareness, joy

You will notice that some of these colours indicate worry or illness. When you use the ball with a sitter, always, always remember your phraseology and think before you speak. It's also true that for you the colour yellow may become synonymous with something completely different such as the chakra emotions of self-purpose, will-power and mental awareness.

Once you have practised a few times with the ball and once you have found that the energies flow well, then you can try having a sitter with you. Make sure they don't touch the ball in any way and again be clear about the fact that you may not receive much information. If you feel that you are having little success, you could always offer them an auric reading or psychometry instead.

Always remember to cleanse properly after every session. When you have finished closing down and protecting yourself, carefully wipe your ball clean with the cloth and then wrap it and place it away safely.

With crystal ball work, you will encounter the area of fortune-telling in a much stronger light. People will expect you to discuss their future and make predictions. They are likely to ask the usual questions about whether they will marry, change jobs or have children. Dealing with this area requires a certain tact and a definite honesty. It's suggested you put it something like this:

'Although I may see possibilities of future events during my work, I must also stress that no one can predict anyone's future with absolute certainty. The reason is because each person has their own free will. Even if it is ordained somewhere on a higher plane that you do a certain something in your life, you actually have the choice to change any pattern at any time. People do it constantly. So although I might say there is a possibility of something happening, it is the way you behave and react that determines whether it will happen or not.'

Your sitter may want to question that further and it may lead to a discussion for several minutes, but it's important that you don't mislead anyone. Possibilities are not the same as certainties. Never offer false hopes; never predict upsetting outcomes. Neither are set in stone.

This same rule applies for the next area we're going to look at: the Tarot cards.

CHAPTER 21

THE TAROT CARDS

The using of cards for divination purposes (cartomancy) has become an increasingly popular practice during the twentieth century. Of all the cards available, Tarot are certainly the best known and most commonly used. It has become more complicated during the last thirty years because an enormous influx of new Tarot cards has come onto the market, making choice extremely difficult. We'll look at the different types of packs that are available a little later.

Have you ever seen a Tarot card or studied one? Most of us have seen or used Tarot cards at some time during our life. Some people have a negative reaction because of their strong images; others immediately identify with them and want to know more. Dependent upon your response, Tarot can be another very powerful tool in psychic development. The detailed and thought-provoking visual images are capable of opening your mind into the realms of higher consciousness. They are often described as the gateway to the soul or a means of uniting the body and soul. As with every psychic tool, some people respond more favourably than others.

The uncertainty concerning their origins only adds to the Tarot's innate sense of the mystical. There are so many theories about the beginnings of Tarot. Some believe they originated from ancient Egypt through the writings of a mystic, Hermes Trismegistus. However, there are also very strong links connecting Tarot and the Cabbala, a form of ancient divination accessed through the Hebrew alphabet. Tarot is also said to have come from the Romany gypsies who spread their knowledge in their journeys from North Africa to Europe; the Hungarian gypsy word 'Tar' means card. Others pose theories involving Tantra (an Indian spiritual movement), medieval Celtic traditions, masters of Atlantis, or Chaldean astrological beliefs. It's also known that, during the Middle Ages, involvement in any form of non-religious meditation or spiritual belief was dangerous; it's thought that the Tarot was a safer way to allow divine knowledge to be passed on, as words were not necessary. As no one knows the truth for certain, one can relate the deeply mystical power of the Tarot to almost any field of spiritual enlightenment. Of course, this is also what makes the Tarot so intriguing.

What is not disputed is the earliest known Tarot in existence. These date back to 1392 but only seventeen remain from the full deck. To find the first full pack of Tarot one has to go forward to Italy in the 1420s. An Italian artist, Bonifacio Bembo, was commissioned by the Visconti family of Milan to paint a complete set of Tarot. They were a wedding gift for the marriage between the Sforza and Visconti families.

Today, the Tarot consists of 78 cards. Each card is called an 'arcanum' which translates as 'mystery' or 'secret'. The pack of cards consists of two parts: the 22 trump cards known as the Major Arcana and a set of four suits called the Minor Arcana.

The Major Arcana is a series of strong pictorial images, each given an individual name and number. Generally, they are said to symbolize the journey of a soul from its birth to enlightenment. Many see the distinctive Fool at the inception and follow through to the final arcanum depicting The World. Each of these 22 cards is intended to be a meditative tool to unlock the subconscious and awaken a deep understanding about different aspects of life. Look briefly at the names of these cards:

Fool, Magician, High Priestess, Empress, Emperor, Pope, Lovers, Chariot, Justice, Hermit, Wheel of Fortune, Strength, Hanged Man, Death, Temperance, Devil, Tower, Star, Moon, Sun, Judgement and The World.

Don't some of the words on their own make your thoughts spiral onto other levels? When used in conjunction with vivid images, it's easy to see how Tarot becomes a powerful tool.

Originally, the Major Arcana were considered the most important part of Tarot, and their meanings and significance were relied upon almost exclusively in readings. For those who become adept with the Major Arcana, the cards of the Minor Arcana offer the opportunity to refine readings and enhance accuracy.

The Minor Arcana consists of four suits of fourteen cards each: ace through to ten, and four court cards of Page, Knight, Queen and King. The four suits are:

Swords
Cups
Wands (also called batons, staves, rods or flames)
Pentacles (also called rings, coins or stones)

These suits have more recently been linked to the four elements of medieval philosophy and modern astrology: fire, water, air and earth.

Although opinion is sometimes divided, generally the suits are attributed as follows:

Swords – Air
Cups – Water
Wands – Fire
Pentacles – Earth

As these Minor Arcana have grown in interpretation and pictorial images, so they have become an even more enlightening tool to aid higher knowledge.

Reading Tarot can be taken at three different levels. On the first level, a reader could quote from a book and take a literal meaning for each card that is shown. On the second, the reader could study each card and see how it relates to the sitter's life; the relation of one card to another may be significant and both psychological and physical events can be drawn on. The third level is that of the psychic, where Tarot can be used as a tool to help trigger insights and achieve higher consciousness. Many people use a combination of all three levels.

The choice of different Tarot sets available makes it difficult for a beginner. The Rider Waite is still the best known and most frequently used of all the packs and it's certainly a good place to start. However, your Tarot cards become as individual and personal an experience as any other form of psychic expression. Therefore, if you are interested in Tarot and want to choose a pack, take plenty of time to make your decision.

Ask friends and relatives if they know anyone who has a set and would let you at least look through them. Alternatively, visit a New Age Shop and you will no doubt find a wealth to choose from. Here's just a small selection: Renaissance, Medicine Woman, Chinese, Egyptian Gypsies, Arthurian, Cat People, Ibis, Hermetic, Orishas (African), Kalevala (Finnish), Native American, Art Nouveau, Angel and St. Petersburg (Russian). There are literally dozens of others. Many shops have a book in which the different packs are laid out for you to peruse. Take your time and really study the different cards. If you stare at a pack and you feel nothing, then it's unlikely to be a good tool for you. If you have a passion for Native American or Russian history, you may find those sets really help your thought processes. Perhaps your ancestors were Chinese or African, or perhaps you have always had a strong affinity with cats or angels. Use your own present state to determine how to move forward. As always, let your intuition guide you. Some Tarot packs can be very disturbing to certain people; make sure you study all the cards in a deck. If you find the Death or the Hanged Man particularly distressing, choose another pack which feels better to you.

When you take your Tarot cards home, you again want to perform your small ceremony to acknowledge their new presence in your life. Use what feels right for you: light a candle or incense, cleanse the pack, imbue it in whatever way feels good with your love and healing. Ask that the pack be blessed and that it helps guide you on your path. Remember to always include a thorough cleansing; you don't know who may have handled them before you purchased them. As with your crystal ball, take good care of your cards. Handle them with respect and care; don't let them become bent or torn. Keep them out of strong sunlight and when not in use, wrap them in something soft and dark and place them in a cool, dark environment. If possible, avoid damp or very dry surroundings. Each sitter will eventually handle your cards during a reading, so you need to remember to keep cleansng the pack after each session.

Before you have your first sitting, however, you need to do some work on your own with the cards. Tarot card sets usually come with their own small leaflet, which loosely describes each card's meaning. Although often shallow in its interpretation, it's a starting point. Study each card individually; memorize the brief interpretation of each. This may take you a while, as you have seventy-eight cards to peruse.

Working with Tarot is not something that can be rushed, so you will need particular patience and perseverance with this form of psychic work. Once you have a cursory understanding of each arcana, then you may choose to find a more detailed book on the Tarot. You may want to learn from a Tarot reader who you may already know. There are also Tarot societies you can contact for further details. As with every psychic society, make sure you feel comfortable with the people and their energies before you affiliate yourself to any one group.

Most importantly, you also need to have quiet meditation time with each card. You may not need to consciously open up when you do this; if the Tarot pack you have chosen is a good tool for you, you may find that almost as soon as you look at a card, it seems to speak to you. Some people feel themselves transported inside the card, as though they too were part of the scene. Others find their thoughts spiralling without personal involvement in the image. It becomes a very individual experience and no one way is right or wrong. All that matters is that you feel comfortable with your own pack and find them inspiring. If your first impressions are positive with the Tarot, then you have the chance to start on a long, exciting journey of ever-deepening discovery. It won't happen swiftly, but it will happen if you continually practice.

Some cards will naturally be more difficult for you to penetrate. This may be because of a feeling of unease or fear regarding such strong images as the Devil, Hanged Man or Death. Others may not disturb you but will seem elusive in quality. Wherever you feel a block, you have to work gently to break through that barrier. Choose to consciously open up and tune in to the card which you find harder to work with. Ask for help from above. Look to yourself to understand why there may be a block. Is it because it seems to represent an area of your own life which is not being fulfilled? Is it because you are tapping into an unpleasant memory when you look at the card? Does it remind you of something which upsets or angers you? Let the process of getting to know your cards be a gradual and pleasant one.

You can also prop a card up in an obvious spot and look at it during the day. You don't need to stare at it under those circumstances; just let your glance fall upon it while you carry out your daily tasks. Then let your subconscious mind continue to work after you have consciously forgotten it. Depending upon other members in your household, you could place several around the house in different areas: by the bathroom sink, near the kettle, on your desk, on top of the television set. You may choose to have your cards for months, or even a year, before you feel you know enough about them to work with them on a practical level. You needn't be in any rush to do anything other than study their images and learn from them.

When you feel you do have a reasonable depth of understanding about your Tarot and you are ready to progress to another level, then you can try doing a 'spread' for yourself. This is how you use the cards for a deeper interpretation of the situation. There are literally hundreds of different spreads; the booklet you got with the cards may have demonstrated several. However, to start with, you may find one called the Chakra Spread to be useful. It's simple in design and because you have now done quite a bit of work on the chakras, it may help your confidence to start at this level.

The spread is easy to do: after shuffling, you turn one card over in front of you. Then turn the next one over and place it directly above the first. You continue until you have seven cards pointing in a direct line away from you. The first card represents the Base, the second is the Navel, the third is the Solar Plexus and so on through to the Crown, which will be the furthest away from you. You should by now have a good relationship with the seven chakras, but if you need a quick guide for reference, then you can use this:

1 – *Present physical and material conditions*

2 – *Sexuality, creative potential and relationships*

3 – *Sense of self and will-power*

4 – *Love and harmony, universal love*

5 – *Communication*

6 – *Psychic awareness and visualization skills*

7 – *Spiritual beliefs and sense of 'knowing'*

You can start by practising a spread on yourself, before you have your first sitter. Many people use Tarot for their own spiritual development as well as others.

TAROT READING
You need to be in your own comfortable space with a clean, bare area in front of you. You may want a table in front of you, or you may prefer to sit on the floor. It doesn't matter which you choose, as long as you are relaxed and focused. Make sure the light is bright enough for you to see the cards clearly and to read from a book if you are still using one, but not so harsh that it distracts your concentration. Place the Tarot cards in front of you.

Now open up in your own time. Go through the usual balancing and grounding techniques. Spend a few minutes concentrating on your breathing at the end. Make sure the white light is flushing through you easily and you have used the earth energies to balance you. Include the Tarot pack in front of you in the white light so that it feels part of you and your circle of light. Connect with your inner self and ask for guidance.

Pick up the Tarot cards when you feel ready. Bless them and thank them for their presence. Now concentrate on a particular focus that you would like to look at in your life. Make it a simple question for your first attempt. You might want to make it an appropriate question such as 'Am I ready for my first sitter with the Tarot?' You might prefer to ask a personal question relating to another area of your life. Form the question clearly in your mind; the more specific you are in your request, the clearer the answer will come. Remain focused on the question and slowly shuffle the cards. Keep shuffling, keeping the question in your mind all the time. Try to focus only on that thought and the cards. When you feel ready, stop shuffling. Don't rearrange the cards after that point. You have stopped there because it was the right place. Turn the top card over and then the following six, to make the Chakra Spread.

You may now choose to consciously lift your energies up to your heart chakra and use that level to help your work. You may find it more helpful to keep all the energies flowing through you, without differentiating between levels. Experiment and see which works best for you.

Start with the first card. What does that mean to you? You might want to look at a book's definition or you may not need to if you have been studying enough already. Look deeply into the card. What is the image saying to you? How does it relate to your present, physical life? Where does that fit into your question? How is it guiding or advising you? Take as long as you like. Then move on to the second one and study it as thoroughly, relating it to your own sexuality and relationships with others. Work your way through all seven, relating them to the chakras. You may want to stop and focus on your own relevant chakra; you may even choose to place the card against the energy centre if it feels powerful. Always remember to cleanse if you pick up anything unpleasant or distressing. Keep asking your inner self for further understanding.

When you have studied all seven individually, then look at them as a collective whole. How does one card relate to the other? Do the first and seventh cards mean something to you when considered together? You may suddenly see a connection between your third and fifth chakras; any combination could lead to a further insight. Keep studying them. If you find yourself drawn back to one card in particular, then really concentrate on the image. Let it speak to you and clarify your question. Keep trusting your intuition and letting it take over.

You may find the Tarot so powerful that you quite quickly feel your mind spiralling onto other levels, guiding you effortlessly into higher awareness. You may know without having to search; the answers may come easily. If you reach a block, then close your eyes briefly and feel the white light washing through you, rejuvenating and refreshing you. Then turn back to your cards and study them again.

When you feel you have gleaned as much as you can from your session, cleanse thoroughly. Remember to include the Tarot in your cleansing process. Then close down and protect yourself well. Wrap that protective cloak around you and feel safe and secure. Take a few quiet minutes to further consider what you have learned from your session. Thank your personal divinity for their guidance and love. Thank the Tarot for being such a helpful tool in your spiritual development. Cleanse again if you wish, then open your eyes. Wrap your cards up in their soft, dark cloth and put them away. Don't leave them out to pick up other energies.

A word of warning about Tarot reading for yourself. Although it may be a useful tool for your own growth, if you use it constantly for your own purposes, it will diminish your psychic abilities to work on other levels. It's like any form of psychic development. Your gift should be shared and used to help others, as well as yourself. By all means, let yourself become familiar with the cards and their meanings by practising alone. However, after a while, you should know when you are ready to work with a sitter. You can listen to your own inner self and realize that the time has come for you to work with others and develop your skills. (As always, this means in an unpaid, voluntary capacity at this stage.) Also, whilst you may get to know yourself much better through Tarot readings, you need the outside influence of others to increase your awareness.

For instance, you may get to know after a few sessions on your own, that when the Lovers card is turned over, it is referring to a specific situation within your own life; the Star, Moon and Sun may also come to have personal and individual meaning for you. However, to expand awareness with your cards, you need to see how they relate to other people. You won't be growing and developing yourself or your abilities unless you bring other people into the equation. So when you know that you have learned enough of the basics to be of value to your sitter, then arrange to share the Tarot.

You will know through practice which spread you want to use. They will vary according to your sitter. Your intuition will guide you as you progress and you may find yourself creating your own spreads that mean a great deal to you. Their shapes may enhance your own psychic abilities. You may find a lot of the ones you read about in books are unsuitable for your method of working. In the beginning, try to make the spread as simple as you can. The Chakra Spread is a good basic start. You may even want to make it more simple and use a spread of three cards, representing the past, present and future. Or you may want to have your sitters choose four and look at what is going on in the four seasons coming up. Don't be afraid to experiment during your early stages and ask your sitter to bear with you through your learning.

Ask your sitter to choose one question to which they would like an answer. Encourage them to make it specific. It needn't be an actual question, of course. It may be a situation which they would like clarified. Just make sure that whatever the area is, they know precisely what it is they want to gain information about. Then ask them to shuffle the cards and think about the question. Don't let them talk during this process. You want them to be as clear and focused as they can be. Tell them to keep shuffling the cards until they want to stop. Then ask them to hand the pack to you.

When you have your first Tarot card sitting, again make sure you explain what is happening so that your sitter is made to feel as comfortable and relaxed as possible. You may discover that they find the Tarot images disturbing; it's your duty to put them at ease. Often if an image such as Death or the Devil is turned over, people may assume the worst. It's extremely important that, before you start the session, you explain the level on which you are working. Explain something like this:

> *The Tarot cards are only a tool that I use to help expand my own awareness of things. They shouldn't be taken literally. For example, if you choose a Death or Hanged Man card, it doesn't mean death is imminent for you or for anybody around you. All the cards are symbolic and meant to be taken on a deeper level. Death, for instance, might mean you have finished one area of your life and are now ready to move on to another new, exciting phase. It can mean a positive influence. Obviously, it's up to me to interpret the cards in the most helpful way possible and that's what I shall try to do.*

Don't ever skip this phase of explaining, even if your sitter says they have had a Tarot reading before. They may not have had it explained to them then or they may have only turned over the less unnerving images on that occasion. Also, always re-iterate what you have learned about predictions for the future, as detailed in the previous chapter, so that they are clear about future patterns changing at any time. Never assume that your sitter knows anything about psychic matters. You know how important it is to consider their well-being and to nurture them as much as possible; never under-estimate how powerful the Tarot can be.

Also, never be tempted to use your Tarot cards in a jokey or irreverent fashion. If you're having a few friends over for drinks, don't be coerced into having a session with the cards when you're under any alcoholic or drug influence. If someone wants to have a laugh over a situation and use the cards for mischievous purposes, always refuse. It doesn't matter if you are seen as a spoil-sport or a stick-in-the-mud. You may be the only person present who fully understands the power and purpose of Tarot. If you use it for less than noble purposes, you are running the risk of calling up all sorts of unpleasant influences and spirits that it can then be extremely difficult to release again.

Never let children see or handle your Tarot cards either. Tarot is an adult tool. Subjecting children to those images could be very distressing and unbalancing for them. Children have enough to contend with if they are allowed to see daily news bulletins, often showing them nothing but the negative aspects of humanity. Dealing with pictorial images that open up a gateway into higher consciousness is dangerous for them; they aren't ready to handle the responsibility until they reach adulthood. Some people never feel comfortable with Tarot cards, irrespective of their age. If you're one of those people, that's fine. It doesn't mean all symbolic images will disagree with you.

You may find the Runes a more gentle and thought-provoking tool.

CHAPTER 22

THE RUNES

The Runes are another form of ancient divination, although they are not as well known as the Tarot cards. The Tarot are more immediately accessible in some ways as their images are so vivid. The Runes are a much more subtle, more elusive form of psychic expression. Whilst the modern-day set of Tarot consists of 78 cards, the modern-day Runes set is composed of 24 different symbols. Instead of cards, these symbols are most often etched or painted onto small, round pebbles. There are usually 25 in a full set, because a completely blank rune is often included.

If you look at page 337, you'll see a set of these Runes, together with a brief name or meaning which is attributed to each. Take a few minutes to look at them. Do you find it difficult to see beyond the obvious, i.e. that some look like the letters B or M or maybe one looks like a fish and another an anchor? These are often people's first impressions. Our understanding of their true significance is buried so deeply within our inner selves that it takes time and discipline to see beyond our initial reaction.

The Runes are much more complex than they first seem and each has to be studied individually over a period of time to develop an understanding and relationship with it. Many believe the Runes can define patterns of divine consciousness and can reveal secrets of the universe that are held deep within the symbols. Of course, it may seem unlikely, as you stare at a squiggle on a stone, that it could end up meaning a great deal. That is why study is needed. As with the Tarot, there are books on the Runes that give a fairly detailed interpretation of each symbol; as with the Tarot, they can only be the gateway into higher consciousness. You have to do some work for yourself.

The origins of the Runes are not certain, rather like the Tarot, but there is plenty of evidence of Runic symbols and letters that have been used in one form or another since the third century BC. The Runes are also called the 'Alphabet of Honorius' and have evolved through the centuries via a combination of Bronze Age carvings, Greek and Latin Letters and the Germanic runic alphabet. One can trace it back even further if you heed ancestral folklore, which talks of an ancient tribe who came from the Far North with the last great Ice Age, before 10,000 BC. They were said to have direct memory of the timeless secrets of the Runes and to have passed them on to the newer tribes. One early piece of known evidence is a bronze helmet, inscribed with text that can be likened to Runic symbols. The helmet has been dated as being from the third century BC. There have been countless examples of these ancient symbols on a variety of objects since: on rocks, stones, weapons, goblets, amulets, rings, brooches, Viking ships and monuments. These discoveries have been made in various places: Greenland, Iceland, Britain, Italy, and Scandinavia, to name but a few.

There is a well-known tale in Norse mythology that decrees the Runes to be a gift from the god, Odin. (You may remember from Chapter 3, that Reichenbach, during his research in the 1800's on energy forms, chose to call his understanding of energy the odic force, after the god Odin). Odin is said to have hung for nine days and nights upon the World Tree whereupon he became dizzy and fell. However, as he fell, he saw the Runes and quickly grabbed them. Odin is then described as being reborn with great wisdom and well-being.

It is unlikely anyone will ever know the Runes' true origins and perhaps that is exactly as it should be. They are intended as a source of inspiration, a means of delving into the mysteries of the higher consciousness. There is no doubt that they have been used in a variety of ways and for a number of purposes for centuries. Ancient tribes relied upon them for guidance in their daily life. Wise men and women (known as Rune Masters and Mistresses) were highly revered within their own societies and would regularly be called upon to cast the Runes

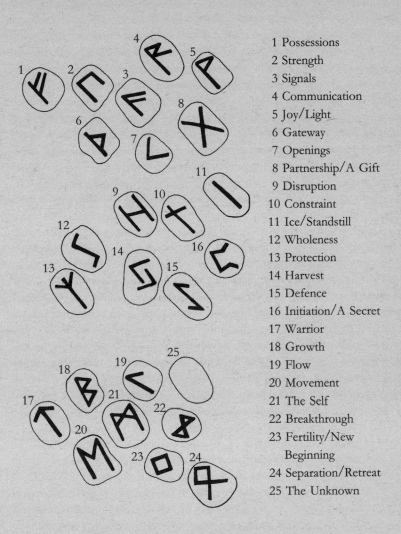

1 Possessions
2 Strength
3 Signals
4 Communication
5 Joy/Light
6 Gateway
7 Openings
8 Partnership/A Gift
9 Disruption
10 Constraint
11 Ice/Standstill
12 Wholeness
13 Protection
14 Harvest
15 Defence
16 Initiation/A Secret
17 Warrior
18 Growth
19 Flow
20 Movement
21 The Self
22 Breakthrough
23 Fertility/New
   Beginning
24 Separation/Retreat
25 The Unknown

The Runes

and thus determine the best action to take in a given situation. This might be in relation to a child's birth, wherein they would ask questions regarding its name and life-path. They would seek guidance for crop planting and how to choose the best locations to ensure the highest yields. They would ask for approval from gods and deities. They used it to assist people passing over to the other side. Seasonal festivals were often accompanied by Rune readings. They were seen as a tool which would help ward off evil and promote health and fertility among their people. Healing was also done via the Runes; they were used as a means of accessing higher consciousness in order to remember the most effective remedies for a particular injury or illness.

It might at this stage be difficult to see how a group of stones with a few markings on them could possibly offer such insights, but you need to remember that the Runes are again only a tool to help minds into higher spheres. Once you gain a deeper connection with the symbols, you can understand how they relate to universal energies, the solar, stellar and planetary systems, the four seasons, the winds and the deities. Each rune is also assigned a mnemonic rune-sound, which is basically a method of uttering a sound and meditating upon it to unlock the key to the prophetic mysteries within that particular Rune. The Runes symbolize a unity, a harmony on a level with which few people resonate in our modern world. In both Celtic and Germanic languages, the word rune translates as a 'mystery' or 'holy secret' that is 'whispered'. You will have to do your own work to start you on your path of Runic discovery. Try the following exercise to begin with:

RUNIC AWARENESS

Choose one of the runes on page 337. Draw a large replica of it on a separate piece of paper and write the word under it with which it is associated. Then close your eyes and sit comfortably. You needn't open up fully if you don't wish to do so, but spend a few minutes focusing on your breath and feeling it relax you. Let the white light wash through you and remember to ground yourself.

Now open your eyes and look at your symbol. What is the first thing you think of? Now think again. What else does it signify to you? Keep gazing at the shape, letting it become hazy in front of your eyes, but don't lift your gaze from the page. How does that shape relate to the world as a whole? What else could it symbolize? (You'll have to do some work at this stage. Insights may not come easily in the beginning.) Refuse to give up. If you've chosen the straight line which is 'Ice', for instance, what does a straight line signify in life? When is it positive? When can it be seen as a negative influence? What do the beginning and end of the line make you feel? Why? You need to really focus to enable your mind to work on higher levels. You will block yourself if you refuse to concentrate. Use the exercise as a test for your endurance. Don't let your mind wander. There are two ends to the 'Ice' line. What else has two ends to it?

Think of the word you have been given with the symbol. In the case of 'ice', what does it mean to you? You may have the obvious thought of cold or rigid, but keep thinking. What are the uses of ice? When is it essential? When is ice a pleasure? Why do you have to live in a world with ice? What other forms can ice take and what happens when it does? What has to happen before ice melts? Keep thinking. Keep expanding on the possibilities of the word.

When you feel ready, withdraw yourself from the word and symbol. See it disappearing off into the far distance. Sit there for a minute, contemplating what you have learned from the symbol. Does it mean more than you first thought? How can you relate it to your own life and what is happening to you at the present?

Now remember that you are sitting in your favourite space and that it's time to return to your present day. Cleanse and close down. Balance yourself. Protect yourself well and wait a minute or two before you open your eyes again.

Did you discover something new from your exercise? If you refuse to give up, if you continue to concentrate no matter how little you are feeling, that patience will be rewarded. Greater awareness doesn't occur over night, but once you open the doors it can start to come into you. Then the more you focus, the more you can absorb. Try meditating on each Rune, one by one, over a period of time. You needn't buy the

Runes at this stage, if you don't want to. You can draw them yourself (see the examples on page 337) and increase your awareness that way.

If, after some work, you feel you want to purchase your own set of Runes, then there are plenty available on the market. Traditionally, as previously mentioned, they are made of pebbles and painted either black or red. There are also more inexpensive sets available, often made of oblong plastic.

You could also make your own, of course, by taking a walk along an area such as a pebbly beach and choosing a set of stones. If you want to do this, make sure you are permitted to take the stones from the beach and make sure it feels right as you pick up the pebbles. Hold them in your hand and feel their energy. Do they feel good? Is it right to take the stones from their natural environment? You also need twenty-five pebbles of very similar shape and size. Otherwise, you may unconsciously learn the shape of certain stones and draw upon them in a reading by touch rather than intuition.

However you acquire your Runes, you again should perform a small ceremony with them. Put on your favourite music, light the incense and candle, and spend a little time with your new psychic tool. Most Runes are kept in a soft, dark-coloured pouch and drawn from that bag as and when they are needed. Keep the Runes and pouch in good condition. Handle the Runes yourself and get to know each one. Especially if they are made of round pebbles, touching them alone is a wonderful experience. Run your finger tip along the symbol. Remember there are chakras in your fingertips. What do they say to you? Don't encourage others to touch them and don't allow others, such as children or animals, to play with them. Cleanse them when you first bring them into your environment and then remember to cleanse them again after your sitters have touched them.

Runes can be used as a spiritual tool for yourself, before you share them with others. Use that time as an initiation for the Runes and as an opportunity to learn more about yourself. As with Tarot, there are many spreads used in the Runes, although now it is described as 'casting'. When you choose your Rune it's important that you place it down on the table without fiddling with it. However it is placed, that's the right way for it to be. Don't turn the Rune the other way because you think it looks better. Some symbols have a reversed meaning. If you've placed it down and the surface is blank, then turn it over. It will either remain blank because you've drawn the blank Rune, or a symbol will be there. Again, don't turn it another way. Leave it as it is. Now you interpret what is there.

Once you have bought a set of Runes, you will have a booklet to help your interpretation, but you may choose to purchase a separate, more complete book as well. There are quite a few on the market but make sure you look through them thoroughly. Choose the book which inspires you the most and whose interpretations you find the most thought-provoking. The books will demonstrate different ways of casting the Runes, although you can simply draw upon one Rune if you wish and then meditate upon it. To get a fuller picture, you could choose to use a simple three-rune casting.

This involves drawing out three Runes, one by one, and placing them in a row in front of you, from left to right. They are then read as follows:

Left (1st) – *the situation as it stands at present*

Middle (2nd) – *the action you need to take*

Right (3rd) – *the final outcome*

When you feel ready, try a full reading as follows:

RUNE READING
Place your bag of Runes in front of you. Close your eyes and go through your opening-up and tuning-in techniques. Ground yourself. Check that you are balanced. Draw the white light and the earth energies into and through you. Say a prayer to ask your inner self for guidance. Bless the Runes and give thanks for their presence in your life.

Now you can choose to lift the energies up to your solar plexus or just let the white light wash through you. Try both and see which produces better results.

Now think of a simple question to ask the Runes. Focus on it for a minute, then pick up your bag and dip one hand into it, without looking at any of the Runes themselves. Let the Runes slip through your fingers as they move around in the bag. Don't rush the process. Keep your eyes closed if you like and simply enjoy the sensation of the soft, smooth pebbles. When one pebble seems to jump into your hands or tingle as you touch it or feel different in some way, then withdraw it from the pouch and place it in front of you. Repeat the process until you have three pebbles lying from left to right in front of you.

Now you have to interpret them. Start with the one on the left, which is the present situation. You may either have a book you want to consult, or you may want to focus and use your higher consciousness to interpret what it means. Remember to keep relating it to the present situation regarding your question. Then repeat the process again with the middle Rune and see how it relates to the action you could take. Lastly, study the third Rune and try to access information about the final outcome. Don't worry if it doesn't seem to make sense. Trying to work with the Runes in a literal sense isn't always inspirational. Keep delving below the surface of what you are reading or seeing; in other words, let your mind spiral higher and higher during the reading. You may find yourself responding to your question in a way that is completely contrary to anything you have considered before. It may initially seem puzzling to you, particularly if insights come in the forms of symbols or patterns of evolutionary behaviour about which you presently know very little. Take what you do know and work with it; then store away any further information that you receive but can't understand and look at it later. You may want to write down any phrases or insights if you are worried about remembering them. Keep a pad and pencil by your Runes for this purpose.

When you feel you have gleaned as much information as you can, close your eyes again and go through your closing down-process. Protect yourself properly and check that you feel well grounded. Remember to include the Runes in the cleansing process and remember to say a small prayer to thank your personal 'god' and the Runes for their assistance. Don't open your eyes until you feel ready to do so.

If you find your first few attempts rather confusing and frustrating, in that you find it difficult to relate the Rune to the question, don't worry over it. This is quite usual. The Runes really are a tool that only work well after considerable time and study. However, they are also a tool that you can come back to whenever you feel ready. Sometimes we try to use them too soon in our development and they leave us feeling inadequate. Wherever you find yourself in your learning process, be gentle and encouraging.

The Runes are also a wonderful opportunity to learn more about the universe. Some of the insights you receive may relate to planetary or stellar systems about which you know little. Try reading more about the world and how it operates. You need to combine literal knowledge with an innate sense of higher consciousness. This usually develops as a gradual merging of beliefs that doubles your own understanding. You can start that process of understanding your world and the people better by taking the practical steps of learning more about the physical way in which we operate. Some of the facts you've read about through these chapters may already have given you food for thought but the more you learn about our world, the more fantastic and inspirational it becomes. Consider a few facts below:

The sun is over a million times bigger than the planet Earth.

The Sahara Desert constantly increases in size by over four million acres each year.

Silk from a spider's web is stronger than any steel thread of the same thickness.

The population of planet Earth is growing by approximately 250,000 people per day.

Swifts (birds) can stay in the air for two to three years at a time without landing.

The sun is just one star amongst another one hundred billion stars in the Milky Way.

Some of those facts may seem quite unbelievable, but then the more you learn, the more you realize you don't know. Learning about the Earth and its relationship to the universe is a wonderful, mind-expanding tool. The more you resonate with universal understanding and knowledge, the more you will be able to tap into the Runes' divine secrets. Whether or not you find the Runes to be inspirational in your psychic development, the fact that they may encourage you to expand your knowledge of the world will serve you well in your spiritual growth.

When you decide that you would like to have your first sitting with the Runes, it's helpful if you explain to your sitter that the Runes are a more philosophical and elusive form of psychic work. This may appeal to some people; others will find it threatening if they don't understand the interpretations. It may make them feel inferior. If you want to use the Runes on a regular basis, you need to find a way of speaking your insights that is easily accessible to people. It's always important that you phrase your words carefully and clearly, but Rune divination requires an extra degree of awareness. You will learn through practice what is the most helpful way to phrase statements about the Rune symbols.

Always have your sitter ask the question while they hold the bag of Runes. Then let them dip their hand into the bag and concentrate on the question as they pull out the required number of stones. Explain to them that they shouldn't turn them around after they have placed them in front of you. When you give a Rune sitting, you may find it more powerful to lift your energies to your solar plexus area. Runes (as well as the Tarot and crystal ball) can be kick-started into action by using your abilities in auric reading. After a few moments, your focus on the

Runes or whatever will take you away from your sitter's aura, but it can be a good confidence tool in your early stages.

Now we're going to look at an area where you can combine a physical knowledge with psychic development: palmistry.

CHAPTER 23

PALMISTRY

Palmistry differs somewhat from the other elements of psychic development which you have so far been looking at and practising. In all the other forms of psychic expression when you used a tool for additional help, you were using an abstract tool, whether it was a flower, crystal, card, stone or ball. That tool had to be interpreted and used in a variety of ways to increase your levels of awareness. There were no set rules about how to do this and it became a very personal experience of discovery.

Palmistry is in another sphere because it relies on a tried and tested means of physical evidence for its information, i.e. formations within a hand. However, where it becomes a powerful psychic tool is when you add your psychic skills to that already established information, and can then offer a much more detailed and thought-provoking reading. A good palmist will combine literal information with higher consciousness. However, it's also true that not all palmists who have set themselves up in business are using their psychic abilities during work. In this chapter, we'll look at how you can tell the difference and ways in which you can develop palmistry as part of your own psychic and spiritual growth.

Palmistry is yet another form of ancient divination whose roots are uncertain. It's certainly true that many cave walls across our Earth are decorated with ochre-painted handprints. Chinese scripts and Indian texts dating back some 3,000 years refer to man's fate being within the shape and patterns of his hand. Aristotle, in a letter to Alexander the Great, discusses his thoughts on hand-reading, gleaned from earlier Egyptian works. Ancient Rome housed many hand-diviners. The Old

Testament states 'God sealeth up the hand of every man; that all men may know his work' (Job 37:7). Later, various books in Latin, Greek, Hebrew, German, and then English talked about the information contained within the palm. It's also thought that wandering gypsies were again responsible for much of the spread of palmistry and its meanings. In Britain, there is evidence that palmistry may date back as far as the Druids, as it's known that they used a form of communication called Finger Ogam. This was a sort of mute speech that was made possible by reference to the palm and certain patterns within it. It was said to be their way of passing on divine messages of cosmic consciousness.

Palmistry is also very much related to astrology. Areas of the palm are designated as mounts which are then named after various planets. For instance, the wedding ring finger is aligned with Apollo, the Sun God. Gold is the metal of the sun and it's said that the ring is placed there because a line of energy runs from that finger direct to the heart.

Some people believe that the palm contains each person's life history: past, present and future. Therefore, some would say that the mysteries of the universe are contained within every person's hand. Remember our Hologram Theory? If the whole of us is contained in every bit of us, does it not make sense that the hand, when touched and studied, will reveal all the information we need to know?

Palmistry is an intricate and complex art. The more you study the physical basics of what each part of the hand contains, the more there is to know. Virtually every line and shape within each hand is relevant and can be interpreted. What you'll study here is a very condensed version that doesn't do justice to the complete technique. However, hopefully it will give you food for thought and whet your appetite for further study.

Start by studying your own pair of hands. Hold them up in front of you. Are your fingers naturally spread wide? This indicates a generous, open person, but you may let opportunity slip through your fingers sometimes. If you've kept your fingers close together, this would show that you are reserved in nature and not particularly confident. Remember, it's your first, spontaneous gesture that you should read.

Now look at your fingers. Are they long and pointed or short and stubby? Have at look at the different fingers shown on page 351. Are yours square, conic, spatulate or pointed? This also tells you something about yourself.

Square: practical, reliable, realistic

Conic: talkative, likeable, imaginative, impulsive

Spatulate: energetic, individualistic, inventive

Pointed: artistic, intuitive, impractical, restless

If your fingers are pointed but your palm itself is square, then this would show a combination of both traits. Each finger also relates to different parts of your personality.

The index finger (Jupiter) is about your self-expression and confidence. If this finger is longer than your ring finger, then you are an extrovert who enjoys holding court. A very short index finger could indicate an inferiority complex.

The middle finger (Saturn) shows your attitude towards responsibility. If it's particularly long, it would suggest that you have a lot of responsibilities and burdens in life. If this finger is short it indicates that you can be irresponsible.

The ring finger (Sun) is about your creativity and success. A long finger points to being a lover of life and excitement. A shorter finger shows that you will not necessarily use your creativity.

The little finger (Mercury) is about communication. A long finger here demonstrates an intelligent and expressive person. A short finger may indicate difficulties in self-expression.

The thumb is often considered the most revealing of fingers. It's about your will-power and your powers of logic. If the spread between your thumb and rest of your fingers is particularly wide, this may show a craving for freedom and a degree of selfishness. A very closed thumb indicates that you're tight with money and reserved in emotion. If your thumb is very large in relation to your whole hand, it may mean a great deal of self-control and strong sense of morals. A small thumb would show you are easily influenced by others.

The above all mention short and long fingers only. If your own fingers are reasonably proportionate in length, then you can conclude that your abilities are reasonably balanced. However, the fingers are also read by looking at the three separate sections or phalanges of each finger. Each relates to different areas and the varying lengths of each is significant. Whether joints are knotty or smooth is also important. In other words, the whole picture becomes more complicated, although there isn't room for full details here. This is just to give you a taste of what can be gleaned.

Now look at the palms of both your hands. How different are the markings within each? Most people have a wide variation between left and right. Each palm has a different story to tell. If you are right-handed, then it is said that your left hand shows what you have been born with and your right hand shows what you are doing with your talents in this lifetime. If you are left-handed, the reverse is considered true.

The palms themselves are a myriad of lines and shapes which can take years to study properly. Let's look at a brief description of a few major lines. You can refer to the diagram on page 353 to clarify which line you are studying.

The life line starts somewhere between the thumb and index finger and curves down in a sweep around the thumb joint. It refers specifically to your physical health and longevity in this lifetime. A strong, clear line which has a wide sweep and is unbroken shows a robust constitution. A broken line indicates some illness or accident. (Remember, it is not your duty to tell a sitter details like that. You need to phrase it in a way that is gentle, such as 'You may need to pay more attention to your health in your later life and remember to slow down, rather than keep pushing yourself.') Marks such as chains or little island-like circles also indicate areas when your health may be in question and when you need to be gentle with yourself. People often anxiously scan their life line to see how long they will live, assuming that unless their line curves right round their thumb and down to the wrist, that they will die young. Most people don't realize that the age of seventy is indicated a good inch above your wrist. Little lines crossing through your life line show worries in your life; an upward swing indicates a healthy response to the situation.

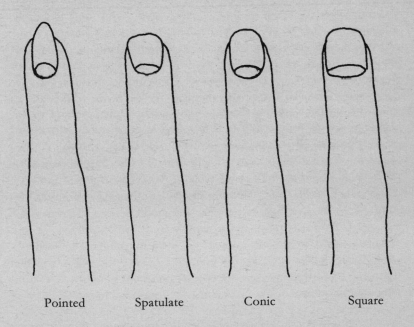

Pointed   Spatulate   Conic   Square

Fingers

The second line is the head line and runs, very roughly, from between your thumb and index finger across the middle of your palm. As the life line was about the physical, so the head line is about the mental. A strong, clean line will indicate an astute intellect. If it is straight, you will be good at concentration and will be very logical and practical in your outlook. A head line that slopes will show that you use your intuitive sense in a constructive way. Many men have a straight head line and many women have a sloping line, perhaps confirming a general difference between the sexes! If the line is wavy, faint, forked or broken, it suggests indecision and possible mental confusion. This doesn't mean a mental breakdown; it may simply indicate a time of confusion in your life.

The third line is the heart line and this deals with your emotional sphere. This starts from about the middle of your first (Jupiter) finger and runs across your palm, above and roughly parallel to, your head line. Many people are particularly fascinated by the heart line as it says a great deal about our capacity for love, and how we treat others. The more chained or criss-crossed the line is, the more difficulty we experience in love and relationships. A number of people don't appear to have a separate heart and head line; they seem fused into one. This shows someone who is intently focused and relentlessly practical but refuses to let emotions into their conscious life. (An exception is Down's Syndrome children who have just one line representing both the heart and heart lines. This appears to confirm that their thinking comes from their feelings rather than rational reflection.) If your heart line sweeps upwards towards your fingers and breaks off into several branches, this means you possess an affectionate nature. Branches which sweep down show disappointment in love. A heart line which is completely broken suggests that you are demanding in love and frequently let down by the experience. A long line, irrespective of its condition, shows you are expressive in love; a short line, again ignoring its state, shows you may be repressed in your emotions.

These life, head and heart lines are considered the major three lines in the hand and their relation to one another is also very relevant to the sort of person you are. Do your life and head lines start as one? This suggests you are a thoughtful person, not given to rash behaviour. If

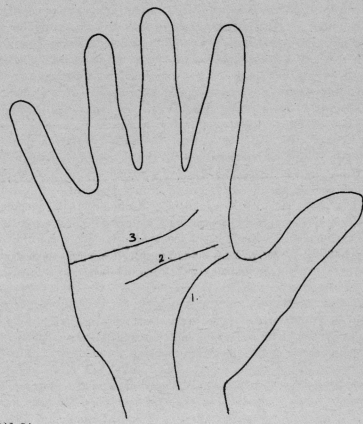

1 Life Line
2 Head Line
3 Heart Line

Hand Lines

your head and life lines stay joined for a short distance in the beginning, however, this could show a tendency not to try new pastures and to remain stuck in uninspiring situations through a fear of the unknown. If your head and life lines are widely spaced apart, then you run the risk of being reckless and easily bored. If the distance between your head and heart lines is wide, then you are said to have a broad outlook on life. If there is little space between your head and heart line, then you may tend to be narrow-minded in some areas. Again, the full information is more complex than this; these are rough guide-lines from which you can start.

Another area about which people are always curious is relationships and/or marriage and children. These can be indicated by specific lines. The lines indicating the number of significant relationships is found at the side of the palm between the little finger and the end of the heart line. The line or lines in between start at the side of palm and curve round, sometimes as far as below the ring finger. The longer the line, the longer the relationship. A light, thin line shows a relationship that was not a serious commitment. The deeper the line, the more intense. A deep line need not necessarily mean marriage, as nowadays so many opt for common-law arrangements whilst still experiencing a committed relationship. The nearer the line is to the base of the little finger, the later in life the relationship occurs. Similarly, if a line is close to the heart line, it suggests a very young affair.

Children are more difficult to discern and you need a good light to see the lines. These are quite light, fine lines that run above and perpendicular to the relationship lines. They are usually found below the little finger and just meet the relationship line or lines, without crossing over them. If the line doesn't meet it may indicate the loss of a child. If the line crosses over the relationship, it suggests that you put more importance on the relationship with the child than anyone else. Where it becomes more difficult, is that people who love children, without wanting or having children of their own, may also possess these fine lines. They could form close bonds with relatives' and friends' children and generally enjoy a good relationship with them. Therefore, it's not easy to accurately predict parenthood. You can suggest possibilities but not absolute definites. As you already know from your study, this is true of all areas of life. You can point out tendencies towards certain personality traits or health trends, but everyone has the ability to change their own destiny whenever they wish.

The details above are the very first basics for palmistry. If you want to consider it more seriously, there is a wealth of books which go into the subject in much more detail. You need to study the mounts of Mercury, Saturn, Jupiter, Venus, Mars and the Sun and Moon. There are also lines relating to Fate, Health, Travel, Sensitivity, Good Fortune, Intuition, Money and Spirituality. The relationships of all these lines to each other are all significant. The shape of the whole hand, the pattern of the individual fingerprint, the nails' texture and shape, the skin colour, the fleshiness of certain parts of the hand – a whole host of factors make up a detailed reading. Do study more on the subject if it interests you.

Now there is also the other area to consider. How can you bring psychic skills into palmistry? In touching the hand during a reading, you have the excellent opportunity for an auric reading. You have a close connection with your sitter's energies and the chance to tune in to their aura and see what you can pick up on that level. You can also use your higher senses to pick up further information during a reading, provided you are fully open and balanced before you start. You may be studying the relationships lines and suddenly 'see' a situation with a partner. You may feel the emotion of what happened. You may look at their life line and understand what an illness or upset was all about. You may see how they could slow down or relax more and alleviate possible further stress. The possibilities of marrying the two skills together make it exciting and powerful.

Of course, it takes practice before you will be able to merge the two together. You need to start by memorizing a few basics. Can you remember which are the life, head and heart lines? What are the different types of fingers? What does each finger tell you about? Where are children lines indicated and why do they not necessarily mean they will have their own children? What indicates a long relationship? If you have the opportunity to read more, incorporate further information into your study. Once you understand some of the physical information available to you, then you need to find someone on whom you can practise. Make sure you have memorized the lines first. If you have to refer to a book for clarification, your energy and focus will dissipate and make receiving psychic information very difficult.

Again, make it clear to your sitter that this is an early stage for you and ask them to bear with you if the information that comes through is slow. Always ask permission before you take hold of their hand and make sure you hold it gently but firmly. Once you start your reading, it will probably help you if you aren't interrupted, so ask if they could please save their comments until you have finished.

PALM READING

Start with your usual opening-up process. Then check that your weight is balanced on the chair and that you feel nicely relaxed. Ask for guidance from your inner self. Take several deep, gentle breaths. When you feel ready, open your eyes.

Firstly ask your sitter which hand they use for writing. Now take that hand in yours and hold it. You may have to practise before you find a position which feels comfortable. Try cupping their hand with one of yours, or place both of yours over their hand.

What is your first impression? How is their hand feeling to you? Cold or warm? Hard or soft? Frightened or relaxed? Do you feel a sense of calm or is there a buzzing feeling of various energies swirling around? Do those energies feel alive and vibrant or fuzzy and clogged? Are you receiving very little?

Now start your auric egg of energy: lifting your own energies to the solar plexus, then reaching out to their solar plexus and pulling some of their energy back into your own aura. What further information are you getting now? How does this relate to your first feeling when you held their hand? Do you suddenly have images of what the hand does during the day? This may tell you about their job or hobbies. Don't spend a long time with your auric reading; this is simply to start your psychic energies working.

Look at your sitter's hand. Study its length and shape and the relation of the fingers to each other. Tell your sitter the information as you receive it. You needn't stop to dwell on certain areas. At this stage, it's enough for you to have the energies flowing, to experience the difference of literal information working with the extra dimension of psychic awareness. As you study the palm itself, ask your inner self for further help when you feel it's necessary. If you see a break or chain or island and feel you need to know what it relates to, so that you can help your sitter, then ask for guidance. You may receive this psychic information in symbols or images, but by now you should be developing your ability to interpret what you receive. Always phrase your words carefully.

Remember to keep lifting your energies to your solar plexus. This is the 'gut instinct' area of us and you need to use both your intuition and inner self to give as full a reading as possible. Keep referring back to the lines in the palm, acknowledging that there is physical information for you to use. Whenever you feel stuck, ask your inner self to refer you to the part of the palm which contains details that you need to know.

If you receive anything unpleasant, always wash it away with your pure light. As you are combining auric reading with palm reading, it's quite possible you may pick up uncomfortable sensations.

If you have spent some time studying palmistry, you may be pleasantly surprised by the speed and clarity with which information comes through. Many people find the experience of combining psychic and literal details to be powerful and liberating. It seems to speed up the psychic energies. Others find it hard to keep a balance between the two and their psychic energies become confused. After a few sessions, you will know what feels right for you. Keep cleansing under your waterfall if you do feel unsure of what you are receiving.

When you feel you have said enough, let your energies drop again to your base. Explain to your sitter that you are going to take a minute or so to balance yourself and ask if they would please sit quietly and consider what you've been saying while you do this. Ask them to especially consider anything you've said which doesn't make sense. Take your time to cleanse and close down. Don't open your eyes again until you feel ready.

During the feedback you receive, try to notice if any inaccurate information was coming through psychic channels or from your sitter's palm. This isn't always easy to remember, but after a few sittings you'll find it less difficult. You need to determine whether you are reading the palm incorrectly or whether you aren't using your psychic energies as smoothly as you could. If you were reading their palm correctly, it's likely that a certain amount of the details will be accurate. It also depends on how much self-knowledge your sitter has. Sometimes, when you gently point out a personality trait, people may not accept it, because they are ready to look at that area of themselves yet. Or they may deny it at the time, but then go away later and think it over. They may then come to the conclusion that you were right after all, although they may never tell you! This is again where you need to leave your own ego out of psychic work. If they deny what you say when you 'know' that it is accurate, never argue with your sitter or try to persuade them that they are wrong. Simply ask them if they would please go away and think about it for a little while. Explain that sometimes they can think more clearly after they have left the reading.

This combining physical information and psychic energies isn't that uncommon. In fact, you are have already been doing this through your psychic development, although you may not have been aware of it. You see, people physical bearing tells us a great deal about them: how they walk, carry themselves, their little mannerisms and speech patterns. Unconsciously, we study all these aspects of people when they come to us for a reading. So, for instance, an auric reading isn't just about psychic energies on their own. The chances are that you will have already sized up your sitter before you started, observing whether they are confident or shy, happy or sad. This isn't because you're 'cheating'; it's because it's a natural part of observing people and getting to know them. A person's smile or lack of it tells you much about their present emotional, physical and mental health. However, to understand what is happening on a deeper level, you must use your psychic gifts. Never be ashamed of using both, however. What you want to avoid is simply looking at a person and deciding what their whole being is like from the outside. That is where you will fall down, because the outer shell rarely reveals their inner spiritual path. Use your own powers of observation and then combine them with higher knowledge, to provide a richer, deeper understanding.

CHAPTER 24

USING YOUR PSYCHIC DEFENCES

Discovering your psychic energies can be one of the most powerful and enlightening experiences of your life. Once you have discovered that you've only been using a small part of yourself and there is much more to explore, the initial feeling is very freeing and exciting. You can compare it to the sensation of learning to drive a car and passing your test; the world suddenly becomes more accessible and you want to drive everywhere, enjoying the new sensation of freedom. However, if you aren't a careful and responsible driver, you may end up in trouble. Unfortunately, this is often hard to accept, until you have an accident, which reminds you that driving can be dangerous. The same is true of psychic development. You are often so busy enjoying your new world, that you can't be bothered to stop and acknowledge the dangers. This chapter is for everyone who hasn't yet fully looked at the problems that can occur with psychic work. This isn't to say that you will automatically have psychic accidents; hopefully, most of you will be going around so well protected and grounded, that nothing unpleasant can affect you. However, the more prepared you are, the less likely it is that you will need to call upon all your reserves of psychic defence.

Why would you need psychic defence anyway? You may be clear that you are using your psychic gifts in the most responsible and careful of ways. You are not using anyone adversely in the process, you are being gentle and supportive in manner, you are constantly seeking guidance and approval from your inner self and higher sources of awareness, and you are trying to leave your ego out of the psychic equation. How could there be a problem, if you are behaving in as healthy a fashion as possible? If you are truly adhering to these principles, then you will have a clear conscience. You will 'know' you are doing no harm and not provoking any difficult karmic reactions.

However, psychic defence isn't about looking at whether you are behaving in as responsible a fashion as possible; it's about how to further protect yourself from other outside influences. You will no doubt acknowledge that with psychic and spiritual development, you are tapping into new, unknown areas of different energies and cosmic influences. You can't possibly understand all these subtle forces and realize their effects upon you. You can only know that there is much that is new and exciting that you are starting to explore. In realizing this, you are opening up your own subtle bodies in a way you have never done before. So, not only are you aware of new energies, you are also opening yourself up to receive more influences into your aura. It's a powerful combination. It can also be very unnerving at times.

Once you start working with other energies and fully opening your own chakras, you will probably notice a change in yourself. This may take place after a few weeks or months, or even a year, depending upon your own level of progress. This change can take different forms. You may find yourself feeling affected by aspects of life that never bothered you before. It might be that music seems too loud in a restaurant or club. Someone whose company you once enjoyed may now seem to jar with you; you may find them more draining or their energies too explosive for you to be able to relax. You might find yourself suddenly feeling more tired than usual. Perhaps you feel like snapping at people sometimes, which is not your normal behaviour. Maybe you are crying more easily. Do you feel as though certain negative experiences keep hitting you, without you having done anything to trigger them off? It's possible you're having vivid dreams and disturbed sleep patterns. You may be walking around, feeling somewhat disjointed and out of focus with life, without understanding why.

The above is just a small sample of what can happen when you don't protect and ground yourself enough, using your own psychic defences. If you continue with psychic development, some of the above will almost certainly happen to you. It's a natural progression and it happens because it's important that you learn how to properly protect and ground yourself. So let's look at various ways in which you can do this. The more prepared you are, the less likely it is that you will ever need to use all the methods described.

First and foremost, you need to pay attention to cleansing under your pure white light/waterfall and closing your chakras. By now, you will have read dozens of references to this. You won't want to be reminded again. You're probably sick of the words 'cleanse and close down'. However, no matter how often you're told about it, the chances are you will reach a stage when you pay less attention than you should to this area, because you're convinced you know it all. You don't. You can't. You can never close down too much. You can never cleanse too often.

Once you work psychically on a regular basis, you will be opening up constantly all day long without ever realizing you're doing it. You may be sitting next to someone on a train or discussing something in a bar with someone and your chakras will suddenly open and your aura expand without your even knowing it. You then absorb the energies of those around you and go home, carrying them all inside you. You then wonder when you get home why you are more tired than usual, or why you snapped at your partner without cause. Close down all the time.

Cleanse every time you leave a crowded environment. If you spend time with someone who is depressed or upset, cleanse and close down afterwards. If you visit someone in hospital, cleanse and close down when you leave. Even if you have a phone conversation with someone which affects you or you've been reading a book about spiritual and psychic growth, cleanse and close when you finish. Before you go to sleep, cleanse and close down. When you get up in the morning, cleanse the night away and close your chakras. (We all dream, even if we don't remember what happened. Those dreams can stay in our unconscious and affect us through the day.) Is your waterfall or cleansing place really clear to you? Maybe you need to visualize it more thoroughly. Make it come alive and become a sanctuary for you.

Also look at your psychic cloak of protection. Is it really helping you, or have you become used to putting the cloak around you, without properly considering whether it is right for you? If you're using light, should you try visualizing fabric instead, or vice versa? Have you really got the best colour for you? Try another colour to experiment, but remember to avoid dark hues.

Are you remembering to ground yourself properly after psychic work, or are you again rushing the whole process, telling yourself you're fine when you're not? Do you really see those long, strong roots growing out of your feet when you need to earth yourself again? Can you really feel them anchoring you deep into the earth's core, making you feel solid and secure again? Do you remember to earth yourself this way if something uncomfortable happens to you during the day? You can think of this at any time, because no one need know what is going on in your mind.

These are the techniques you already know about, but need to keep practising. Constantly. Now let's look at other methods you can use to help yourself.

Your cloak of protection is a quick way of making yourself feel shut off from unwanted influences, but you can use other images. Create a solid crystal around you and your aura. You can see out, but nothing can touch you. The special properties of the crystal will create added protection. If you find a crystal too claustrophobic, then try creating a fine filter screen all around you. This is to prevent any negativity invading, whilst allowing other, wanted influences to penetrate. You might prefer to place yourself inside a golden egg of light which has solid edges that cannot be permeated. If the egg-shape doesn't feel right for you, try using the shape of a pyramid or a pentagram, both considered strong images for warding off unwanted energies. It doesn't matter which shape you put around you, so long as it makes you feel good.

If you want to feel completely cut off, try jumping into a shiny, clean dustbin and pulling the lid over you. If you want to use a colour, make the bin a shade of grass-green to envelop you in love. This will give you a moment of completely being on your own. Use this when you need a moment's respite but try not to see it as a constant solution.

You may end up simply cutting yourself off from others, rather than addressing the issue in hand.

If you are in someone's presence and they are extremely angry, directing abuse towards you, then you can use a couple of methods to help ease the situation. Receiving a barrage of fury from someone can be deeply upsetting. Next time it happens, take a few deep breaths, ground and focus yourself, consciously retract your aura so that it is smaller and tighter, and then imagine holding up a mirror in front of them. This psychic mirror has the effect of re-directing the anger back to the other person. You don't need to articulate what you are doing and you don't have to mime holding up anything; the thought process alone creates the power. It's probable that they will take a step backwards or suddenly slow down in their tirade. They won't understand why, but it doesn't matter.

There is another very strong visualization technique you can use to deal with another person's anger, but it takes personal strength to do this. Try sending the person waves of love and light from your own solar plexus. This won't work if you are deeply angry yourself because you will only be directing more angry energy to them. You have to be in a position where you can accept their frustration and not react to it. If you can attain this higher level of understanding and empathy and can then use love as a means of healing and helping, it's wonderfully powerful. You may not succeed at this for a while, but if you keep practising the act, there will come a time when you may be able to love unconditionally, rather than subjectively. It is something to aspire to, rather than to expect immediately.

There are also quick physical tools you can use to help you when you feel vulnerable. If you feel you are being bombarded by unwanted energy when you are with other people, cross your ankles and fold your arms across your chest. This is a physical cutting off from others than can maintain your own energy supply and help deflect energy away from you.

Using stones and crystals is also a popular method, as you know from your study of crystals. If you feel you need to strengthen your psychic defences, then try wearing a stone around your neck, or have one near you during the day and/or night. There are so many stones that are used for protective and strengthening purposes, but here's a quick run-down of some you might like to try:

For General Protection: tourmaline, flint, tiger's eye, amethyst, jet, turquoise, golden topaz.

To Draw Out Negative Energies: amber, malachite.

For Grounding: carnelian, hematite, granite.

You may find others work better for you. Again, this becomes a personal choice as you get to know yourself, and crystals, better.

Talismans are also popular means of protection. Whether they work or not is up to your own individual relationship with symbols and what they mean to you. For many, the sign of the cross or the Star of David signifies protection and purity. For others, the Chinese yin-yang symbol is spiritually sacred. There is also the Moslem moon, the Ankh, the 'Isis' Buckle, the Eye of Horus and the Caduceus. You will find examples of these symbols opposite. If any of them make you feel secure, try wearing one around your neck. If you're artistic, draw a symbol and place it near you at work or by your bed. You might prefer the figure of Buddha or an angel or god with whom you feel an empathy. Some find their image of a protective animal such as an elephant or lion far more powerful. It doesn't really matter what you use. It's what makes you feel good that matters. Do you feel a respect and love for the cat kingdom? A tiger or lion may be a good symbol for you. Do you feel more at home with Egyptian mythology? You might choose Sobek, a crocodile guardian and protector. If you spend some time studying any ancient mythology, you will find your own natural protector and guide.

If you still find your own body and your space is being invaded by unwanted energies, you can choose further means of cleansing yourself.

A very effective method is to take a bath using a recognized cleansing herb or remedy. Any good health shop should be able to advise you,

Goddess Isis Buckle

Ankh

Caduceus

Eye of Horus

Yin-Yang

Moslem

Star of David

Protective Symbols

but if you want to try a simple method, just use sea salt and baking soda.

CLEANSING BATH

Put six tablespoons of sea salt and six tablespoons of baking soda into a bath of running water. Don't have the bath water too hot and avoid this method altogether if you suffer from low blood pressure. Soak for up to twenty minutes before you get out and dry yourself thoroughly. Although this is a terrific way to cleanse your entire body of negative energy, it will also leave you feeling tired afterwards. It would help if you could then lie in the sun for twenty minutes afterwards to re-energize yourself. Of course, watch the sun's intensity and always use sun-screen lotion. Don't choose to do this if you have a busy day ahead of you. Wait until you have the time to relax and be gentle with yourself.

Another powerful tool is auric brushing. Just as you brush your hair to keep it clean and untangled, so you can brush your aura to remove unwanted particles and revitalize your energy. You need to do this with someone else who is sympathetic to psychic work.

AURIC BRUSHING

Both parties should keep their eyes open throughout to avoid feeling off-balance and dizzy. One person stands with their arms by their sides and their legs slightly apart. The other needs to imagine that their fingers are growing longer and longer. Now they use their extra-long fingers to brush through the other person's aura. They need to do this in one long, firm sweep, starting from above the head and brushing all the way down the body, finishing up a few feet away from their feet. If it's not done as one movement, some of the debris may be left where they stopped the movement, just as tangles can't be removed properly from the hair without going through the whole hair from top to bottom. The brusher needs to move all around the person and brush from every side. When the brusher has finished, it may feel right to psychically sweep up the debris from around the feet and place it in a rubbish bin. Then repeat the process, reversing the roles. There's a wonderful sense of peace and well-being after this takes place.

You can also use a smudge-stick (a form of incense) to clear a room of atmosphere. These smudging sticks are available from health and New Age shops in a variety of scents. In the chapter on crystals, you read about burning sage-grass to cleanse your crystal. This also has a positive effect on your aura and the room. Keep doors and windows open whilst the smoking process takes place. Other incenses and aromatherapy oils can be just as effective. Again, experiment and choose what works for you. What one person finds wonderful as an odour, another will find quite repulsive. Eucalyptus, peppermint, pine and juniper are all very good for clearing unwanted energies from a space. Others, such as marjoram, clary sage and jasmine can work wonderfully well on a more personal level.

You can also imbue a room with your own energy and love. If you're having trouble making your space feel as if it's really your own, or if you feel the energies have been disturbed by a particular person's presence, then you can use your own vibrations to make a difference.

CLEARING A ROOM

Sit quietly in the middle of your room when no one else is around. Put on your favourite music or burn your chosen incense. Open up and ground yourself.

Now increase the image of the white light so that you can feel it streaming down from above, through every single pore in the ceiling, becoming richer and brighter all the time. Feel the white light cascading down and filling your room, washing away any unwanted residue. Feel it pouring in endlessly, and let it continue until you feel the whole room has been washed clean. You should actually feel and smell the new, fresh air before you continue.

Then feel your aura expanding with warmth and love and breathe in the colour green for a few minutes, until you feel as though you are pulsing with loving vibrations.

Now send those vibrations outwards to all the corners of the room. You may want to focus on one corner at once and work your way around, or it may feel more powerful to imagine that your whole being is exuding this love and spreading out from every part of you at once. Make sure you really fill the room with your energies. Feel the love going all the way up to the ceiling, into each far corner, under and over and around and through everything in the room.

Visualize green streamers of love if this helps, or see it as a golden light filling the entire room. Let its strength wash away any other uncomfortable images or feelings. Know that your love is more powerful than any other force. Bless the room and its purpose. Ask for help from your inner self to protect this space and for others who come into it to be enriched by its atmosphere.

Feel the visible pulsing of loving energy in the room. Check that you have properly filled the space and that is feels comfortable, before you gently withdraw your energies. Feel your aura gradually contract back towards you.

When you feel ready, cleanse yourself under the waterfall. Include your room under a giant flow of water or white light. Then slowly close down and protect yourself again. Put an extra cloak of protection right around you. Ground yourself well before you open your eyes.

You should now feel a tangible difference in your room. You should feel comfortable sitting there, knowing that it feels right now. You may want to repeat the process again when you feel the need.

Lastly, always look to yourself for understanding of your reactions to influences around you. Is there something you need to learn from the energies that you are being bombarded by? It may simply be that you need to learn how to shut off and protect yourself. You may be too open to everyone and everything. Being receptive to life is a wonderful quality but it will harm you if you don't learn when it's appropriate to open up and when it's essential to close down.

When you first discover abilities to help and heal others, you naturally want to share it with as many people as possible. You may be walking down the street and pass by a homeless figure whom you long to heal.

You may send out loving vibrations, unconsciously using your own energies in the process because you won't be properly opened up and tuned in to do so. Unfortunately, your own desire to help is not enough and you may damage your own energies in your rush of enthusiasm. Remember that the only condition for healing is that the other person be willing to open their mind to the possibility of change. Sadly, many people aren't. You can't force people to accept healing or nurturing, unless they want it. If you try to force what you think is helpful advice onto them, they will only back off further. People come to psychic work when the time is right for them. Learn to be discriminating in your work, as this will protect you. Always ask permission and be responsive to their reaction.

There's another valuable lesson to be learnt with psychic defence techniques, too. You have to learn to know when it is right to shut off and when you are shutting yourself off from a learning experience from which you could benefit. If you are in doubt, always ask your inner self for guidance. If you are in a situation and you feel uncomfortable, but aren't sure whether you need to practise some withdrawal method, or whether you need to learn something further about yourself, then ask yourself what is happening. If you are focused and pure in your intent, you will be given advice. Just because we are developing our psychic and spiritual awareness does not in any way make us superior to others. We are part of a constant learning cycle and sometimes we don't want to learn certain lessons. If you find yourself feeling unpleasant emotions, is it because there's an element of yourself you aren't willing to face and deal with? This degree of sensitivity will grow in time. If you are in doubt or distress, choose the psychic defence mechanism which works best for you. Later, you can then look at what happened and decide if you were the victim of someone else's negative energy, or if you had something to learn from the experience.

If, at any point, you know yourself to be psychically attacked by some outside force and you cannot control the level of what is happening, with manifestations which are outside your power causing mischief, then you need outside help for this work. You may have unwittingly caught the energies of some unhelpful force whose intent is to cause distress on some level. An experienced psychic will know how to deal with this, so do contact a local psychic college or institution and seek advice. The vast majority of the time, no harm is actually done by these disembodied souls and there is little to fear, except your own fear of fear itself! Whilst there is no reason for you to tolerate these unpleasant influences, there is an important lesson to learn. You have only drawn them into your energy by being too vulnerable in the first place, so you need help to increase your own psychic defence mechanisms to ensure that it never happens again.

There's no need for you to be alarmed by the above paragraph; for the majority of psychics, this unnerving experience never occurs in the first place. It should never occur if your intentions are always pure and good and you keep yourself well protected and grounded.

Remember to always practise psychic defence under everyday conditions. Never under-estimate its importance, and that will ensure you can enjoy your psychic and spiritual development to the full.

CHAPTER 25

THE FUTURE

What sort of future does psychic work have as part of our planet's evolvement? The answer must surely be, 'Psychic awareness has a significant future, if human life is to survive.' We can no longer ignore that we are swiftly destroying our Earth's natural resources whilst, at the same time, many human relationships are suffering and conditions of chaos are reigning in many areas across the planet. Unless humans discover their own spirituality and how it relates to everyone and everything, we are in grave danger of continuing a downward spiral to self-destruction. Fortunately, the twentieth century has also seen a great growth in conscious awareness and it is steadily growing, almost daily. This book is a small attempt to continue spreading the possibilities of what human beings can accomplish and how we can reverse negative trends, learning from our mistakes and moving forward as a result.

Enormous change starts from small changes within us that grow and expand. You cannot truly be successful and fulfilled in your life's work unless you know that you are working to your true capacity, paying heed to your inner self and levels of higher consciousness that will guide and advise you.

The people whom we call 'saints' nowadays would appear to do just this. When Mother Teresa was asked why she did the extraordinary work she did and why she touched the hearts of millions of suffering souls, she was reported to have replied something simple along the lines of, 'Because I am meant to do this work.' She made no bones about the hours she spent in prayer with her God and how she was guided by his teaching. Her own ego didn't seem to play any part in the equation. She followed her life's destiny with quiet assurance, not seeking approval or praise from anyone. Unassuming dedication on such a level is still rare and something to which many could aspire. You cannot accomplish this unless you 'go within' and discover the intended path of your own soul. Only then will you be of the utmost help to those around you.

This does not mean you should ever ignore your own physical state or the physical needs of those around you, particularly dependants. You've been considering the concept that you chose to have your soul put into a physical body in this incarnation to learn from the experience. You won't learn if you disregard your physical existence. This is one of the most difficult aspects of psychic and spiritual development: learning how to put everything into practice so that it becomes balanced and healthy. Spending all day meditating probably won't further other areas of your life, but moderate, daily sessions of quiet contemplation may yield insights and understandings which will enable you to live your physical life in a much fuller realm.

It may help you a great deal to keep considering the Hologram Theory and how it relates to your life and everyone else's place within the universe. We need to see everything as part of the whole and to always consider others, whilst still acknowledging the necessity to work upon our own personal journeys. Our own paths are part of the whole cosmic pattern and we can only resonate fully with all the energies available to us when we open ourselves to spiritual growth and enlightenment.

You may read through this whole book and still be in a state of indecision over what you really think and feel about 'the meaning of life'. You may have always held very opposite views and find these hard to digest. You may want to believe but find it a struggle to try to do so. You might feel some of it makes sense but there is so much you still don't understand and that it won't fit together in your mind. This is a very natural state to reach. Any moment of change or growth is almost always preceded by a time of confusion or anxiety. Don't pressure yourself into feeling you have to make any decisions or come to any firm conclusions. Just quietly continue thinking and expanding your awareness of people and the universe.

In time, your thoughts will crystallize and you will follow what feels right for you.

You have started the beginning of an infinite journey. Hopefully, this book will have whetted your appetite for further knowledge, for opportunities to keep expanding your consciousness and to learn more about how you can function in a truly holistic sense. There are so many more concepts to grasp, so many levels of higher consciousness which you have not yet even considered. Do you remember the very first visualization technique which you tried back in the Introduction? Can you remember if you found the endless skyscraper daunting but exciting? Now it's time to try the Exercise again.

EXPANDING YOUR THOUGHTS NO. 2

Close your eyes and settle yourself in your safe space. Now open up properly. Take your time and remember to breathe as deeply as you can, without feeling uncomfortable. Balance yourself and feel yourself connect with the Earth's energy via your feet. Wait until you feel cleansed and rejuvenated by the white light before you continue.

When you're ready, see the tall building in front of you again. Does the image seem stronger now? Look up and see it stretching away into the far distance. Perhaps it feels different now: no less exciting, but easier to understand and accept. Do you feel a closer affinity with the building?

Walk through the open door and enter the ground floor level. Notice how solid your feet feel on the ground. You feel comfortable, heavy, earthed. The surroundings feel clean and familiar. You go over to your lift (or stairs) and enter it. You look at all the buttons on the lift panel and understand why there are so many. You look at the basement button but know that you have passed the stage of wanting to even visit that level. You have moved on to other pastures now. You decide to revisit your first and second floors.

The lift glides smoothly to the first floor and opens. You see your

375

friends and family again. This time it feels different. Their images are clearer, you can feel their energy and see them for what they really are. You realize you are now looking at people in a different way. You see them as whole souls, not disjointed, flawed people. You realize you are learning to love unconditionally. You can feel the love from your aura reaching out and mingling with theirs. Take a good look around the room and really appreciate each and every person. Acknowledge new people that are now there for you and give thanks for their presence. Enjoy the feeling of love which emanates from them. Give a last smile to everyone before you close the lift door and move up to the second floor.

The lift door opens again and you are now confronted with your working environment. How much has that altered since your first visit? For many people, this is slow to change. People are hesitant to consciously bring their spiritual beliefs into work. That is fine. Now look a bit deeper into this room. Have changes occurred without you really noticing it? Have others benefited from your increased awareness, without you having to discuss matters with them? Is there someone to whom you were able to give some absent healing? How do they look now? Has your attitude changed to areas of your work? Walk slowly around your work place. What else is here for you to learn about? Do you see a possibility that you hadn't considered before? Is there a person smiling at you whom you hadn't communicated with much before? Let yourself be guided by what is shown to you. Remember what happens, so that you can think about it further at a later time. When you feel ready, return to your lift.

Press the button for the third floor and feel the lift glide upwards. When it opens, you step out into your own personal space, exactly as you have created it and know it already. Walk around it and enjoy it once more. Are there some differences in this room once you examine it more closely? Look closely, feel and smell the room. Note any changes and decide if you would like to try them yourself. Notice how vibrant, bright and beautiful the energy is in this room. It has a purity, an intensity, that invigorates and uplifts you. Stand in the middle of your third floor and take several deep breaths. Bless this heavenly sanctuary and resolve always to keep it clean and pure.

Now return to your lift and press the button for the fourth floor. This time the lift moves easily and takes you upwards. When the fourth floor opens, you see your own level of spiritual advancement. This is personal to you and will be different for each person. You may find your spiritual helpers or your protective guide waiting for you. You may see a special gift just for you, lying in the middle of the room. You may be told which area of psychic development you are meant to study next. It may be a powerful insight that comes to you, or a flash of understanding from a higher level of con-sciousness. Whatever it is, it is your own personal acknowledge-ment of your very individual path towards enlightenment. It doesn't matter how small or large that experience is, because we all work at our own pace. The fact that you have reached the fourth level shows that you are starting your journey. Give thanks for this wonderful new step and vow that you will continue to work with love in your heart and a willingness to learn from and to trust your inner self.

When you return to your lift, the doors close of their own accord and gently lower you to another floor. This will again be personal to you, according to your own development. When the doors open, you are led to whichever area of your life you need to look at next. Trust your inner self in this journey. It will probably lead you to an area of your life that you either feel reluctant to look at or haven't even considered before. If you feel confused after you've been led in a certain direction, ask your inner self for some help. Ask what the lesson is that you need to learn. When you're ready, return to the lift.

Press the ground floor and let the lift return you to your roots. As soon as you step out on the ground level, you again feel secure and safe. Your body feels heavy and comfortable. Walk through the open door and enjoy the feeling of warmth that envelops you from the comforting sunshine outside. Turn one last time and look up at your tall building. Look forward to the journey you have started.

Know that it will take you a while and that the path may not always be easy, but know also that it is going to be a constantly expanding and exciting process.

Now walk back to your own chair and feel your weight resting on the seat. Feel your feet resting firmly on the ground. Take several minutes to ground yourself again. Now cleanse thoroughly under your waterfall and carefully close all your chakras, one by one, slowly and firmly. Swathe yourself in your protective cloak and thank your inner self for your experiences. When you feel ready, open your eyes. Sit quietly for a few minutes before you get up.

How different was that for you from your first attempt? Your changes may be subtle or dramatic, depending upon your own personal feelings about psychic development. Whatever happened for you, it was right. If little changed, that is fine. Acknowledge the little that was different and learn from that. If everything felt very different, concentrate on the area that you were led to last of all. Know that this is the area that you need to look at in your life now. You can always return to your tall building whenever you feel ready in the future.

In fact, all the Exercises are meant to be used at different times and more than once. A complete list of them appears in the Contents at the front of this book so you have easy reference at any time to whatever Exercise you think you need most. If you have embraced karma and re-incarnation, return often to the Karma Exercise and learn more about some of your relationships that way. If you develop a close affinity with your bird or fish, return to them often, to learn from them. Keep working on your different chakras. You can never learn too much about them and about how your own energy centres are opening. They change just as your aura constantly changes. If working with a candle inspires you, keep using different candles and keep practising.

Don't be afraid to change things within your own space, either. Move the furniture, alter the lighting, use different incense or music. Put up different drawings or posters. Try another plant. Move crystals into different locations. Don't let the energy become stagnant. Keep it moving and keep renewing the vibrations. Welcome change and learn from it.

Every day, spend some time on your breathing. Your breath is your gateway to higher consciousness. Learn how to have it become your greatest friend and aid. Gradually learn how to breathe more deeply and yet remain safe and protected. Know from your breathing whether you are properly balanced or not. If you listen to yourself, you will always know what your body is telling you. Learn how to balance yourself and ground yourself quickly and easily. Cleanse so often and so thoroughly that it becomes as natural as blinking your eyes. Make sure it's a powerful process. This can only happen with continual practice.

Let yourself practise different forms of psychic work. Even if you feel a quick affinity with psychometry, for example, do try flower reading, healing, auragraph work and dowsing. Again, don't let your energies become stale. Even if you prove inaccurate in other psychic work, you will still have changed your energies and expanded your awareness. Embrace new possibilities and accept that you can't excel at everything but that everything has something to teach you.

Always treat your sitters with the deepest respect. Always remember to thank them for their time and never be tempted to charge them for your services. Your early stages are a learning process during which you will no doubt make some mistakes. Appreciate their part in your progress and try to always leave your sitters on a positive note that will inspire and uplift them.

Also, read as many other books on psychic and spiritual development as possible. Everyone teaches differently and has a different approach to their work. Try other ways and see what feels right for you. Something else may strike a deeper cord of recognition for you. It doesn't matter which method you use, as long as it is powerful for you and as long as your intentions are pure and honourable. Never forget that personal ego and psychic development are incompatible.

Apart from reading, attend as many lectures, fairs and courses as you possibly can. There is a wealth of opportunities out there for everyone;

observe and participate in everything, provided it feels right for you. This doesn't mean you should let yourself be coerced into any society or any set of beliefs if you don't feel good about it. Remember to keep asking your inner self and trusting your own instinct and intuition. If a group or individual makes you feel uncomfortable or threatened, they probably aren't meant for you. You are free to make your own decisions without outside influence. Learn to trust yourself. The world of psychic phenomena can also attract some very unbalanced souls and you need to make sure that you remain protected and grounded, so that you can be the best judge of what is right for you.

There are so many other forms of psychic and spiritual development, many of which you may not have yet dealt with. See how many of these names are familiar to you: Alexander technique, Qigong, Theosophy, Reiki, Acupressure and Acupuncture, Shamanism, Bioenergetics, Core Energetics, Homeopathy, Reflexology and Graphology. The above are just a small selection of alternative and holistic belief systems that offer powerful help to millions of people. You won't know if they might be beneficial to you without exploring some of them for yourself.

If you are clear that you really want to further develop your own psychic potential, then the single, most positive step forward for you is to join a development circle. This is a group of people who meet together regularly and practise psychic development together, whilst under the constant guidance of a fully trained psychic. There are many development circles that sit regularly across the world; any reputable psychic association will be able to give you details. Again, this is a very personal choice. The energies within a given group may be suited to one person and not another. It may take you some time and some searching before you find the one that is right for you. Don't be so enthusiastic in your approach that you take the first development circle that becomes available to you. Always meet the teacher first and use your intuition to tell you whether this person is meant to be a psychic guide for you. They may be wonderful at their work, but their energies may still not be compatible with yours. You will also find that the teacher will be quick to suggest if they don't feel they are suitable for you either.

Sitting in a development circle may accelerate your progress but, more importantly, it will afford you greater protection. You will be surrounded by your teacher's guides as well as your own. You will also be supported and encouraged in a way that working on your own can't offer you. The energies of a collective group of people can be much stronger, lighter and brighter than your own, assuming the teacher has brought together the right group of people. You can support one another during classes and also learn to appreciate how unique everyone is when they work psychically. You can gain a true understanding of how you are meant to work at your own level, without comparing and judging yourself or others.

You will probably also be given the opportunity to have sittings with a variety of different people, many of whom will be complete strangers, chosen by your teacher. This also increases your abilities, as you learn the benefits of leaving all conscious knowledge of your sitter behind and working fully on a higher realm.

If you want to continue working on your own spiritual development outside a psychic circle, that is fine, too, but you should be aware that your progress may be slower, unless you seek other guidance and help. Remember, no one book can offer you everything you need to know.

As your understanding develops and expands, try to share it with others when you know it is appropriate. You will soon know whether someone wants to listen or not. If they scoff or are unnerved by your conversation, don't force your thoughts or beliefs in any way. They will find their own path to tread when the time is right for them.

Sometimes, it feels easier not to say anything, rather than risk ridicule. The difficulty with taking that stance is that you also may lose the opportunity to spread some thought-provoking concept which could enrich somebody else's life. If you can again leave your own ego out of the equation and not mind another person's reaction to what you say, you will be in a far healthier state. When you do find someone who is genuinely interested and wants to talk, remember to let them have their say too! Psychic and spiritual development creates such a uniquely energetic field that it is often very hard to remember to stop and listen to someone else. You won't help them if you start a long speech about its benefits; people need to discover this for themselves. Your role is to encourage mind expansion, not bombard them with information that they can't yet access.

It's also important to consider the words you use, just as you do when giving a sitting. Constant references to 'subtle bodies', 'vibrating auric fields' and 'resonating with cosmic consciousness' are likely to put most people off. Use simple, honest language that people can understand as it will therefore make them feel secure. This doesn't mean talking down to anyone; it means learning to tune in properly to their aura and to find the best way of communicating. There will be times when, no matter how you phrase concepts, people will laugh at you and turn away. Use that moment as a lesson for yourself to help you deal with others as compassionately as possible.

Humans constantly limit themselves through fear. Fear comes from facing the unknown. Psychic and spiritual development is all connected with breaking through the fear barriers and realizing, through that process, that fear is completely unnecessary. It is the block which stops our energies from flowing holistically. Every day, in a small way, try facing a little fear that you know you don't need. Meditate upon it, do something physically to alleviate it, or use a psychic defence mechanism to let go of it. Keep practising the process of letting go of fear so that it becomes a natural part of your life. Start with the small areas and gradually build up to your larger blocks. Ask your inner self for guidance throughout. You will soon realize that other people's unpleasant reactions all stem from fear. Arrogance, bullying, anger, frustration, aloofness; any quality we find difficult to accept in others is almost always based on fear. Sometimes that fear is so deep-rooted that it takes a great deal to sift it out and let it go. It's said that people can't generally do this in one life-time; they need to keep returning to Earth to work through the problems. That's why it's so important that we use all the time we have in our lives to enrich our souls and let them grow and expand.

However you choose to work on your own soul path, let yourself be guided only by truth and purity of the highest vibration. Let the brilliant white light radiate down with such clarity and intensity that the only thought forms which can penetrate come from the highest of sources. Then you will know that only good can come from your experiences, and you will spread positive, loving and helpful messages with everything you do. Respect and cultivate your relationship with your inner self and your personal 'god'. Let them show you the way when you need help and acknowledge their unique strength and purpose.

Above all, enjoy your new awareness and nurture it gently every step of the way. Know that its possibilities are infinite, as indeed are your own capacities for loving and giving. May the realms of highest consciousness bless you and protect you always.